Eradicating Extreme Poverty

ERADICATING EXTREME POVERTY

Democracy, Globalisation and Human Rights

Edited by
Xavier Godinot

Translated by
Angela Cady and Andrew Hayes

Additional editing by
Judith Stone

PlutoPress
www.plutobooks.com

First published in French 2008 by Presses Universitaires de France
English edition first published 2012 by Pluto Press
345 Archway Road, London N6 5AA

www.plutobooks.com

Distributed in the United States of America exclusively by
Palgrave Macmillan, a division of St. Martin's Press LLC,
175 Fifth Avenue, New York, NY 10010

British Library Cataloguing in Publication Data
A catalogue record for this book is available from the British Library

ISBN   978 0 7453 3198 0   Hardback
ISBN   978 0 7453 3197 3   Paperback

Library of Congress Cataloging in Publication Data applied for

This book is printed on paper suitable for recycling and made from fully managed
and sustained forest sources. Logging, pulping and manufacturing processes are
expected to conform to the environmental standards of the country of origin.

10   9   8   7   6   5   4   3   2   1

Designed and produced for Pluto Press by Chase Publishing Services Ltd
Typeset from disk by Stanford DTP Services, Northampton, England
Simultaneously printed digitally by CPI Antony Rowe, Chippenham, UK and
Edwards Bros in the United States of America

Contents

ATD Fourth World

The international movement ATD Fourth World is a non-governmental organisation with no religious or political affiliation which engages with individuals and institutions to find solutions to eradicate extreme poverty. Working in partnership with people in poverty, ATD Fourth World's human rights-based approach focuses on supporting families and individuals through its grassroots presence and involvement in disadvantaged communities, in both urban and rural areas, creating public awareness of extreme poverty and influencing policies to address it. It brings together people from all walks of life, starting with people living in the most extreme poverty and has a presence on the ground in 30 countries on five continents. Through its 'Permanent Forum on Extreme Poverty', an international network of anti-poverty organisations and human rights defenders, it maintains links with people and associations in 155 countries. Florianne Caravatta, Marilyn Ortega Gutierez, Alasdair Wallace, Patricia and Claude Heyberger, Rosario Macedo de Ugarte and Marco Aurelio Ugarte Ochoa, who authored this book, have been full-time volunteers in this movement for many years.

Trained in politics and economics for 40 years, Xavier Godinot, who coordinated the book, has combined academic and grassroots approaches in the fight against extreme poverty. He directed ATD Fourth World's research institute for twelve years. He then ran anti-poverty projects in Madagascar, with families living in rubbish dumps. He is now working at the headquarters of ATD Fourth World in France where he is coordinating an action research project in eight countries to evaluate the Millennium Development Goals.

Preface to the English Edition

Xavier Godinot

Three years have elapsed since the French version of this book was published by the Presses Universitaires de France. I spent most of this time in Antananarivo, the main town of Madagascar, as Regional Coordinator for the Indian Ocean region of the International Movement ATD Fourth World, a non-governmental organisation dedicated to combating extreme poverty and exclusion in both the northern and southern hemispheres through partnerships with people in extreme poverty.[1] It was an outstanding position from which to expand my knowledge of what it means to live in extreme poverty, and how to fight against it in different contexts. This preface reflects a lot of what I learnt in these three years.

In Antananarivo, my wife and I did not stay in any of the wealthy and gated communities used by mostly white foreigners. For three years, we rented a flat in a working-class neighbourhood, close to the shanty town of Antohomadinika, at the north-west limit of the capital. With French and English colleagues from the same NGO, we were the only white inhabitants in the area. We were lucky enough to have electricity, cold water and toilets in our flat, which was a luxury in a town where 75 per cent of the inhabitants have none of these facilities. We learned a lot from some inhabitants of Antohomadinika and Andramiarana, who had worked closely with our predecessors for years. Eventually, we delivered a collective report to the World Bank on 'The Urban Challenge in Madagascar: When Destitution Wipes Out Poverty'.[2] It was presented to a large and diverse audience, including families in extreme poverty, in October 2010, on the occasion of the International Day for the Eradication of Poverty, providing these families with a platform to voice their daily struggles and concerns.

The shantytown of Antohomadinika III G Hangar is a maze of shacks and alleys inaccessible to cars and invisible from the main road. It comprises more than 9,000 inhabitants, of whom 70 per cent are under 18 years old. Its population has increased by more than 50 per cent in 14 years. An additional estimated 10 per cent, who did not register at the city council mainly because of their poverty, should be added to this count. Most people survive on precarious and informal work, and most of the households, comprising on average six people, live in wooden shacks of between four and eight square metres with dirt floors, built on land that is flooded during the rainy season. Within their shacks, they may paddle in water for weeks. During a meeting in the area in January 2010, convened for the preparation of our report to the World Bank, a group of inhabitants shared their concerns, including Mrs Mamy who said 'When it rains, dirty water flows into the houses. Then, we put the beds up on bricks.' Most families rent their shacks and struggle to pay the landlord, leading to the constant risk of eviction. As only five public water taps are available, people have to queue for hours to bring home the buckets of water they need for the day. 'Personally, I go to the tap at 4.30 a.m. to get water, and I come back at 5.50', said Mrs Hanitra. The sanitation and waste collection are very poor: only two garbage skips and three toilet blocks, which residents must pay to use. As this area has the highest prevalence of severe food insecurity and monetary poverty in Antananarivo, few people use the toilets.

The living conditions on the garbage dump of Andramiarana, ten kilometres north of the capital, are worse still. More than 650 people stay here, making a living as waste pickers. Among them, 63 per cent are under 20 years old. Most households are homeless families who have been evicted from place to place for years, eventually ending up at the dump. All of them strive to survive in dire straits. The poorest live in shacks made of plastic bags and wood, that one can enter only on all fours. Before starting a cash transfer programme funded by UNICEF, we found out that 70 per cent of them were not registered at the city council, which means that they had no legal existence, no citizen rights, and that their children could not enrol in school. Mrs Hanta, a single mother of four living on the dump, told us in July 2009: 'The biggest injustice we suffer is ignorance. Here, people had no schooling and are abused, since they dare not confront those who are educated. We dare not and cannot voice our ideas to those who are educated. This is why we get only precarious and low paid jobs, that comply with no legal standard.'

How many tens of thousands of people throughout the world are too poor to be captured by statistics on poverty? If 'people are the real wealth of a nation', as stated in the first Human Development Report in 1990, the fact is that this wealth is too often ignored, despised and wasted.

Our proximity to these areas of extreme poverty helped us imagine the intensity of the hardship and indignity that is hidden behind a recent assessment of the Millennium Development Goals:

> The number of urban residents living in slum conditions is now estimated at some 828 million. In the developing world, it is actually growing and will continue to rise in the near future ... The practice of open defecation by 1.1 billion people is an affront to human dignity ... and the root cause of faecal-oral transmission of disease, which can have lethal consequences for the most vulnerable members of society – young children.[3]

It must be stressed that resisting such conditions of deprivation and exclusion demands a lot of resilience, which can be observed in the slums of Antananarivo. Mrs Hanta, to take one example, a dump resident quoted above, works endlessly to send her children to school so they will not end up illiterate. The intense structural violence that is embedded in inhuman and indignant living conditions could constantly erupt into brawls or riots. It rarely does, thanks to the many slum dwellers who are true peace-makers, through daily gestures that build up friendship, forgiveness and solidarity.

Thanks to my work, I had many opportunities to visit areas of extreme poverty in the islands of Madagascar and Mauritius. According to the Human Development Index, Madagascar ranks among the least developed countries, with a low human development, Mauritius among countries with a high human development.[4] I tried to understand how these countries tackle extreme poverty, and how they were impacted by the recent economic, food and environmental crisis.

In 2007, the housing bubble burst in the United States, as a result of bank behaviour based on unconsidered risks and the search for easy profits: in other words, as a result of irresponsibility and greed. Millions of lower-middle-class American households could not pay their debts and lost their houses. Their subprime mortgages, that could not be reimbursed, were classed as 'toxic assets'. In September 2008, the Lehman Brothers investment bank, that held a lot of these toxic assets, went bankrupt. However, toxic assets had been incorporated in derivatives and sold to foreign banks, causing a huge crisis of confidence. The subsequent paralysis of the global financial system became an economic and labour market crisis that plagued the world throughout 2009, forcing millions of people out of work. As jobs were lost, more workers had to resort to vulnerable forms of employment, as the ranks of the working poor swelled.

This crisis illustrates how harmful a deregulated global financial market can be, which backs what is said in Chapter 6 of this book, that the process of deregulation must be reversed. A few steps have been made by governments in this line, yet much remains to be done. As a response to this global crisis, the United Nations system launched a host of joint initiatives, including the Social Protection Floor initiative, aiming at extending at least a minimum level of social security to all, especially in developing and emerging countries. In fact, social protection measures are decisive in mitigating the impact of economic crises and responding to demands for social justice. Cash transfers have appeared as a new effective tool,[5] since they have proven successful in alleviating the poverty of tens of millions of people through renowned programmes like 'Oportunidades' in Mexico, launched in 2002, and 'Bolsa familia' in Brazil, launched in 2003. The Social Protection Floor initiative is gaining momentum, with the support of the World Bank[6] and the likely support of the European Community,[7] which has become the biggest provider of development aid in the world.

World food prices increased dramatically in 2008, causing hunger riots in around 20 countries. Since the early 1990s, many poor countries' food bills have soared five- or six-fold, owing not only to their population growth, but also to their focus on export-led agriculture. Combined with the global financial crisis, this resulted in an increase of undernourished people, whose number was estimated to exceed 1 billion in 2009.[8] Yet food prices plummeted in 2009, and spiked again in 2010. Though weather-related events – droughts, floods, tropical cyclones – are a major cause of price volatility on agricultural markets, the United Nations Special Rapporteur on the Right to Food insists that hunger is not a natural plague and does not result from a simple shortage of food at the global level.[9] Increasing industrial agricultural output alone results in more environmental damage, while food prices remain unstable, and rural poverty and hunger persist. Political causes of hunger have to be tackled, including the lack of investment in agriculture that feeds the local communities in many poor countries, the lack of regional food reserves, the massive deregulation of commodities-derivative markets that must now be reversed, the land grabs that benefit foreign markets, not local communities, and the insufficient organisation of small farmers, who should be supported to improve their bargaining position.

During our three-year stay, Madagascar was hit by several tropical cyclones that devastated parts of the east coast and claimed many lives, and by several droughts that provoked famines among peasants in the south. There is little doubt that these weather-related events are linked to climate change and to the severe deforestation of the island for decades. Around 300,000 hectares of forest are estimated to disappear each year, critically endangering many native species of its fauna and flora, much of which is unique to the island and to the world. Since February 2009, Madagascar has been in the throes of a political crisis that has led to a decline in economic activity, exacerbated by the negative impact of the global financial crisis on export-oriented activities. Yet, an exceptional rice harvest in 2009, up by 40 per cent from the preceding year, proved the resilience of agriculture.

As people in extreme poverty live in a situation of constant crisis, it is sometimes believed that one more economic or political crisis makes no difference. Not in Madagascar. The loss of thousands of formal jobs pushed workers into the informal labour market, increasing competition to the detriment of the less skilled and those in poor health, whose small earnings decreased. The same occurred for the waste-pickers of Andramiarana: the closing of factories that disposed of their waste on the dump led to a decrease in recycling, and a decrease in recyclers' earnings, that has hardly enabled them to survive.

Each time I took the plane and landed in Mauritius, a tropical archipelago of 1.3 million people, 800 kilometres east of Madagascar, I was struck by the incredible difference between the two countries. All the more incredible since Madagascar was said to be wealthier 50 years before. Nobel Prize economist Joseph E. Stiglitz recently pointed out some factors of 'The Mauritius Miracle'.[10] First, its people have spent the last decades successfully building a diverse economy, a democratic political system, and a strong social safety net. Second, unlike most countries, Mauritius has decided that most military spending is a waste: it has no army, only a few coastguards and a police force. This makes a capture of the state by the elite much more difficult, and saves money to invest in people, since the small island has few exploitable natural resources. Third, given its potential religious, ethnic and political differences, the country invested in two crucial fields for social unity; a strong commitment to democratic institutions and cooperation between workers, government and employers, and education for all. This is not to say that Mauritius is without problems, or without poverty. According to the National Empowerment Foundation, 229 pockets of poverty remain, with 7,000 families surviving in dire poverty. However, the proportion of young illiterate people in Mauritius (5 per cent) is six-fold smaller than it is in Madagascar (30 per cent). Less than 1 per cent of the population is deemed to live in extreme poverty. The extent of the problems in its larger neighbour, Madagascar, is far from inevitable, and concerted action on all fronts, and by all actors, could remediate it.

In the field of research, a significant trend of 'rethinking poverty' has appeared for some time. The UN Department of Economic and Social Affairs (DESA) contends that current poverty measurements are problematic and controversial, and urges going beyond the dollar-a-day poverty line, that ignores non-monetary factors such as deprivation, vulnerability and exclusion. Although the world has made considerable progress in reducing poverty since 1990, the progress has been very uneven, with China and East Asia accounting for most of it. DESA urges promoting structural transformation to bring about 'inclusive development' that benefits all citizens, including poor people.[11] Tools for the measurement of poverty have continued to improve, with the design of new multidimensional indices, among which is the multidimensional poverty index, which considers multiple deprivations and their overlap at household level, including health, schooling and living conditions. In 2010, half of the world's multidimensionally poor lived in South Asia (844 million people) and more than a quarter in Africa (458 million).[12]

Yet, if we really are to combat poverty, we need to redefine wealth and prosperity as well, and to question the primacy of economic growth at all costs. Tim Jackson, the economics commissioner on the UK government's Sustainable Development Commission, makes the case for 'Prosperity without Growth',[13] arguing that if the idea of a non-growing economy may be anathema to an economist, the idea of a continually growing economy is anathema to an ecologist, since we live in a finite planet. Improving our wellbeing in a sustainable way implies moving away from consumerism and valuing a type of prosperity which encourages simpler ways of living, investing in relationships and the meaning of our lives.

The debate amongst economists about the ways to fight global poverty, broached in Chapter 6, has moved away from the controversy between defenders and adversaries of foreign aid. A new type of economic research on poverty has emerged, shifting from looking for universal answers to more limited and concrete problems, through randomised controlled trials. Esther Duflo and

Abhijit V. Banerjee, of Harvard University, who together founded the Poverty Action Lab in 2003, are prominent figures in this new approach.[14] They focus on the world's poorest, contending that poor people are just like the rest of us in almost every way, having the same desires and weaknesses, but not the same possibilities to reach their goals: 'The poor are not less rational than anyone else, quite the contrary. They have to be sophisticated economists, just to survive.' The authors considered the challenges poor households face in escaping their condition, and listened to them about what they thought, they did or wanted to do. They rigorously assessed anti-poverty programmes that worked, or not, in areas including education, health and governance, comparing costs and benefits. They make clear that development is a very complex and slow process, requiring patience and humility, where 'hope is vital, and knowledge critical'.

I suggest that the methodology we used to write the four life stories, in Part One of this book, is as rigorous as that of the Poverty Action Lab, and that both are complementary. Obviously, the role of practitioners is to take action with people trapped in chronic poverty, not to run randomised controlled trials which they are not trained for. Yet practitioners are also researchers, trying to find out the most effective ways to help people move out of extreme poverty. People living in extreme poverty are also researchers, as we all are, in striving to improve their lives and, still more, those of their children. Evidence exists that the cross-fertilisation of knowledge does not lead to less rigour or a less scientific approach; quite the contrary.[15]

If we are to eradicate extreme poverty, there need to be changes in local, national and global governance so that the knowledge of the slum dwellers in Antohomadinika, Andramiarana and elsewhere around the world is taken into account. As this book demonstrates, they challenge us to implement personal, professional and institutional change, towards a governance where decision-making is centred on real participation of people in extreme poverty, and goals are centred on the eradication of extreme poverty.

NOTES

1. For more information visit www.atd-fourthworld.org/
2. Mouvement ATD Quart Monde, *Le défi urbain à Madagascar. Quand la misère chasse la pauvreté*, Antananarivo: ATD Quart Monde, 2010.
3. United Nations, *The Millenium Development Goals Report, 2010*, New York: United Nations, pp. 61, 62.

4. United Nations Development Programme, *Human Development Report 2010*, New York: UNDP, 2010, pp. 143–5.

5. Joseph Hanlon, David Hulme and Armando Barrientos, *Just Give Money to the Poor: The Development Revolution from the Global South*, London: Kumarian Press, 2010.

6. The World Bank, *Building Resilience and Opportunity: The World Bank's Social Protection and Labour Strategy 2012–2022*, Concept Note, May 2011.

7. Robert Schuman Centre for Advanced Studies, European University Institute, San Domenico di Fiesole, *European Report on Development 2010*, Florence: European Communities, 2010.

8. United Nations, *The Millenium Development Goals Report, 2010*, p. 11.

9. See the website of Olivier de Schutter, United Nations Special Rapporteur on the Right to Food, www.srfood.org/.

10. Joseph E. Stiglitz, *The Mauritius Miracle*, article appearing on *Project Syndicate*, 7 March 2011, www.project-syndicate.org/commentary/stiglitz136/English.

11. United Nations, Department of Economic and Social Affairs, *Rethinking Poverty : Report on the World Social Situation 2010*, New York: United Nations, 2010.

12. United Nations Development Programme, *Human Development Report 2010*, pp. 7–8.

13. Tim Jackson, *Prosperity Without Growth: Economics For a Finite Planet*, Earthscan, 2009.

14. Esther Duflo and Abhijit V. Banerjee, *Poor Economics: A Radical Rethinking of the Way to Fight Global Poverty*, New York: Public Affairs, 2011. This approach is also implemented by Dean Karlan and Jacob Appel, *More Than Good Intentions: How a New Economics is Helping to Solve Global Poverty*, New York: Dutton, 2011.

15. Fourth World – University Research Group, *The Merging of Knowledge: People in Poverty and Academics Thinking Together*, Lanham, MD: University Press of America, 2007.

Foreword

Christopher Winship
Diker-Tishman Professor of Sociology, Harvard University

The economic crisis of 2008–10 should be sufficient to wholly undermine the neoliberal belief in the superiority and infallibility of markets. Behind the often almost religiously held belief of the neoliberals are two key assumptions:

- the autonomous nature of the individual as an actor
- that a free market, unencumbered by regulations, is the most efficient and effective way to organise society.

Long before 2008, however, there were vehement criticisms of neoliberalism. These focused almost exclusively on the neoliberal belief in the superiority of the market, not on the neoliberal concept of the individual. The accusation, often repeated, has been that pure market structures necessarily lead to unacceptable levels of economic inequality and leave vast number of individuals in economic poverty.

Eradicating Extreme Poverty tells the story of four families and their valiant struggle to deal with poverty. The stories come from four parts of the world: Burkina Faso in Africa, France in Europe, Peru in Latin America and the Philippines in Asia. Despite the diverse locales, these stories have much in common.

First, and most obvious, is the severity of the economic destitution that they experience. In each case, families are struggling from one day to the next to meet their basic needs.

Second, although their experiences are different in important ways, all these families are severely challenged in trying to manage their day-to-day lives. They are simultaneously embedded in a complex and demanding network of relationships with other individuals who, like them, are excluded from mainstream society. There are no well-off extended family members or friends who can, or will, help these families manage their lives.

Third, there is the constant concern of respect. More accurately, there is a lack of the respect and recognition that these families hunger for, but are denied by their broader societies. Although their struggles against poverty are impressive and valiant, society writ large sees them as living lazy and immoral lives. More generally, they are simply not considered worthy human beings.

Why are the stories of the four families important? Obviously, they deserve our empathy and concern. But what is to be learned? In Part Two, Xavier Godinot argues that we need to understand extreme poverty in a deeper and more comprehensive way. Importantly, what these stories illustrate is that poverty is not just a matter of economic destitution, but also of social exclusion and denial of respect. Although the economic woes of the poor are a considerable challenge, society as a whole neither thinks that they are worthy of help nor that they should be recognised for the considerable efforts they expend attempting to create viable lives for themselves and their families.

So what constitutes being in extreme poverty? For organisations like the UN or the World Bank, individuals are in extreme poverty if they are living on less than some minimal amount. The figure 'less than $1.00 a day' is often used. The Millennium Development Goals specify the threshold as $1.25 in 2005 dollars. Obviously, this definition is purely economic. If we were to look back hundreds of years ago, much of the world by this definition was living in extreme poverty.

In *Eradicating Extreme Poverty*, Xavier Godinot defines extreme poverty as being both economically destitute and suffering from social exclusion (with the associated loss of respect and recognition). Although the idea of poverty as social exclusion has gained much currency in liberal policy circles in Britain in recent years,[1] and is currently receiving increased attention in the US, ATD Fourth World (of which Godinot is a member) and its founder, Joseph Wresinski, have been arguing since the 1960s that poverty needs to be understood not just as a problem of economic deprivation, but also – and fundamentally – as a problem of social exclusion and lack of recognition.

Why is this important?

A useful place to look for an answer is to the work of the German philosopher, Axel Honneth, and his seminal work *The Struggle for Recognition: The Moral Grammar of Conflicts*.[2] In this book, he builds on the early work of Hegel and the famous American sociologist George Herbert Mead. Honneth develops an extended argument that the need for social recognition is a primary, if not *the*, core need of humans, and it is the lack of social recognition, that is, respect, that is at the heart of most social conflict. In making his argument he focuses his criticism on the conception of the individual in philosophical liberalism – roughly that individuals can be understood as autonomous moral agents. For Honneth (as originally for Mead), the self is intersubjectively understood. We understand who we are in and through our relationships with others.

The roots of philosophical liberalism go back at least to the Renaissance. It is commonly associated with writings of Kant, Locke, and John Stuart Mill. By a wide margin, its assumptions underlie most present-day Western philosophical and political thought. It is, however, distinctly different from neoliberalism. In fact, many individuals who would subscribe to philosophical liberalism would strongly reject neoliberalism's assumption about the superiority of markets. However, philosophical liberalism does share with neoliberalism the assumption about the autonomy of individuals.

In the last several decades, philosophical liberalism has come under sharp attack from a group of philosophers known as communitarians. Prominent names are Charles Taylor, Alasdair McIntyre, Michael Walzer, and Michael Sandel. Sandel's book *Liberalism and the Limits of Justice*[3] provides that definite critique of philosophical liberalism.

More important to *Eradicating Extreme Poverty* is Charles Taylor's work on the self and the importance of recognition. In *Sources of the Self*,[4] Taylor argues that our identities are deeply moral; that, in essence, to understand who we are is to understand ourselves as moral beings. Key to being a moral self is the recognition by others that one is a worthy human being – exactly what individuals and families in extreme poverty are denied. As Taylor states in his justly famous article 'The Politics of Recognition', 'Due recognition is not just a courtesy we owe people. It is a vital human need.'[5]

What we see is that in the context of Honneth's work, and communitarianism thought more generally, *Eradicating Extreme Poverty* provides a more basic and deeper criticism of neoliberal thought. The standard criticism of neoliberalism focuses on its complete belief in the superiority of markets. *Eradicating Eextreme Poverty*, and indirectly Honneth and more generally communitarianism, argue that in addition neoliberalism has grossly misunderstood the nature of man. Rather than conceiving of humans as autonomous individuals, they need to be understood as essentially social. As such, poverty involves not just a lack of the necessary material resources needed to survive, but also the social resources – or more accurately put, the social relationships – needed to live a full and dignified life.

Does the broader conception of poverty described in *Eradicating Extreme Poverty* have policy implications? First and foremost, it indicates the insufficiency of standard economic approaches to alleviating poverty: food stamps, housing vouchers, clothing drives or simple cash transfers. Although such responses may help alleviate the material deprivation of the poor, they do nothing to end their social exclusion or experience of indignity. They may, in fact, accentuate these problems by creating the social stigma of being seen as a person 'in need'. As Joseph Wresinski, who grew up in extreme poverty, often said of his mother – 'she had no friends, only benefactors'.

The question of how to deal with poverty as social exclusion in terms of policy represents a significant challenge. Glenn Loury provides an in-depth analysis of the issues involved, not just in the context of poverty, but also race, in his book, *The Anatomy of Racial Inequality*.[6] Loury focuses his book on Erving Goffman's notion of 'stigma', the concept that one has a 'spoiled' identity. His concern is that discrimination can result from a stigmatised identity.

Loury distinguishes between two types of discrimination: 'discrimination in contract' versus 'discrimination in contact'. He argues that government and specifically legal intervention works best when the issue is 'discrimination in contract' – the failure of institutions and people to abide by formal laws in areas such as employment, housing, and voting. When the issue is 'discrimination in contact' – that is, the stigmatisation of their identity and resulting social exclusion – the problem is considerably more difficult. How is government to legislate on who one's friends are, who one has to dinner, or more generally to accept as a member of one's social circle? Here what is needed is as much a change in the attitude of the non-poor as in their behaviour. Certainly, policies that prevent discrimination in areas such as employment and housing are helpful in that they make it illegal to exclude others in the most transparent and obvious ways. However, they fail to ensure in any way that the poor (or minorities) are given the respect and dignity they deserve and need.

Eradicating Extreme Poverty certainly does not provide the last word on the nature of extreme poverty, much less definitive policy proposals for how it can be eradicated. It does, however, through the four stories it offers, provide us with insights into the complicated and difficult lives of those living in extreme poverty.

Most importantly, it shows us how those living in extreme poverty are socially excluded and the consequences in terms of denied recognition and dignity of extreme poverty. This is important, for it is in understanding the lives of others that a basis is formed for creating an inclusive community. Shared stories as such are a critical part of the democratic project. All humans have not just political rights – to participate in the political and civic structure of their communities, and economic rights – to have the opportunity to achieve a viable standard of living. They also have social rights – to be included as full members of the community as a whole.

Although a just society must demonstrate political and economic solidarity, there also must be social solidarity – where all are included and given due recognition and dignity.

NOTES

1. For example, see *The Politics of Inclusion and Empowerment*, ed. J. Andersen and B. Siim, New York: Palgrave, and in particular, Ruth Lister's essay therein.
2. Axel Honneth, *The Struggle for Recognition: The Moral Grammar of Social Conflicts*, Cambridge, MA: MIT Press, 1996.
3. Michael Sandel, *Liberalism and the Limits of Justice*, New York: Cambridge University Press, 1998.
4. Charles Taylor, *Sources of the Self: The Making of the Modern Identity*, Cambridge, MA: Harvard University Press, 1989.
5. Charles Taylor, 'The Politics of Recognition', in Amy Gutmann (ed.), *Multiculturalism and The Politics of Recognition*, Princeton: Princeton University Press, 1992, p. 26.
6. Glenn Loury, *The Anatomy of Racial Inequality*, Cambridge, MA: Harvard University Press, 2002.

Acknowledgements

To all those who made this book possible, I wish to express my gratitude. First and foremost, to Eugen Brand, Bruno Couder and Susie Devins for their support over a period of four years. Sincere thanks to Yvette Boissarie, Angela Cady, Andrew Hayes and Bruno Langlais who worked regularly on the project for two years.

PART ONE

The four accounts were originally written in different contexts. The versions published here have been edited and abridged. Names of people and places have been changed to protect the privacy of the individuals featured in the stories.

The World Bank commissioned the Research Institute of ATD Fourth World to contribute to *Moving Out of Poverty* – a research study which aimed to identify the processes at work in the lives of the families faced with extreme poverty.

The first versions of the monographs on Burkina Faso and Peru were financed by the Belgian Poverty Reduction Partnership Programme and the World Bank in 2004 and 2005, thanks to the efforts of Patti Petesh, Deepa Narayan and Quentin Wodon.[1]

The Story of Paul in Burkina Faso was written by Patricia and Claude Heyberger, with the assistance of Paul S, Bruno Bambara, Professeur Amadé Badini and Guillaume Charvon.

The Story of the Rojas Paucar Family in Peru was written by Rosario Macedo de Ugarte and Marco Aurelio Ugarte, with the help of Alicia Paucar, Benigno Rojas, Marguerita, Laura, Miguel and Fernando, Anne-Claire Brand, Jean-Marie Anglade and Cristina Diez.

The Story of Mercedita and her Family in the Philippines was written by Marilyn Gutierrez, with the collaboration of Mercedita Villar Diaz-Mendez, Maritess, Juanito, Roselina, Rowena and Rosana, Alasdair Wallace and Andrew Hayes. She was the subject of a book published in that country in October 2006.[2]

The Story of Farid, Céline and Karim in France and Algeria was written by Floriane Caravatta, with contributions by Farid and

Céline Koffic, Gérard Bureau and Sophie Muguet, specifically for this publication. It was completed at the end of 2007.

ENGLISH EDITION

Project coordinator: Matt Davies
Translation: Angela Cady and Andrew Hayes
Editor: Judith Stone
Proofreading: Angela Cady, Charlotte Spring and Detrich Peeler

SEMINARS

My thanks go to Deepa Narayan, Patti L. Petesch and Professeurs Christopher Winship, Amadé Badini and Nicolas Lynch for their comments on the first drafts of the monographs during the seminar organised in Méry sur Oise (France) in October 2004.

Special thanks go to Luca Barbone and Quentin Wodon, who organised the seminar *Attacking Extreme Poverty* at the World Bank in Washington in October 2005, during which the monographs on Burkina Faso and Peru were presented.

Special thanks also to Jean-Michel Séverino and Joseph Zimet, who organised the seminar *Extrême pauvreté et développement* at the Agence Française de Développement in Paris in June 2006, during which the monographs on Burkina Faso and Peru were presented.

PROOFREADING

Sincere thanks to Thierry Viard, who coordinated the proofreading of the final version, and to all those who made contributions or helped with the proofreading: Lovelaine Basillotte, Valérie Brunner, Gérard Bureau, Alberto Chavarro, Ronan Claure, Françoise Coré, Régis De Muylder, Cristina Diez, Michel Faucon, Daniel Fayard, Elena Flores, Catherine Fotiadi, Wouter Van Ginneken, Jean-Pierre Gollé, Michèle Grenot, Elisa Hamel, Paul Harris, Sarah Kenningham, Christian Miranda and Janet Nelson.

EDITING OF ENGLISH EDITION

Special thanks to Judith Stone who worked tirelessly to edit the English version for publication and without whose help this edition would not have been accomplished.

NOTES

1. International Movement ATD Fourth World, with the support of the Belgian Poverty Reduction Partnership Programme and the World Bank, *Contribution to the Moving Out of Poverty Study: Family Monographs from Burkina Faso and Peru*, Fourth World Publications, 2005.
2. Marilyn Gutierrez, *Gold Under the Bridge: A Story of Life in the Slums*, Anvil publishing, Manila, 2006.

Introduction:
Insecurity, Poverty and Extreme Poverty

Xavier Godinot

I am one of those who believe and affirm that it is possible to destroy extreme poverty.
Make good note, I am not saying 'reduce', 'lessen', 'limit', or 'control', I am saying 'destroy'. Extreme poverty is a disease of the social body in the same way leprosy is a disease of the human body. Extreme poverty can disappear just as leprosy has disappeared. Yes, it is possible to destroy extreme poverty.

(Victor Hugo, addressing the Legislative Assembly, 9 July 1849[1])

Eradicating extreme poverty may appear to be an extraordinarily naive or pretentious goal in a world where 925 million people suffer from hunger, 1 billion people do not have access to clean water, 900 million adults do not know how to read or write, 100 million children of primary school age do not attend school. Nevertheless, it is reaffirmed repeatedly in major international documents.

The preamble to the 1948 Universal Declaration of Human Rights says:

> The advent of a world in which human beings shall enjoy freedom of speech and beliefs and freedom from fear and want has been proclaimed as the highest aspiration of the common people ...

The Millennium Declaration, adopted by 180 heads of state and government at the General Assembly of the United Nations in September 2000, makes this commitment:

> We will spare no effort to free our fellow men, women and children from the abject and dehumanising conditions of extreme poverty, to which more than a billion of them are currently subjected.

Eradicating extreme poverty has been held up as an ideal for centuries. What is new is that we now have the material means to realise this ambition; the United Nations Development Programme continues to declare that extreme poverty could be eradicated within one generation. At the same time, new risks of economic and social hardship and pauperisation have appeared, including the AIDS pandemic and climate change, all of which threaten populations in less developed countries in particular.[2]

The economic and financial crisis has led the World Bank to estimate that about 40 million more people became hungry in 2009 and 64 million more people were living in extreme poverty by the end of 2010.

SUSTAINABLE DEVELOPMENT

The eradication of extreme poverty is part of a search for a more just, equitable and sustainable development model. The Brundtland report, published in 1987, now a worldwide authority, gives this definition:

> Sustainable development is a development that meets the needs of the present without compromising the ability of future generations to meet their own needs.

The follow-up to this definition, adopted by the international community in Agenda 21 at the Rio Conference in 1992, is less well known:

> Two concepts are inherent in this notion: the concept of 'needs', in particular the essential needs of the world's poor, to which overriding priority should be given, and the idea of limitations imposed by the state of technology and social organisation on the environment's ability to meet present and future needs.

Themes for the Rio+20 Conference in June 2012 include a focus on the green economy in the context of sustainable development and the eradication of poverty.

'Another world is possible' declares the alter-globalisation movement. This search for an alternative development model involves scientific knowledge and technical and political progress; it asks fundamental questions about where our priorities lie and our attitude to our natural and human environment. Today, a better perception of the damages and risks of climate change is encouraging a growing awareness of how our individual and collective behaviour must change with regard to our natural environment. In the same way, better knowledge of the damages and risks of economic and social insecurity and poverty could lead to greater awareness of how we must change our individual and collective behaviour towards people living in those situations.

AN ENCOUNTER WITH EXTREME POVERTY

A United Nations report insisted that any serious approach to extreme poverty, and to those who experience it, must be based on an initial, fundamental observation:

> The poor make up a sector of the population we know nothing about; worse, we do not know how little we know. If we are forced to it, we have to acknowledge how hard we have tried not to know. The huge walls around the suburbs in many of the world's great metropolises (which, by the way, cost far more than the countless dwellings they conceal are worth) show it.[3]

Encountering extreme poverty is always a shock. In 1958, Geneviève de Gaulle Anthonioz was invited to visit the emergency housing camp at Noisy-le-Grand near Paris by Father Joseph Wresinski. More than two hundred and fifty families awaiting housing had been living there for several years in 'igloos' – fibrocement shelters with rounded roofs. Her personal account relates it to her own experience in a Nazi extermination camp.

> When I first entered this huge shanty town at the end of a mud path, I thought of that other camp, Ravensbrück ... This landscape of low, corrugated iron roofs, from which grey smoke rose, was a separate world, removed from everyday life. On their faces, the inhabitants wore the signs of distress which I knew so well and which, no doubt, had been my own. At his request, a family opened the door of its 'igloo' to Father Joseph who introduced me to them. In the darkness, I saw the sad and weary eyes of the father, who brought forward two boxes for us to sit on. The mother appeared from the back of the room carrying a small baby in her arms. She was young and attractive despite her thinning hair... It was really very cold, more so than outside, and I was astonished to hear Father Joseph ask them for a cup of coffee for us. How could he do this when surrounded by such destitution? The children disappeared while the water was boiling and came back quickly carrying two glasses holding coffee

and sugar. We drank our coffee by the glow of a candle set in a bottle ... We took our leave, thanking them for the coffee, and I could not help thinking about the small ration of bread we used to share in Ravensbrück. 'What is worse than not being able to give anything', said Father Joseph, 'is that you are never asked for anything.'[4]

Geneviève de Gaulle Anthonioz tries to make the reader understand the extent to which her entire being was shaken to its foundations by her encounter with extreme poverty and its victims. Her senses were assaulted by the sight of children and adults in extreme destitution, the cold that seized hold of her, the cries and lamentations that filled the chapel for the funeral of two children who had been burnt alive in their igloo, the unbearable odour of bodies and the bitter taste of a coffee that had to be begged from the neighbours.

Economic growth is said to be the solution to extreme poverty, yet this was happening in an economically-booming industrialised country.

POVERTY AND EXTREME POVERTY

It is important to distinguish between *poverty* and *extreme poverty* without setting one against the other. We will examine two approaches:

- poverty as a deprivation of basic capabilities, as maintained by Amartya Sen
- poverty as a violation of human rights, as argued by Joseph Wresinski.

Poverty as a Deprivation of Basic Capabilities

Amartya Sen, winner of the Nobel Prize for Economics in 1998, has had a lifelong interest in extreme poverty and famine. He believes that 'economic unfreedom, in the form of extreme poverty, can make a person a helpless prey in the violation of other kinds of freedom'.[5]

Born in Bengal, at the time a part of British India, Sen lived with his family in Dhaka, today the capital of Bangladesh. He describes seeing the 1943 famine in Bengal during which, according to present-day estimates, approximately 3 million people died:

It was a terrible ordeal which occurred so suddenly that I was unable to understand it.

I was nine years old at the time and a pupil at a rural Bengali school. Among the people that I knew at school and their families, there were no visible signs of distress, but, in fact, as I would discover thirty years later when I studied the famine, the majority of the population of Bengal experienced little deprivation during the entire period of the famine.

One morning, a very thin man appeared at our school; he was behaving strangely, which – as I would learn later – is a common symptom of long-term food deprivation. He had come from a distant village looking for something to eat, and he was wandering about in the hope of finding some help. During the days that followed, tens, thousands and then an endless procession of people passed through our village, emaciated beings with hollow cheeks and wild staring eyes, many of whom were carrying children in their arms who were nothing more than skin and bones ...

Later studies revealed that the total amount of food available in Bengal at the time was not particularly low. Therefore, it was utterly intolerable to have had to witness this degree of social failure. Those who died did not have the means to obtain the food that, nevertheless, was there.[6]

Sen based the innovative concept of 'basic capability' on the observation that they did not have the ability to gain access to the food that was available.[7] He believes that 'poverty should be understood as a deprivation of basic capabilities'.[8]

Sen is interested in the real opportunities that individuals have to live the life they want. He first considers the 'primary goods' that an individual has at his disposal – income, education, health, civil liberties, and so on. All of these constitute a means to help him to pursue his goals freely.[9]

However, these primary goods are not necessarily a measure of a person's liberty or wellbeing. Human beings differ greatly from each other in terms of age, energy, gender, physical needs, vulnerability to illness, tastes, the environment in which they live, and so on. Given the diversity of ways in which people convert primary goods into the freedom to pursue their respective goals, these goods cannot be used to measure the full extent of this freedom.

Instead of focusing on the resources that individuals have at their disposal, the analysis must focus on the actual lives that individuals may choose to live – namely the different methods of 'human functioning' and the varying degrees of importance individuals may attach to them. Some methods of functioning are very basic, such as being well fed and in good health; others are more complex, such as having self-respect. Some people will be more materialistic, attached to having material goods; others will be more spiritual, more interested in having time for meditation and contemplation.

Therefore, in order to define the real opportunity that an individual has to live the life that he chooses, not only must the primary goods that he owns be taken into account, but also his way of functioning. The wealthy person who decides to fast has the same level of nutrition as a person who is reduced to famine. However, the former may choose to eat a little, a lot, or even to gorge himself on food, choices which do not exist for the latter. The capability of the former is high, whereas the capability of the latter is non-existent. Therefore, it is not possible for the person living in poverty to be fulfilled according to his own goals.

Sen believes that the attention given to inadequate incomes in the debate on poverty masks other forms of deprivation. He questions the validity of income thresholds or nutritional requirements as a criterion for evaluating the degree of poverty or malnutrition. The variability of people's needs, and the differences in their capabilities for transforming a financial or nutritional resource into wellbeing, makes it impossible to standardise an evaluation. Working with Mahbub ul-Haq at the United Nations Development Programme in the 1990s, they created a new indicator – the human development index (HDI) – designed as an alternative to the gross national product (GNP), which had been used as the principal indicator until then.

Extreme Poverty as a Violation of Human Rights

In the winter of 1954, Abbé Pierre revealed to France and Europe that a huge population of 'homeless people' were in danger of dying of cold. Father Joseph Wresinski decided to live among the camp families in Noisy-le-Grand, Paris, until they were all re-housed. When he arrived there in July 1956, he had the impression of 'entering into evil'.

Social workers and political and trade union activists saw nothing but 'welfare cases', 'social misfits' and even 'social outcasts' in the emergency housing camp; Wresinski felt that he was dealing with a population whose historical identity had been ignored.[10] He identified with them because he had also known extreme poverty throughout his own childhood. With them, he created the 'Action, Culture and Re-housing Group for the Provincials of the Paris

Region', which later became the International Movement ATD Fourth World.

In 1960, with Alwine de Vos Van Steenwijk, a Dutch diplomat on assignment in Paris, he created the ATD Fourth World Research Institute. There was 'an atmosphere of general incomprehension' because – with the exception of the United Kingdom – research on poverty in Europe was almost non-existent at the time.[11] The institute carried out research and organised international seminars, publishing the book *L'exclusion sociale* in 1965.[12]

Rather than viewing them as misfits, Wresinski increasingly used the concept of social exclusion to describe a cultural process of sidelining poverty-stricken people.[13] The European Commission and then the International Labour Organisation adopted the concept. Sociologists started to use the term at the beginning of the 1990s to characterise the change or breakdown in ties that link the individual to the community and give him the means to access his fundamental rights.

The sociologist Manuel Castells gives this definition of social exclusion:

the process by which certain individuals and groups are systematically barred from access to situations that would enable them to earn an autonomous livelihood according to the values and the social standards formulated by institutions in a given context.[14]

Serge Paugam prefers the concept of social disqualification, which highlights the stigmatisation and humiliation of people confined to welfare, as well as their resistance to this situation, within an overall context of a lack of employment security and the weakening of social ties.[15]

The heritage of poverty

In the 1960s, the work of the Research Institute on the persistence of extreme poverty in France helped to verify the hypothesis that it was a heritage of the past. In fact, most of the families relegated to the emergency housing camps of the Paris region had not fallen into extreme poverty but had always lived in extreme poverty.[16]

Joseph Wresinski became convinced that in order to place a disqualified population – the target of indifference and contempt – at the heart of the world's concerns, it was necessary to show that extreme poverty was a negation of the great ideas of humanity and a violation of human rights. In 1969, he invented the term 'Fourth World' to give a name to an underprivileged population in rich countries and to allow that population to be identified as an active participant.[17]

Wresinski petitioned French, European and international authorities relentlessly. In February 1987, the French Economic and Social Council adopted the report *Chronic Poverty and Lack of Basic Security*, now often referred to as the Wresinski Report. On 20 February 1987, he made a statement during the 43rd session of the United Nations Commission on Human Rights in Geneva,[18] paving the way for two decades of work. This concluded with the adoption of *Draft Guiding Principles on Extreme Poverty and Human Rights*[19] by the sub-commission on human rights in August 2006. Also, based on the Wresinski Report, in 1994 the Council of Europe initiated a project entitled *Human Dignity and Social Exclusion*, which led to the adoption in 1998 of a report proposing guidelines for an intersectoral approach to social rights by Member States.[20]

MEASURING EXTREME POVERTY

In the wake of the Wresinski report, the French Economic and Social Council adopted this definition of insecurity or deprivation and extreme poverty:

> A lack of basic security is the absence of one or more factors that enable individuals and families to assume basic responsibilities and to enjoy fundamental rights. Such a situation may become more extended and lead to more serious and permanent consequences. Chronic poverty results when the lack of basic security simultaneously affects several aspects of people's lives, when it is prolonged, and when it severely compromises people's chances of regaining their rights and of reassuming their responsibilities in the foreseeable future.[21]

This definition is still used as a reference in many research projects on economic and social insecurity and poverty.[22] It has the advantage of defining both the condition of extreme poverty and the process that leads to it, without pitting those suffering from insecurity against those suffering from extreme poverty. Rather, it makes clear that they are both victims of the same process of exclusion.

Statisticians, who attempt to understand *insecurity*, the *accumulation of insecurities* or *multiple deprivation* and the *persistence* of poverty among households, question the relevance of the commonly used monetary evaluations of poverty. In particular, they show that the annual income declared by households is disconcertingly unstable in the short term and cannot be used as a reliable indicator of the annual movement into and out of poverty.[23] Many organisations are now attempting to implement multidimensional approaches to poverty.[24]

In view of this research, the major failings of present-day evaluations of poverty are evident. Eurostat, the European Union's statistical body, uses a relative monetary poverty indicator, evaluated on the basis of income level: below 60 per cent of the median national income, a household is said to be poor.[25] This hybrid indicator, which is 'not really a poverty indicator or an indicator of inequality',[26] remains unchanged if the income of all is doubled during a period of prosperity or halved during a period of recession. According to Amartya Sen, this type of indicator shows, quite simply, that poverty cannot be eradicated and that programmes designed to combat poverty can never really succeed.[27]

For developing countries, the World Bank uses an absolute poverty indicator evaluated according to a level of consumption: the ability to buy a supply of essential goods (food, clothes) to which is added a set of essential services (housing, transport, etc.). The poverty threshold is set at $2 per person per day with the extreme poverty threshold set at $1.25 per person per day. Between 1990 and 2005, the number of people throughout the world living on less than $1.25 a day fell from 1.8 billion to 1.4 billion.[28] However, the bank acknowledged that 'there is no certainty that an international poverty line measures the same degree of need or deprivation across countries'.[29] In June 2007, the United Nations announced that 'new measures of the relative cost of living among various countries will require a revision of the international poverty line and may change our understanding of the extent and distribution of global poverty'.[30]

A further limit to most present day statistical analyses is that they do not include the most marginalised populations. They only count households living in standard housing, automatically excluding homeless populations as well as people living in community housing, shelters, prisons, psychiatric hospitals, retirement homes, and so on, as well as illegal immigrants. Yet, many of the poorest households are among these population groups.[31]

DEFINING EXTREME POVERTY

When defining poverty, Amartya Sen employs the concepts of the individual and liberty. Wresinski employs the concepts of person, family and human dignity; people exist within a family or other groups that constitute the centre of their identity. Their dignity requires them to assume their responsibilities and to enjoy their fundamental rights. In June 1996, the United Nations Commission on Human Rights accepted the approach of the Wresinski Report when it adopted Leandro Despouy's final report on human rights and extreme poverty which said that extreme poverty was 'the new face of apartheid'.[32] This report also affirmed that:

> this accumulation of misfortunes and deficiencies in health, education, housing, participation, etc., which continually plagues the lives of those enduring extreme poverty, has a precise and clearly defined name in standard legal terminology: absolute denial of the most fundamental human rights.

The relationship between Wresinski's definition and the one given by Eugène Buret a century and a half earlier is striking. In his survey on extreme poverty among working classes in England and France in the nineteenth century, Buret writes:

> Poverty represents a condition of non-satisfaction of a series of needs, extreme poverty, a non-satisfaction of needs which, when extended over a period of time, leads to suffering, ill-health and, sometimes, even death... We will use the term extreme poverty to describe extreme hardship that requires the assistance of public or private charity. According to us, man is suffering from extreme poverty when he is no longer able to bear his own poverty and that of his loved ones, when he is in danger of collapsing under its weight if nobody comes to his assistance.[33]

Both definitions make much of the continuity between poverty and extreme poverty and highlight the three main characteristics of extreme poverty. These are:

- an accumulation of deprivation in several areas of life
- the persistence of this situation makes the effects devastating by weakening the person concerned and reducing their capacity for autonomy

- people are unable to gain access to their fundamental rights or to assume their responsibilities without external help.

These two definitions present the archetype of an impoverished human being as someone who has nothing, who is nothing and who has nobody on whom they can rely. They have nothing, because, over time, they have accumulated insecurities in all areas of their life. They are nothing, in their own eyes and in the eyes of others, because they are incapable of assuming their responsibilities. There is nobody to pay them respect and help them to gain access to their rights.

Wresinski explains:

> What he is unable to accept, despite everything, is being shamed. 'We are not very much, we are poor people, but we are not animals.' It is in order to avoid being shamed that, little by little, the person who has fallen victim to extreme poverty breaks off contact with the world around him.[34]

MATERIAL POVERTY AND SOCIAL EXCLUSION

Sen and Wresinski developed complex and multidimensional approaches to poverty and extreme poverty that influence each other. This can be seen in the United Nations Development Programme's 2000 Human Development Report, entitled *Human Rights and Human Development* which was inspired by Sen's ideas on development and considers poverty to be a denial of human rights.

However, Sen mainly employs the concept of poverty, and Wresinski that of extreme poverty. Are these terms indistinguishable? There is constant confusion between them. The heads of state present at the Copenhagen Social Summit in 1995 undertook to 'eradicate poverty', whereas those at the Millennium Summit in 2000 simultaneously affirmed the wish to 'free our fellow men from extreme poverty' and 'create a climate favourable to development and the eradication of poverty'.

There are strong arguments in favour of making a clear distinction between poverty and extreme poverty.

Relative Poverty and Extreme Poverty
Relative poverty

The first argument emphasises the difference in nature between relative poverty and absolute poverty. Sen recalled some of the important steps in the debate on this subject between economists and sociologists in industrialised countries over more than a century.[35]

In the United Kingdom at the end of the nineteenth century, the work of Benjamin Seebohm Rowntree on the domestic consumption budgets of poor households in York, and that of Charles Booth in London, led them to define absolute poverty levels according to a basket of food goods and non-food goods (clothing, hygiene, heating, etc.) required for daily survival.[36] By using the same poverty indicators in 1936 and 1951, Rowntree concluded that, between these two dates, the proportion of the working class living in poverty in York had fallen from 31 per cent to 3 per cent as a result of a high level of employment and the setting up of social benefits as recommended by the Beveridge report.[37] This change was so great that, in its 1950 election manifesto, the Labour government stated that 'extreme poverty has been abolished'.

In reality, many people still did not have what they considered to be the basic goods they needed to live. In 1960, Peter Townsend used other indicators and showed that one Briton in seven was living in poverty, and argued that:

> Any rigorous conceptualisation of the social determination of need dissolves the idea of 'absolute' need. And a thoroughgoing relativity applies to time as well as place. The necessities of life are not fixed. They are continuously being adapted and augmented as changes take place in society and in its products.[38]

Sen recognises the progress made as much by the absolute approach as by the relative approach to poverty, but challenges both of them when they become too rigid. With a 'rigidly relativist' approach, poverty cannot simply be eradicated, because there will always be people who are relatively poorer than others. If poverty is solely a relative notion referring only to the fact of being at the bottom of the social ladder, wanting to eradicate it does not have much meaning. Despite unanimous agreement in support of an entirely relative concept of poverty, 'there is a good case for an absolutist approach ... to poverty related to the notion of capability'.

Sen focuses his attention on the capabilities of individuals more than on the goods and services they have at their disposal. The capability to live without shame, of being able to participate in community activities or of having self-respect, requires resources that vary greatly depending on the time and the place.

One or two hundred years ago, the Central African pygmy was able to live half-naked without any feelings of shame, take part in his tribe's activities without any need for a vehicle and have self-esteem without knowing how to read or write. In order to have the same 'capabilities' today, an individual in an industrialised country must have radically different material and cultural resources. Thus, 'an absolute approach in the space of capabilities translates into a relative approach in the space of commodities and resources' and 'poverty may be seen as a failure to reach some absolute level of capability.'[39] Therefore, Sen defines an absolute socio-historical poverty.

Extreme poverty

Wresinski argues that extreme poverty prevents people from assuming their responsibilities and is thus a violation of human rights. He also expresses the viewpoints of those who are unable to speak for themselves and affirms that extreme poverty is intrinsically linked to shame and scorn – and this is what distinguishes it from poverty.

Extreme poverty is the combination of material poverty and social exclusion. It is 'the condition of the man to whom his brothers have not left the basic means allowing him to feel and to show himself to be a man'.[40]

In 1969, when Wresinski had just left the Noisy-le-Grand camp where he had lived for more than a decade, he wrote:

Damaged in his heart and in his soul as much as in his body, the poor man is only able to accept the judgment that others have of him. He is a poor man, and nothing is worth the trouble, even the attention that he might give to his own body, his clothes, or the image that he offers to himself and presents to those around him. This is where the self-negligence comes from which repels us and forces us to turn away, although it is nothing other than the acceptance of a man who has been impoverished by a society that has treated him continually with nothing but contempt.[41]

In one of his last texts, he wrote:

The worst blow of all is the contempt on the part of your fellow citizens. It is that contempt which stands between a human being and his rights. It makes the world despise what you are going through and prevents you from being recognised as worthy and capable of taking on responsibility. The greatest misfortune of extreme poverty is that for your entire existence you are like someone already dead.[42]

Extreme poverty is a permanent denial of human dignity as defined, for example, by the sociologist Vincent de Gaulejac:

> Dignity is what an individual feels and what is accorded to him when he belongs to the community of men and is treated with the respect that he is due as a human being. It is based on two aspects of identity: self-respect and the respect granted by others.[43]

Majid Rahnema explores the various forms and meanings of poverty and extreme poverty in different civilisations at different times.[44] In all the major religions – Judaism, Christianity, Islam, Buddhism and Hinduism – the search for inner fulfilment has driven great spiritual leaders to opt for voluntary poverty in order to free themselves from all enslaving forms of material dependence. For the 'voluntary poor', the limitation of material riches is a condition of freedom – a means of reaching higher levels of human and spiritual riches. For them, poverty is characterised by the absence of all that is superfluous. Extreme poverty, on the other hand, is the deprivation of what is essential.

The advent of a global economy has created abundance but also scarcity and extreme poverty, because the growth of this type of economy is based on the infinite creation of new needs that the very poorest are unable to satisfy.

Rahnema joins Wresinski in his call for a profound transformation in ways of living: a reinvention of voluntary poverty – which could more readily be referred to as frugality or simplicity today – to combat extreme poverty. It is vital to differentiate properly between poverty and extreme poverty, or relative and absolute poverty: one may be adopted and even desired, while the other must be destroyed.

A further argument for the need to distinguish between poverty and extreme poverty is the need to attract attention to situations of extreme deprivation. Often, the observation of human groups does not extend to their very poorest members – those who are not integrated into the community – who are rarely included in censuses and statistics. Invisible in statistical analyses, excluded from decision-making processes, they are also overlooked by government policies. Focusing on extreme poverty is vital to understanding the intensity and the scale of the inequalities among any human group and the situations in which human and civil rights are not respected.

COLLABORATING IN THE FIGHT AGAINST SOCIAL EXCLUSION

Economic and social deprivation, poverty and extreme poverty have been differentiated, not to set them against each other, but to connect them to each other. It is necessary to pursue the goal of reducing poverty, which is relative, and of destroying extreme poverty, which is absolute.

The fight against extreme poverty must not be confused with the fight against inequalities; both are often the result of a refusal to accept the most blatant injustices.

In constantly changing societies, eradicating extreme poverty requires long-term action on several levels:

- those suffering from extreme poverty must be able to escape from it
- those who are on the brink of destitution must be helped to avoid falling any further
- everyone must be protected from extreme poverty.

Fighting poverty and extreme poverty obviously implies fighting economic and social hardship and insecurity, as well as all the forms of exploitation and exclusion that lead to it.

In general, these different types of action complement one another, sometimes brought together under the term 'the fight against social exclusion'.

Reducing poverty and eradicating extreme poverty are huge challenges which require specialists in every field to share their knowledge. A unique study by the World Bank, conducted in 50 developing countries, argues that:

There are 2.8 billion poverty experts: the poor themselves. Yet the development discourse about poverty has been dominated by the perspectives and expertise of those who are not poor – professionals, politicians and agency officials... The bottom poor, in all their diversity, are excluded, impotent, ignored and neglected; the bottom poor are a blind spot in development.[45]

Three types of knowledge, outlined by Wresinski, need to be combined:[46]

- *Academic knowledge*, which remains 'partial, indirect and purely informative'. It does not mobilise or encourage people to commit themselves in the name of others.

- *Knowledge gained from life experience* of people in extreme poverty, whom Wresinski considered to be the leading experts on poverty; they have lived through it and know what it means in terms of suffering and what changes need to be undertaken to improve their situation. Often, this knowledge is sidelined, crushed and stifled by academic knowledge.
- *Knowledge gained by professionals* who have committed themselves to the cause of the deprived.

Each of these areas of knowledge must be developed independently and then combined with the others to produce a more relevant and more effective approach to the fight against poverty and extreme poverty. Unfortunately, too many works on poverty continue to be the product of a research process designed to achieve goals that are defined by others, in which the most unfortunate are simply used as informers or are totally excluded. Research on poverty may well reinforce social exclusion by leaving those living in poverty without a voice and without power, rather than providing an opportunity to build a partnership with them through a participative approach. Sharing and building expertise with those who are living in extreme poverty necessarily implies starting from their concerns – not from theoretical questions over which they have no control. It is only when their suffering and aspirations are heard and their resistance recognised that their experience can raise more theoretical, institutional or political questions.

This participative approach has inspired this book. The first part, 'Resisting extreme poverty every day', presents four life stories drawn up in close collaboration with people experiencing extreme poverty on four different continents: Europe, Asia, Africa and Latin America. The second part of the book, 'Human rights and responsibilities', analyses and discusses the issues.

NOTES

1. Victor Hugo, *Combats politiques et humanitaires*, texts published by Gérard Gengembre, Paris: Pocket, 2002.
2. Pierre Jacquet and Laurence Tubiana, *Regards sur la terre*, Paris: Sciences Po Les Presses, 2007.
3. Leandro Despouy, *The Realisation of Economic, Social and Cultural Rights: Final Report on Human Rights and Extreme Poverty*, Economic and Social Council of the United Nations, E /CN.4 /Sub.2 /1996 /13, p. 38.
4. Geneviève de Gaulle Anthonioz, *La Traversée de la nuit*, Paris: Seuil, 1998. She was sent to Ravensbrück concentration camp for having chosen to resist the Nazi occupier and its totalitarian ideology.

5. Amartya Sen, Autobiography, www.nobel.se/economics/laureates/1998/sen-autobio.html

6. Amartya Sen, *L'Economie est une science morale*, Paris: Éditions La Découverte, 1999, p. 44–5.

7. The first text in which Sen introduced and defined the concept of 'basic capability' was the conference 'Equality of What?' given at the University of Stanford on 22 May 1979. In it, he emphasised the inadequacies of utilitarian, libertarian and Rawlsian approaches to equality.

8. Amartya Sen, *Development as Freedom*, Oxford: Oxford University Press, 1999.

9. This notion of 'primary goods' is borrowed from John Rawls, *A Theory of Justice*, Cambridge, MA: Harvard University Press, 1971.

10. Gilles Anouil, *The Poor are the Church: A Conversation with Fr. Joseph Wresinski, Founder of the Fourth World Movement*, Mystic, CT: Twenty-Third Publications, 2002, p. 48.

11. For further information on this history, see Xavier Godinot, *Recherche scientifique et libération des plus pauvres: le questionnement de Joseph Wresinski*, in *La connaissance des pauvres*, under the direction of Pierre Fontaine, Louvain-la-Neuve: Éditions Academia Bruylant and Travailler le Social, 1996, pp. 193–207.

12. Jules Klanfer, *L'exclusion sociale. Etude de la marginalité dans les sociétés occidentales*, Paris: éditions Aide à Toute Détresse – Science et Service, 1965. This book gives an account of the work of a symposium on 'Les familles inadaptées' organised by the ATD Fourth World Social Research Bureau.

13. For the history of this concept and its dissemination in France, see Emmanuel Didier, 'De l'exclusion à l'exclusion', *Politix*, Vol. 9, No. 34, (3rd quarter of 1996).

14. Manuel Castells, *End of Millennium*, Oxford: Blackwell, 1998, p. 71.

15. Serge Paugam, *La disqualification sociale, Essai sur la nouvelle pauvreté*, Paris: Presses Universitaires de France, 1991.

16. Jean Labbens, *L'héritage du passé*, Paris: Science et Service, 1965.

17. Louis Join-Lambert, 'Quart Monde', in *Encyclopédie Universalia, Themes et Problemes,* April 1981, pp. 341–4.

18. Joseph Wresinski, *La grande pauvreté, défi posé aux droits de l'homme de notre temps*, E/CN.4/1987/NGO/2.

19. Emmanuel Decaux, member of the sub-commission on human rights, 'Une pierre blanche sur un long chemin', *Revue Quart Monde*, No. 200 (November 2006), pp. 27–9.

20. See www.coe.int/T/E/Social_cohesion/HDSE/

21. Joseph Wresinski, *Chronic Poverty and Lack of Basic Security: The Wresinski Report of the Economic and Social Council of France*, Paris: Fourth World Publications, 1994, p. 1.

22. Pierre Concialdi refers to the definition of hardship and poverty in the Wresinski Report as being 'the most commonly used' in his book *Non à la précarité*, Paris: Éditions Mango, 2007, pp. 28–30. Patrick Cingolani considers that the Wresinski Report 'marked a turning point', *La Précarité, Que sais-je?*, Paris: Presses Universitaires de France, 2005, p. 16.

23. Stéphane Lollivier and Daniel Verger, 'Trois apports des données longitudinales à l'analyse de la pauvreté', *Economie et Statistique*, Nos 383–384–385, December 2005, p. 247.

24. Daniel Verger, 'Bas revenus, consommation restreinte ou faible bien-être: les approches statistiques de la pauvreté à l'épreuve des comparaisons internationals', *Economie et Statistique*, Nos 383–384–385, December 2005, p. 31.

25. The median income is that which divides a population into two equal parts, with half of this population having a higher income and the other half having a lower income. In France, the National Institute for Statistics and Economic Studies (INSEE) defines the poverty threshold at 50 per cent of the median income.

26. Daniel Verger, 'Bas revenus, consommation restreinte ou faible bien-être: les approches statistiques de la pauvreté à l'épreuve des comparaisons internationales', p. 15.

27. Amartya Sen, 'Poor, Relatively Speaking', *Oxford Economic Papers*, Vol. 35, No. 2 (July 1983), pp. 156–7.

28. International Bank for Reconstruction and Development and World Bank, *Global Monitoring Report 2011: Improving the Odds of Achieving the MDGs*, Washington, DC: International Bank for Reconstruction and Development/ World Bank, 2011.

29. World Bank, *World Development Report 2006: Equity and Development*, World Bank and Oxford University Press, 2005, p. 286.

30. United Nations, *Millennium Development Goals Report 2007*, New York: United Nations, 2007, p. 5.

31. This is what is highlighted by the French National Observatory on Poverty and Social Exclusion (ONPES), which believes that, at present, these households represent 2 per cent of the French population. ONPES, *Report 2005–6*, p. 43.

32. Despouy, *The Realisation of Economic, Social and Cultural Rights: Final Report on Human Rights and Extreme Poverty*, p. 37.

33. Eugène Buret, *De la misère des classes laborieuses en Angleterre et en France : de la nature de la misère, de son existence, de ses effets, de ses causes*, Paris: Paulin, 1840, cited by Majid Rahnema, *Quand la misère chasse la pauvreté*, Paris-Arles: Fayard/Actes Sud, 2003, pp. 228–9.

34. Joseph Wresinski, preface to Jean Labbens, *Le Quart Monde, la condition sous-prolétarienne*, Paris: Éditions Science et Service, 1969, p. 17.

35. Sen, 'Poor, Relatively Speaking', pp. 153–69. The lines which follow are a partial summary.

36. B.S. Rowntree and G.R. Lavers, *Poverty and the Welfare State*, London: Longmans-Green and Co., 1951; Charles Booth, *Life and Labour of the People of London*, London: Macmillan, 1903.

37. *Social Insurance and Allied Services* (The Beveridge Report), November 1942.

38. Peter Townsend, *The Development of Research on Poverty*, cited in Sen, 'Poor, Relatively Speaking', p. 155.

39. Sen, 'Poor, Relatively Speaking', pp. 163–8.

40. Joseph Wresinski, *Les pauvres, rencontre du vrai Dieu*, Paris: Éditions du Cerf, 1986, p. 137.

41. Joseph Wresinski, preface to Jean Labbens, *Le Quart Monde, la conditions sous-prolétarienne*, Paris: Éditions Science et Service, 1969, pp. 16–17.

42. Joseph Wresinski, *The Very Poor: Living Proof of the Indivisibility of Human Rights*, Paris: Éditions Quart Monde, 1994, p. 19.

43. Vincent De Gaulejac, *Les sources de la honte*, Paris: Desclée de Brouwer, 1996, p. 137.

44. Rahnema, *Quand la misère chasse la pauvreté.*

45. Deepa Narayan, *Voices of the Poor: Crying Out for Change,* Oxford: Oxford University Press for the World Bank, 2000, pp. 2, 264.

46. Joseph Wresinski, *A Knowledge that Leads to Action,* December 1980, available for download at www.joseph-wresinski.org in the 'Anthology' section. All the quotes which follow are taken from this text.

Part One

Introduction: Resisting Extreme Poverty Every Day

Xavier Godinot

All too often, the victims of extreme poverty do not speak; they are spoken about. They are distorted through the way they are represented by those who are more affluent. The historian Arlette Farge points out that the failure to listen to what the weakest themselves have to say about their existence is nothing new:

> It was affirmed constantly by the elite that all ideas and opinions given by the common people were mad, inept, impulsive and lacking in intelligence. In 1776, Condorcet defined popular opinion as 'that of the most stupid and poorest section of the population'.[1]

The thoughts and ideas of the most disadvantaged about their lives are just as inaccessible today as they ever were. Michèle Perrot poses the question to historians and sociologists: 'How can we write the history of poor people when those who write about them and tell us what they have to say do not belong to this group?'[2]

The life stories in part one of this book feature families in four different countries whose experiences illustrate the difficulties and efforts of many families faced with extreme poverty in those regions. They are able to tell us themselves about their lives and to express their own thoughts and ideas.

THE NARRATIVE PACT

Traditional methods rarely reach the poorest members of society, who have many reasons not to open up to outsiders, because it is very difficult for researchers to win their trust. Each of the following accounts is the outcome of the commitment and support of members of the ATD Fourth World volunteer corps, who established a relationship of great trust with the families over many years.[3]

The involvement of the families themselves in the process of writing their stories required agreements – 'narrative pacts' – between the writers and the central characters. In the writing process, the families and members of the ATD Fourth World volunteer corps tried to develop an honest and equal relationship in which they learned together how to tell the truth; each individual was allowed to express their own point of view and was questioned by others. The goal was to find appropriate words to show them in their world, where they experience powerlessness and suffering – but also desires, joys, efforts and successes.

Although the accounts were written down by others, the central characters had some control over the writing process and monitored the results. The writers of the life stories from France and the Philippines read the accounts back to the central characters in full so that they could correct them. In Burkina Faso, Paul was given a summary booklet so that he could check the text, because he was not able to read the full version. A similar approach was used in Peru.

Given their close relationship with those living in extreme poverty, the writers had to add an element of objectivity. A seminar was therefore organised, bringing together professors and academics from the University of Ouagadougou, the University of Lima and Harvard University, to produce a valid analysis of the issues.

LEARNING FROM LIFE STORIES

In ATD Fourth World, work on the writing and publication of 'family monographs' of those in situations of extreme poverty began in the early 1970s and has been constantly updated.[4] In the 1980s, Gaston Pineau introduced the use of autobiography as a means of self-training to strengthen people's capabilities.[5]

Patrick Brun attempted to analyse how the writing of biographies as part of a group could have an emancipating effect on their authors.[6] By allowing people to 'explain themselves in the full sense of the term, namely to construct their own view of themselves and the world', Pierre Bourdieu learned that individuals occupying an inferior and obscure position in society found that this extreme 'poverty of position' had a greater impact on their lives than the more extreme 'poverty of condition'.[7]

In agreeing to tell the stories published here, all the adults insisted that they should contribute to the fight against extreme poverty:

'Yes, as long as it brings poverty to an end', said the Rojas Paucar parents from Peru, who are still prisoners of chronic extreme poverty.

For Mercedita, whose family in the Philippines is still living in poverty, the main objective was to help the mayor of her town 'understand the poor better' – avoiding the extremes of overwhelming sensitivity on the one hand and insensitivity or indifference on the other.

For the Koffic parents in France, and for Paul in Burkina Faso, who are clearly on the road to escaping extreme poverty, the accounts bear witness to the fact that it is possible to escape.

These accounts, and many others, confirm that 'for the very poorest, the goal of knowledge is to eradicate extreme poverty'.[8] This is why socially excluded families have taken the risk of revealing themselves and contributing to an account of their lives.

NOTES

1. Arlette Farge, 'L'existence méconnue des plus faibles', *Etudes*, Vol. 404, No. 1 (January 2006).
2. Cited in Mouvement international ATD Quart Monde, *Démocratie et pauvreté: Du quatrième ordre au quart monde*, Paris: Éditions Quart Monde et Albin Michel, 1991, p. 641.
3. For more information about the Fourth World volunteer corps see the section 'Reaching out to and representing the poorest' in Chapter 6.
4. International Movement ATD Fourth World, *This Is How We Live: Listening to the Poorest Families*, Paris: Fourth World Publications, 1995.
5. Gaston Pineau and Michèle Marie, *Produire sa vie: Autoformation et autobiographie*, Montreal: Éditions St Martin, 1983, p. 424.
6. Patrick Brun, *Emancipation et connaissance: Les histoires de vie en collectivité*, Paris: L'Harmattan, 2001, p. 285.
7. Daniel Fayard, 'Livres Ouvertes: La misère du monde', *Revue Quart Monde*, Vol. 148, No. 3 (September 1996).
8. Louis Join-Lambert, 'Reconnaître l'autre comme chercheur', *Revue Quart Monde*, Vol. 140, No. 3 (September 1991).

1
The Child who Walked with Death:
The Story of Paul in Burkina Faso

Patricia Heyberger and Claude Heyberger

Paul was living on the streets of Ouagadougou, the capital city of Burkina Faso, West Africa, when he first met Claude Heyberger and Bruno Bambara from ATD Fourth World in 1996. For the next eight years, Claude and Bruno offered friendship, support and help to him and his family.

Claude Heyberger and his wife Patricia, both French, had been members of the ATD Fourth World volunteer corps since 1979. When this story started, they were living and working for ATD Fourth World in Burkina Faso. Bruno Bambara, a Burkinabé, was the founder and director of a large school in a district of Ouagadougou where school enrolment is a major problem. Bruno was a friend and supporter of ATD Fourth World.

Paul was already about 16 years old when they first met him, but he is described as a child throughout this account; in the culture of Burkina Faso a person is regarded as a child as long as their father is still alive.

THE STORY BEGINS

It was a Wednesday evening in September 1996, around 8.30 p.m. It had been dark for more than an hour and all was quiet, unlike the bustle from the Great Market nearby during the day. Keeping a sharp lookout, Claude Heyberger and Bruno Bambara rode slowly along on a scooter beside the walls of the Great Mosque of Ouagadougou. Suddenly they found what they were looking for: a small group of children and teenagers sitting on the ground, eating rice out of tomato tins. As they approached, the children leapt up and greeted them loudly: 'Claude, how's it going?' 'Hey, man, how's things with you?' Some were surprised, 'Is it Wednesday already? Have you brought us some books?' There was much shaking of hands and laughing and talking. The children finished their rice, then chose a streetlight nearby and found a piece of cardboard for everyone to sit on. Claude and Bruno opened up their bag of books and the 'streetlight library' could begin.

The children they had come to meet lived and slept on the streets. Since 1983, successive teams of ATD Fourth World volunteers had focused their action on the most vulnerable children. Claude and Bruno devoted one evening every week to running the 'streetlight library' for these children. The library provides the means for them to meet and get to know each other. Through the books, the children discover new horizons and can start to satisfy their thirst for knowledge.

Seated in the glow of the streetlight, Bruno and the children pored over a book. As usual, he asked questions, encouraging them all to talk. Following the illustrations and Bruno's questions, the children traced the story of *Yacouba*,[1] a young boy sent by his family to hunt a lion; in the end, he saves it instead. The children were quick to react: 'If someone has no pity in his life, he is not good', exclaimed the child they all called 'Chubby', even though he was not particularly fat. He was placid, quiet and pleasant. This was not the first time he had come along to the street library and at the end of the session he told them that his name was Paul.

Little by little, over the next eight years, Claude and Bruno were to learn where Paul had come from, and why he was living on the streets in Ouagadougou. At the end of this journey together, they suggested to Paul that he should write his story. More than ten working sessions followed, during which Paul tried to make sense of the path his life had taken, took an active part in the writing process and checked that the text reflected exactly what he wanted to say. His story is told in his own words as often as possible.

This is how Paul remembered these first meetings:

It was near the Great Mosque, next to the Great Market, where Claude and Bruno used to come at night. We'd talk about things and look at books: there was a book where they farmed with a donkey, books about men in olden times, books about animals. We'd learn about things we didn't know from the past ... If we came to listen we could learn something new. We talked about life: if you do this it's good, if you do that it won't work ... I'd come just to talk. I believed them because if they said they'd come and talk to us on that day, then they'd come that day.

PAUL'S FAMILY

Paul belongs to the Mossi tribe, the largest tribe from central Burkina Faso. He was born in 1980 in the family home belonging to his paternal grandfather in a district of Kobodogho,[2] a small town 50 kilometres west of Ouagadougou towards Bobo Dioulasso. No birth certificate was issued at that time. The document issued by the prefect of Kobodogho on 13 January 1998 in lieu of a birth certificate, reveals that his name is Baowenisom Paul. Baowenisom is a traditional name, meaning 'Seek God's blessing'. Paul is the fourth of six children.

Paul's father, Joseph Koudougou, is a farmer. His grandmother said she did not know her own age or Joseph's. Paul's mother is a 'housewife' according to her administrative documents but, like all women in rural areas, she spends a lot of her time working in the fields. She speaks very little, even when her husband is not there. However, it is clear that both she and Paul's grandmother play a vital role.

Paul's maternal uncles are a dominant presence in his activities in the village. Within Mossi society, the maternal family is the focus for affectionate attachment with the child, whereas the paternal family represents the figure of authority. The term 'uncle' does not always mean a brother of Paul's father or mother; it may mean a more distant relative who does not necessarily have any responsibility or authority.

The Family's History

Joseph's mother gave him the name of Koudougou. Joseph often went to the Côte d'Ivoire when he was young and spent five years there after he married. A friend started teaching him how to read Mooré, his mother tongue, when he worked on a plantation in the Côte d'Ivoire. He subsequently took lessons in Abidjan.

When he left the Côte d'Ivoire, he came back to the village with his wife and their first two children: Marcel and Madeleine. Paul and Albert were born in Kobodogho.

Joseph began to attend catechism at the Côte d'Ivoire. Later he was baptised and became 'Joseph'. The White Father of the Catholic mission in the village noticed that he could read the Bible and invited him to help with the catechism classes.

On the Move

Subsistence remains difficult for farming communities in Kobodogho, although its position on a major thoroughfare provides an important opportunity for trade development. Paul was probably five years old when, weary of meagre harvests, the family joined one of their uncles in the more fertile land of Borapo, 130 kilometres to the west.

Paul talked about life in Borapo:

> In Borapo, even if you just farmed a little, you could harvest a lot. You just needed to work to earn what you wanted: money, food, clothes. We had animals in Borapo. In the morning we would let out the sheep and goats, together with our uncle's. Then we would take the cattle out. I liked doing that. There was a large forest and we had fun playing in the bushes with friends from the district who came with their family's cattle.

Return to Kobodogho

When Joseph's father died at the beginning of 1990, the family moved back to Kobodogho. Paul was ten or eleven years old. He remembered:

> I was happy to come back because I'd never lived here. I wanted to get to know my village. Once we'd been here a while, we could see that it wasn't the same as Borapo: there's not enough rain and the land is no good. Even if you farm a lot, it doesn't give a lot. We had no cattle. The two years I lived in Kobodogho, before going to the city, were quite good. If there were problems we knew how to solve them. I farmed with my parents. On market days, I went to help my uncle look after his clothes stall. He'd give me 200 or 300 FCFA[3] for helping him.

THE CHILDREN'S EDUCATION

Not all children go to school in Burkina Faso. What may be perceived as an injustice should rather be seen in the context of the duty to 'give back' to the family: each child who has had the opportunity to go to school 'owes' to their siblings and their parents the chance to benefit from the opportunities they have received. However, it cannot be denied that schooling often weakens the ties between the child and their community.

Paul's father believed that schooling is really important. He made great efforts to send his children to school however much it cost him in terms of time, energy and money. And yet the results were not very promising: none of his children went to school for long enough to improve their situation.

The eldest child in Paul's family, Madeleine, was refused entry to school, as she was too old. Marcel was therefore sent to school instead of Madeleine, but he did not like it and left.

Paul started school in Borapo when he was seven. He says:

> At the time, most parents didn't let their children go to school. The other children helped with the work in the compounds. I went to primary school in Borapo with one of my cousins till the fourth year. I was the only one in the family who went. I wanted to learn to read and write. In the village, you can be asked to read or write letters. If you know how, it's easy.

According to Joseph, Paul began to lose interest in school when the family returned to Kobodogho. The teacher advised him not to force a child who did not want to go to school. Joseph recalled that Paul completed his fourth and fifth years in Kobodogho, got his primary school certificate and passed the entrance exam for high school. Paul says that when he was in the fifth year of primary school, he practised for the Primary School Certificate but never actually took the test. At the start of the next school year, Paul refused to return to school.

Nevertheless, Paul learned how to read, write, count and speak some French while he was at school. His father believed that this enabled him to get a job years later.

PAUL LEAVES THE VILLAGE

Paul left his village and his family to go to the capital when he was 14 years old. His father, his grandmother and Paul himself each have different memories of the situation at home before he left.

Looking back years later, his father says, 'Paul did not like working in the fields, he didn't like to sweat.' His grandmother cannot remember any major problems:

> Paul helped his parents and his brothers with small chores. If we sent him to do something, he would do it. I never saw him sick, he was a healthy child. He worked with his parents in the fields. I don't think he was really naughty. Everything comes from the heart: when the heart is happy, all is well. Paul never gave us any heartache.

Paul remembers his final day in the village like this:

It was in 1994, during the rainy season, at planting time. I had even helped a little with the planting. I was with my younger brothers and we were carrying water in a drum and going to the fields. Halfway there, I wanted someone else to take the drum, but they all refused. I put the drum down and went home.

It was market day. When I arrived at the market, I ran into an uncle who said he had to go to Ouagadougou. I told him that I wanted to go too, because I wanted to find a job. We took the bus together.

At the time, I wanted money to be able to start trading. A relative who lived in the city, told me: 'There is a lot of work in the city!' In the village, if you only earn a little bit you go through it all. You have to give some to your younger brothers, you have to buy your shoes and clothes. In the city you only get paid for your work once a month so you can't spend it all.

The Mossi Tradition of Travel

Mossi wisdom teaches that 'a boy is not born a man, he becomes one' by assimilating the traditional system of values transmitted to him by the elders. The act of leaving one's family is part of a defined cultural framework: a child is free to leave when he feels capable of doing a job, such as trading in salt or cola, or working on a plantation. He returns to the village with new knowledge to be shared. The Mossi still say, 'It is not the oldest who knows the elephant, but he who has travelled.'

Nevertheless, Paul's departure did not correspond to traditional Mossi values. He left his village without telling his family; he was not sent by them and did not go to live with relatives.

PAUL TELLS THE STORY OF HIS LIFE IN THE CITY

It was the first time that I'd been to Ouagadougou. There was electricity and light. At night, you could go where you wanted, you could go for miles. There was light, so you weren't scared to walk anywhere. In the village, you couldn't always do that if there was no moon. The houses were close together, there were also a lot of people, there were cars at the traffic lights, and some could go and some couldn't. It wasn't the same as the village! But there were a lot of accidents and a lot of thieves. When you sold something, they could cheat you and take your money. They make like they're going to buy what you're selling but your money goes into their pockets, and you don't see a thing.

When I reached Goughin market, I found a woman who was walking with a bag. I asked her for work. She was going to the market to buy flour to make cakes. She asked me to come to her house, which was on the edge of the market. In the morning, I would take the cakes and walk around selling them in the city. She gave me 75 FCFA in the morning and 75 FCFA in the afternoon to pay for food. In the evening, I ate at her house.

While walking around selling the cakes, I met someone who ran a kiosk that sells coffee and snacks on the side of the road in Bilbalgho, a district in the centre of town. He wanted someone to work with him. I gave up selling cakes after 22 days and went to work at the kiosk.

I worked there for eight months. Every month I was paid 3,500 FCFA and I ate at the kiosk. One day, while I was washing up, I broke five glasses. The boss said he was going to cut into my money. I didn't agree and we had an argument. The boss said that if that was the case, I had to leave the job. I left that same day. I came back for my money later and he paid me.

I didn't go back to see my family during this time. I wanted to go home, not for good, just to see my father, my relatives and my brothers again. I didn't have enough money to go. I was earning money, but I was going through it, buying clothes and playing the National Lottery.

I wasn't alone. In Goughin, I found 'brothers' from my village who were also working for other people. My father came especially from the village to see where I was working. He never told me to come back to the village.

When I left the kiosk, I went back to the city centre and looked for work near the Great Market, the main market in Ouagadougou. But I didn't find any. When night came, I slept outside a tall building. I slept there for twelve days. There were other children even younger than me who came to sleep there as well. When there wasn't anything to eat, we went around to restaurants and ate leftovers.

After twelve days, I went to the house of a woman who cooked rice in another market in the centre of town. I asked her for work, and she told me to come with her. I fetched water at the fountain, we pushed the cart with the rice, we went to the market and we washed the dishes. There were four of us. I met the others there. I slept at the woman's place and I got 2,500 FCFA a month. I stayed there for five months. I left that woman to look for another job.

I returned to the Great Market area in the city centre. I asked where I could find work, either in the kiosks, in the markets, or in courtyards and houses, sweeping and cleaning. I didn't find any work. So I joined the children that I was with before. They still slept near the same building. We went to the same restaurants to get food. That lasted for eight months.

They were little thieves, about the same age as me. There were four of them: Moussa, Amédée, Amidou and Salif. They'd go into the Great Market to steal things from people and the traders. At the time, I just went around with them. I didn't want to steal; I wanted to work.

One day, a woman came along to the Great Market. She asked me if I wanted to work. I said yes. We left together that day for Sankariaré, another district in Ouagadougou, where she lived. She wanted me to work in her courtyard: sweeping and cleaning. It was big and there was a big house. She was a wealthy woman. She worked with Blaise's wife at the palace (Mr Blaise Compaore, president of Burkina Faso). I got 3,500 FCFA a month and I ate lunch and dinner there. I slept in a little house on the side of the same courtyard. Another kid came to ask for work and they gave him water to sell. We shared the same room at night and stayed there for about seven months.

One day, we had a fight with a girl who worked there and the owner's daughter. I insulted them. When the owner's wife arrived, she said there was no problem. But her husband said that I couldn't stay and continue to work there. So I left.

It was nice there; I would've liked to have stayed. I didn't go into the centre of town during that time. I left a bit of money with the woman every month, 2,000 FCFA. When I left, I bought some shoes and clothes with the money.

I went back to the Great Market to find my friends. We still slept near the same building. I started stealing with them because I couldn't find work. At the Great Market we stole cloth, shoes, boxes of Nescafé, chains, watches… Sometimes, we would hide in the gutters because one of them had grabbed a woman's handbag. If you weren't fast enough, they could catch you. I only did it once and it worked. We'd go out at night, too. We'd go into people's courtyards in the various districts. We'd go in two at a time, so as not to be scared. We'd take whatever we saw, radios, money and shoes, and sell them at the Great Market.

I was sniffing.[4] If you sniff, you can do things, you can steal what you want, and if you don't, you can't, you'll get scared. We made money but, as there were four of us, we went through it all. That's why I stayed with them. We paid for our food, we paid for the drugs we smoked and the rubber solution.

Sometimes, when we had money, we wouldn't go out to steal or go wandering around the districts. We'd just eat for three or four days. That was what was good about being with them: we earned money and we did what we wanted. We had enough to eat, we had clothes. There were no fights between us. If someone started a fight with me, the others would come and stand up for me.

Once I was hanging out with the thieves, I never went back to work. I didn't want to work any more. I wanted to go back to the village, but as I didn't earn any money I couldn't. I didn't go back to my family and I never saw anyone from my village. I stayed with my friends for three or four years.

We never talked about our villages or our families amongst ourselves. All I did was go along with them. I wasn't like them because sometimes I thought about returning to the village; they didn't. As they'd spent more time in the city than me, they only thought about earning money. But I wanted to go home. I wanted to go and work with my family. But there wasn't enough paid work.

STREET CHILDREN OF OUAGADOUGOU

In 2002, a study[5] estimated that there were more than 500 young people living on the streets of Ouagadougou, but this number is undoubtedly well below the actual figure. They are mostly poor, orphaned or abandoned, and come from rural areas. Every day they find themselves victims of physical and psychological ill treatment – from adults, drug addicts or older children. They are subject to police harassment. A 2005 statistical study[6] of 275 children on the streets of Ouagadougou showed that 62 per cent did not feel safe, especially at night when they have trouble finding places to sleep. Of the 38 per cent who had dealings with the police, 80 per cent had been to prison. Many complained of loneliness, which leads them to form loose groups or highly organised gangs. As many as 7 per cent appear to have little or no contact with their families.

Help for Street Children

Paul sometimes went to a centre for helping and guiding children living on the streets. The centre had been set up by the Action Educative en Milieu Ouvert (AEMO), under the Ministry for Social Action, to provide educational activities in an open environment.

Although a counsellor met Paul regularly to encourage him to change the way he was living, he did not seem to be influenced by her.

Sometimes we'd leave money there, but we'd soon be back to pick it up. We could wash and leave a change of clothes. There was a lady who used to talk to me and give me advice. We got on all right. She told me I was a good-looking boy and that all I had to do was find a job. But at that time, I was hanging out too much.

The Courtyard of a Hundred Trades

Created by ATD Fourth World in 1983, the Courtyard of a Hundred Trades organises workshops run by local craftsmen for children living on the streets, giving them the opportunity to develop specific skills. At the same time, it offers a haven where the children can talk about their future and their ties with their families.

By the end of 1996, Paul had become a regular presence at the streetlight library so the team at the Courtyard invited him to join a week of workshops to be held there. It took him several months to make the decision to take part in a full-time workshop but, in the meantime, he took part in several sessions of a workshop weaving a 'Cloth of Strength'. These sessions were less demanding than a full workshop and allowed children to participate for an hour or two, or even for half a day, and come back when they wanted. When it was completed, the 'Cloth of Strength' was carried on a march from Ouagadougou to Manega, 55 kilometres away, and held aloft at an event organised by the State of Burkina Faso and the United Nations Development Programme for 17 October, the International Day for the Eradication of Poverty. Paul was proud of taking part and of holding the cloth with his friend at the Commemorative Stone.

In November 1997, Paul and four other youngsters gathered around Master François, a stonemason and friend of ATD Fourth World, who had been running masonry courses for more than ten years. They were there to participate in a week-long workshop to renovate the library of the Courtyard of a Hundred Trades. The atmosphere was peaceful. By undertaking to stay for the whole week, Paul and the other children would have the satisfaction of seeing their work through to the end. Like the others, Paul arrived early in the morning and worked the whole morning under the direction of Master François. Claude also worked with them and they shared a meal together every lunchtime. After having a wash, the children returned to the city until the next day. At the end of the week, the children received a small wage. All the children were asked what they were going to do with their earnings. Paul chose to leave his money at the Courtyard of a Hundred Trades, saying that he wanted to use it to return to his village. Claude set a date to meet him at the Courtyard and plan for this return.

PAUL'S FIRST RETURN TO HIS VILLAGE

Paul described his decision to go back to his village:

> I saw that what I was doing on the streets was no good. You shouldn't leave your family like that. You should help your parents when they no longer have the strength to work, as well as your younger brothers. I listened to what they said at the Courtyard of a Hundred Trades. They told us that if we returned home, we'd have to eat what the parents ate. If we worked, we could have a wife and a home. One day I said: 'I'm going to return to the village.' Claude said that he'd come with me and told me to come to the Courtyard on a particular day, but I didn't come on that day. I didn't have the money to leave.

When several weeks had gone by with no news from Paul, Claude went to look for him around the Great Mosque. He found Paul completely intoxicated from sniffing glue. Paul promised to come the following Monday.

Keeping his promise, Paul came to the Courtyard with the firm intention of preparing for his return home and asked for a date to be set before the Christmas holidays. To encourage him, Claude offered to go with him. Paul accepted. They decided that Saturday 20 December would be the day.

Early that day, without any luggage, but dressed in a shirt and jacket, Paul arrived at the Courtyard. He had the money he had earned from the Courtyard workshops in one pocket, and his photos of the weaving of the 'Cloth of Strength' and the events of International Day for the Eradication of Poverty in the other.

Claude set off with him on the team's motorbike. Paul had said that he lived in Kobodogho itself. When they arrived in the village he indicated a right turn. The tracks became increasingly narrow until finally there was no track left, just fields, but Paul kept showing the way. After a few hesitations, and almost four kilometres later, he saw his family's compound. Surrounded by dry countryside, it was a modest compound, in good condition even though it did not appear to have been renovated in a while. Paul went ahead on his own. Children appeared, an old woman greeted Paul and Claude, and then his father, Joseph, arrived. He showed Paul no emotion, but he was deeply moved when he greeted Claude.

Joseph took Claude to see his storehouse made of clay, covered with straw and firmly closed by a clever system using a plastic bottle crate. The storehouse appeared to be full but, as Joseph put it, there were many mouths to feed. Claude then saw him signal discreetly to the children. Two minutes later, they brought out a white rooster for him and, despite its energetic protests, attached it to the back of the motorbike.

Bruno and Claude visited the village about a month later. Five children came running to welcome them and said their parents were at the market but that Paul had not been home for the past three days. So Claude and Bruno headed towards the market, led by the eldest child on a bicycle. When they found Joseph, he told them happily that his son had been working for the past few days selling petrol. Little by little, Bruno and Claude came to understand that Paul no longer slept at home with his family, but was working with an uncle in another village.

To think about the next steps, and show the father that he would be involved from the outset, Claude suggested getting Paul interested in farming and household chores. Joseph showed immediate enthusiasm. He hoped that Paul would come back to help him farm during the rainy season (from June to October in the Ouagadougou region).

Claude and Bruno then went to see Paul at the market where he worked, some 20 kilometres away. Paul was standing by a stall where petrol was sold in bottles, calm and gentle. He was holding a radio and wearing the same shirt and trousers that he had been wearing on the day he left the Courtyard of a Hundred Trades. Paul was always rather reserved, and he did not say much when Claude and Bruno told him about the discussion they had had with his parents. He ran to get his uncle who seemed surprised at first, but then pleased, by their visit. After Claude and Bruno had thanked him for the trust he was showing in Paul, the uncle explained that they were sharing the money made on the petrol, and offered them a drink to thank them for coming.

Paul said:

It was my uncle who suggested to my parents that I should come and sell petrol with him. He's my mother's brother. I sold petrol and diesel. Every month, I was paid 2,500 FCFA and, if we made a profit, my uncle would give some to me. I slept at the market in a little place we had for storing goods, and my uncle paid for my food at the market.

By the time of Claude and Bruno's next visit, Paul had added a coffee table – a place to sell coffee, tea and buttered bread – to his uncle's petrol business. He did not know when he would go back to live with his family.

Readjusting to Village Life

Parents usually recognise that life on the streets of the city has changed their son and he needs time to readjust to village life when he returns. Very often his family has a simpler life style than he had in the city. For instance, rice is only eaten on special occasions in the village, whereas in the city they are able to find rice every day, even if it is just leftovers. He has also had a taste of the complete freedom to come and go as he pleases, had more money in his possession than ever before and has learnt to enjoy the delights offered by electricity.

His parents, like the community as a whole, no longer understand what their son is ready to accept and are concerned that he will entice other children away to the city. Sending a child into the care of a member of the extended family, like the uncle selling petrol, is often a first step in their return, as the parents can observe him from a distance and begin to trust him once again.

Paul's generation was no longer naturally proud of being a farmer. When Claude asked Paul what his father did for a living, he answered, 'Nothing'. Claude insisted, asking if his father was perhaps a farmer, and Paul answered 'Oh! Yes!' For this reason, parents are no longer certain whether or not to pass this way of life on to their children.

Paul never put roots down again in the village: he was not really living in the village, and he was not really living with his family, since he slept in a storeroom at the market.

PAUL GOES BACK TO THE CITY

In May 1998, Claude received a short letter from Paul's father:

Mr Claude, I am writing to find out about your health. It is really raining here. I would like to ask you to let my child Paul come and help me with the work here. You must give him permission to come. Thanking you in advance. Mr Joseph, father of Paul.

So Paul was no longer with his uncle, but had not returned home either. Claude then realised that Joseph thought of him as Paul's 'guardian'. Claude, however, did not seek any authority over the boy that might undermine his parents in any way.

Paul explained why he had never returned to the village. 'You can't go back to the village without money. It's hard, people talk about you: "He's come back, but he hasn't given us anything: what was he doing over there?"'

No one heard from Paul for the next five months or so.

Back on the Streets

In January 1999, a year after he left the Courtyard of a Hundred Trades to return to his village, Paul reappeared at the Courtyard. He had grown; he looked well and cut a fine figure in his new clothes.

During the past eight months, he had been living in a shelter for children and young people run by Spanish Protestant missionaries on the outskirts of Ouagadougou. But he had no intention of returning there and had not joined up with his street friends again. He said:

It was nice there, we could stay as long as we liked, and they taught us right from wrong. There was nothing bad there: we didn't smoke and we didn't drink. Every morning and evening, we said prayers.

I'd been put in charge: we watched over the courtyard and in the morning we sent everyone off to work. We checked everything to be done. The people running the shelter also brought prisoners to sleep and work there; some of them came to finish their sentences. One day, they broke into the equipment store. A little kid told the other person in charge that I'd told them to do that. Then they took us to another centre where I was no longer in charge. I left.

Claude told him that his father had come to the city to look for him and that they had to think about how to contact him. Claude suggested to Paul that he should go away and think about whether he wanted to go back to the village. They did not hear from him again for nearly two months.

In March, Paul came back to the Courtyard of a Hundred Trades. He said he had been in the city, but that he wanted to return home. However, he did not go.

In April, Paul called out to Claude at an intersection near the Great Mosque. He was minding scooters to earn some money so that he could return to the village.

At the beginning of May, like the year before, a letter arrived at the Courtyard from Joseph, along with the first rains:

Dear Friend, the beautiful weather today has given me the opportunity to write and inquire about your health. As for me, I am very well. A little while ago, you asked me if I wanted help. As you know, I have a plot of three hectares. Could you send me a bag or two of peanuts to plant, as I know how to grow peanuts very well. I will pay you back after the harvest. That is all I have to tell you. I would very much appreciate your help. Thank you and see you soon.

Before replying, Claude and Bruno looked for Paul to remind him just how much his family needed him. The found him in the same place, still minding scooters. He had shaved his head and was hardly recognisable. He was with some tough-looking youngsters and the small pavement where they slept at the side of the road was covered with lids from tubes of rubber solution. Paul was visibly drugged. Finding it impossible to talk, they invited him to the Courtyard of a Hundred Trades the next day, but he did not come. However, a few days later, he came to the Courtyard, where he washed his belongings and rested. He once again spoke about his intention of returning to the village.

PAUL'S SECOND RETURN TO HIS VILLAGE

Throughout June, Paul came regularly to the Courtyard of a Hundred Trades, to talk and to leave shoes and clothes for his return to his family. However, he never set a date. On 2 July 1999, he arrived at the Courtyard early in the morning, saying that he wanted to go home that very day. He had waited several weeks to get back the savings he had given regularly to a shopkeeper for safekeeping.

Claude dropped Paul off on the outskirts of Ouagadougou with enough money to take the bus to Kobodogho, a letter for his father, and two measures of peanut seeds for him to sow with his father. Paul explained later why he had waited so long to return home:

When you come back to the village, there are a lot of friends who'll say that you came back, but you didn't bring them anything. However, with the rainy season, there weren't too many friends around because they'd all gone to work in the bush.

Support for Paul and his Family

During this phase of Paul's return, after careful consideration, the ATD Fourth World team began to offer some financial support to the family. This deliberately remained very modest so as not to usurp the role of the village community. It was also important not to introduce the notion of assistance into Claude and Bruno's relations with Paul's family. Experience with many other families had shown them that a microgrant at the right time could boost a family's confidence; they feel that their effort is recognised. Free from having to pay back a loan, the family can move forward at its own pace and seize any opportunities that arise.

Paul's First Season as a Farmer

For the next three years Bruno and Claude went to the village to see Paul and his family every six to eight weeks. The first visit was at the end of September 1999, once the roads were passable. Paul took Claude to see the field he had farmed. It was about six kilometres away from the compound. Only the experienced eye could see where the fields ended and the surrounding bush began. Claude estimated, however, that it probably spanned half a hectare. The millet had grown in patches and the heads were puny. Nevertheless, Paul said that it had been a good year. There were so few beans and their pods were so small that they were almost invisible.

Paul then took Claude to see the peanut field. It was a beautiful field that had been well looked after. He explained that he and his father had sown beyond the area where the weeds had been cleared because they did not have the strength to hoe any more, so the rest would have to grow amongst the grass.

Paul's mother told them that all the chickens had died. Claude and Bruno gave her 1,000 FCFA, in front of Paul, so that they could buy two or three young chickens. They hoped that this small gesture would demonstrate their support for the activities that Paul and his family had undertaken together. As they were leaving, Paul offered them a large bundle of corn and millet.

Claude and Bruno's next visit was at the end of November 1999, after the harvest. They noticed a small building of banco (a mixture of clay and straw) – no doubt for the chickens – still under construction. On the other side of the compound, a new storehouse had been added to the existing ones. They were all full. The harvest must have been as good as Paul had predicted. Hens ran in all directions, followed by their chicks. A small hut stood on one side of the compound, its door covered in drawings. This was where Paul slept.

Paul arrived, smiling and happy. He spoke of his plans. He was busy building a henhouse, and wanted to grow cabbages and onions. But he still had to fence off the field, a long and difficult task, even if there were enough millet stalks and thorn branches to make the fence.

When Claude and Bruno visited the field, they saw silty soil and a brick well with a broken pump. The water was not far down, but a piece of the cement coping needed to be moved to draw it. Paul had already begun digging a new well. Although he was 19 years old and had the maturity to start the projects he had set his mind on, it was obvious that he could not complete this project on his own.

There was a small building lying in ruins in the family compound. Paul told them that it was a pigsty, but the family had not kept pigs for a long time. His uncle was selling piglets at affordable prices. This gave rise to the idea that Paul should be allowed to try his hand at raising a small pig. Claude and Bruno visited the uncle and paid him 2,000 FCFA for a piglet. Paul would come and collect the piglet when the pigsty was ready.

Becoming a Gardener

When Bruno and Claude visited Paul more than two months later (February 2000), he was still with his family. He looked good in his jeans and fitted shirt with a trendy haircut. The henhouse had been completed but the pigsty still lay in ruins.

Normally not very talkative, Paul initiated the conversation by saying how happy he was to be working in his uncle's garden – the one who had sold him the pig. In return, he was allowed to use a plot in the garden for his own benefit.

I went to help my uncle Philippe water his garden. If we produced something to sell, he'd share the money with me and his three children. One day, he told me to find something I could plant for myself in his garden. He gave me tomato plants. He showed me how to plant them and when to water them. I learned lots of things, like how to treat diseases. To grow things, there are days when we need to plant or to add fertiliser. He showed me everything. I watched, but he explained things, too.

The garden was a ten-minute walk from their compound. It was a nice piece of ground surrounded by a straw fence, with cabbages and onions growing in silty soil. There was a good well lined with cement and laterite stone, with water at a depth of less than five metres. A pile of leftover tomato plants showed what Paul had grown earlier and probably sold.

Relations between Joseph and his children had become strained. The question of the pig they had bought during their last visit came up. Joseph said he felt hurt because the pig and chickens had been bought during previous visits without consulting him. Paul said that the pig was still with his uncle even though everything needed to look after a pig was already there – even the bricks to repair the pigsty. Joseph also said that Paul had sold the peanuts he had harvested and had not shared the money, nor had he shared the money from the sale of the tomatoes.

Claude and Bruno replied that Paul had come back and was working in the village, and that young people also needed to do something for themselves if they were to stay. They thought that Paul should be encouraged, even if he made mistakes.

Paul remained relaxed during this discussion. He tried to defend himself, but without becoming aggressive towards his father. Finally Joseph said that Paul could carry on gardening but should also take an interest in everything else. Claude and Bruno approved and, in front of everyone, handed the father some money for the purchase of cabbage seeds.

Joseph had been appeased. He said how happy he was that communication had been restored between him and his son.

Paul Supports his Family

When Bruno and Claude went to Kobodogho about six weeks later, they found Paul bent over his vegetables, preparing the beds for planting. The cabbages had been harvested and immediately replaced by eggplants. Paul showed them the little nursery of cabbage seedlings that he had grown, from the seeds they had bought for him.

His uncle Philippe – the owner of the market garden – had died about ten days before and Paul was helping Philippe's children to continue with the gardening. He had planted peppers with his cousins and had sown beans to sell the leaves. He also planned to start growing kumba, a traditional African eggplant.

As before, there was tension when Joseph arrived back from the market. According to Paul, this happened only on market days, when he had drunk too much dolo, the traditional Burkina beer made from millet. Bruno and Claude took the time to smooth over the differences between father and son and, as a show of trust, they openly handed Mr Joseph 3,000 FCFA to contribute to the purchase of products for Paul's gardening and the breeding of the father's chickens. There was a risk of things going badly between them because of the way the money was used, but Claude wanted to show them that he hoped they would continue to work together.

The pig was still at the home of Paul's late uncle, Philippe; he preferred to wait to take it back home until the beginning of the rainy season, when it would be easier to find food. Claude and Bruno encouraged him to put his pig with his father's so that they could be raised together. This time, Claude and Bruno simply left money with the father for a male pig to put with the other two.

On Claude and Bruno's next visit, Paul claimed that he had been working in the fields with his family. However, they found his attitude less frank than usual. They asked him about his pig. He said quite simply that he had sold it because he intended to go to the Côte d'Ivoire. Like many in his family, a whole generation of the Burkina population were attracted by the opportunities offered by the economic development of the Côte d'Ivoire. However, the money he had made from the sale was not enough to pay for the ticket. Claude and Bruno thanked Paul for his honesty.

For the first time, Joseph spoke positively about Paul's market gardening, 'If Paul plants in September, his work could bring in money by the end of the year.' Paul, for his part, had new ideas: he had identified a spot for planting mango trees. Claude and Bruno saw this as a sign that he was putting down roots. Because it was difficult to find mango grafts in Kobodogho, they promised to bring him some. At the beginning of August, Claude and Bruno brought Paul the mango trees. They noticed that kumba and rice had been planted as planned.

Failure of the Rainy Season

When they visited the village at the beginning of October 2000, Claude and Bruno were surprised to see that the land along the village roads, all the way to the family's district, was unusually dry: they did not see one puddle of water and the hollow that was usually full during this season was empty.

When they arrived, they saw Paul in the distance, walking through the fields without a shirt, and covered in sweat and mud. He was busy making bricks out of banco for his house. He had grown into a good-looking, muscular young man, a far cry from the way he had looked in the city.

It had not rained in a month and there was no water to be found in the compound. The surrounding landscape was depressing: a slap in the face after all their efforts to do a little more and a little better.

Paul took them to his plantation to see his mango trees. The first tree was beautiful, shaded by thorn branches. The others had suffered although it was obvious that they were watered daily.

The kumba plants that Paul had been cultivating with his father had grown well, but had produced very little fruit. The millet had survived but was sparse. Everything was already yellow. The entire rice field was desolate. After all the hard work Paul had done to prepare the ground and plant the seeds with his mother, there was not even a single ear of rice.

Before leaving, Bruno and Claude handed Paul the seeds they had brought: tomatoes, courgettes, eggplant, peppers and lettuce.

By December 2000, the mango trees were still being cared for, but were struggling to survive. In the garden there were several fine patches of vegetables.

Paul wanted to build his own home close to his parents' compound and was still building his hut in February 2001. The garden had several beds of different vegetables: carrots, peppers, squash, tomatoes and eggplants. Joseph confirmed that Paul was doing well on his own. Bruno also met Safi, Paul's girlfriend.

Everything had changed by the time Claude and Bruno returned at the beginning of May 2001. There was no longer enough water to go around and the vegetable garden was bare. Paul's parents wanted him to help them farm a field six kilometres away, where it had already rained, but he thought it was too early because rainfall was unpredictable in June.

There had hardly been any rain by mid-June 2001, and the bush around Kobodogho had all dried out. Few people were working in the fields, and nothing seemed to have grown.

Paul had decided to go back to work at the market: he was helping a friend to sell oven-baked pork.

Nevertheless, a month later Bruno found Paul working in the fields with his family. They had even started growing a field of tomatoes and kumbas together. They were also intending to grow rice, so Bruno left them a small contribution for the purchase of seeds.

Paul was now involved in activities that gave him a place in society and enabled him to look after himself. Claude and Bruno began to space out their visits.

VILLAGE LIFE

At the beginning of 2002, Paul had been off the streets for nearly three years. He had spent them in the village with his family. He was involved in activities that gave him a place in society and he seemed to have found his bearings again within his community.

Paul had not seen Claude or Bruno since the beginning of October 2001, a vital period for getting the market garden started. Yet he had shown himself able to assume his responsibilities and had learned to work without their support. When Bruno visited Paul in January 2002, he was welcomed by Joseph and, for the first time, invited inside the compound. Joseph told him that the harvests had been better that year. Bruno met an uncle who praised Paul for his hard work. Paul had succeeded particularly well with peppers, onions and eggplants.

Paul later explained:

> When my uncle Philippe – the one who had given me the plot of land – died, I took care of the whole garden. The garden made a profit. When I sold things, I'd share the money I made with my family: I'd give my father 1,000 or 2,000 FCFA and my mother 1,500 to 2,500 FCFA. As it was my mother that prepared the meals, she could buy rice. During the rainy season I could buy enough food for my parents with the money from the garden and I'd still have 3,000 or 3,500 FCFA left over. I bought myself some clothes and shoes. I also bought some chickens at the market and two pigs.

Although very modest, this garden was a genuine project and represented all of Paul's hopes of being able to contribute to the life of the family, and also of laying foundations for his future.

Counter-season Market Gardening

Counter-season market gardening is undertaken during the dry season between November and May. It has developed a great deal in Burkina Faso over recent years due to the creation of reservoirs, known as 'micro dams'. Even on a small scale, this activity is enough to ensure economic stability for many young people living in rural areas. If the conditions are right, it is an affordable and attractive alternative, because it takes over from the traditional counter-season activities that no longer employ them – such as weaving, basket-making and pottery – and therefore maintains the cycles of their community.

PAUL DESCRIBES HIS VILLAGE PROJECTS

On market days, I would go to buy chickens in the morning with the money I'd earned from the garden. Then I'd go and sell them to the traders who came from Ouagadougou. We'd buy the chickens for 850 FCFA and we'd sell them for 1,000 or 1,500 FCFA. Sometimes the traders would give us the money in advance and then we'd go and buy chickens for them. The traders would give us enough money for 15 or 20 chickens, and we could earn 1,500 to 2,000 FCFA from that. The traders did not trust everyone, only those they knew. I had an uncle on my mother's side who sold chickens and he agreed to introduce me to the traders, along with two friends.

When I had finished paying for the chickens, I would go and sell clothes for another uncle on my mother's side who had a secondhand clothes stall in the market. I would eat with him and in the evening he would give me 200 or 300 FCFA. My uncle explained the price of clothes to me. When I sold them for more, I would keep the profit. On market days I could earn up to 1,000 or 1,500 FCFA. With the chickens and the clothes, I could earn up to 2,500 or 3,000 FCFA. Then I'd put some aside to give to my younger brothers and my mother.

I also made bricks out of banco. Early in the morning, I'd go and work in the garden and then make bricks. It brought in money. I didn't do it every day; there were times when I just couldn't make any more because there was no water.

A friend gave me a goat and some chickens. When they grew up and had young, we shared them. We fed the chickens on water and a bit of millet in the mornings. For the pigs, we had to buy spent dolo grains (animal feed made from the solid residue of the millet) and I was the one who paid for them. As for the goats, two of them belonged to me. We sold them to pay for the marriage of my older brother.

My uncle has 50 head of cattle and a tractor. I don't know where his wealth comes from; that's how I've always known him. I worked for him eight or nine times, along with his sons. We'd take the tractor to the other villages and we'd stay there for up to two weeks. The people would bring us their millet and we'd drive over it. We'd keep 1,000 FCFA for ourselves and we'd give the rest back to the uncle. He supplied the diesel.

When the corn was harvested, we'd go to the fields to fetch it. My uncle could have as many as 130 bags of corn and millet.

When I got back to the village, I saw friends I knew there. We'd hang out together but there were no thieves amongst us. We never did anything stupid because we talked to the old people. Three or four of us would go and sit with men older than my father. They'd give us advice about things we didn't know: they'd tell us how to make money, how to find a wife, how to get married ... I have good friends in the village. Salif's an uncle who's the same age as me. If there's a marriage in his compound, I can help with the serving. During the rainy season, he comes to do some farming with me and I go to his place to farm too. There are also Saïdou, Adama and Blaise, who live next door to us. When I started working on my garden, they came every day to help with the watering. Now, when I have money, we'll go to the market and I'll buy them something to eat.

Village Life and Customs

There are family totems that mustn't be dishonoured. If you dishonour them, it's very serious. The old men and women taught me, for example, that there are animals we shouldn't kill. There are ceremonies that they took us to see. For instance, there are ceremonies for the rainy season, for when the rain doesn't come. They are for the whole family, whether you're Muslim or Christian. Often there are things in a ceremony that only children can do. If there are no children, then it's difficult. We'll be taking over from the older generation, so we have to learn.

In the family, you have your brothers and sisters who are very happy to be with you. You get up in the morning and they're the first people you see. In the rainy season, my parents gave me some rice and some peanuts to plant, and some money to go to the market. They did it so I could stay in the village because the work was easier for them when I stayed at home.

In the village, there are friends and relatives who advise you to work. They call you for small jobs. You can help them and that's good. The fact that I worked with members of the family changed their opinion of me. They told me I'd changed. They said, 'He's a good boy.' If you work well and if you don't hang out too much, except during rest time, then it's ok. If you hang out too much, talking to your friends, you can make mistakes and say things that hurt someone and start a fight. To avoid these kinds of problems with people, I preferred to go and work in my garden. The garden was a reason for me to stay.

It's hard to live without your family. If you have marriage problems or health problems, it's your family you have to talk to. That's where you'll get advice that teaches you about life today. If you go to see a relative, you talk about a lot of things with them. It's not like in the city. In the city you talk, but it's only for fun – it's not the type of talk where you get advice like in the village. In the city you can have friends, but they're not like the friends you have in the village. In the city you only know each other, but in the village you know your friends' relatives, their mothers. If something happens in their family, you go to visit them. That's what encouraged me to stay.

Another reason I didn't go back to the city was the old women and old men who advised me to stay in the village. I listened to them because my friends had told me exactly the same thing. They also told me to stay with my parents. When I had a fight with my father, the old women advised me not to make a big deal of it, and not to leave the village because of it. They told me to go to a friend's house, and when I came back it was over. I could also go to my friend Blaise's place and he would go and see my father to smooth things over.

Life in the village isn't hard for me because I know how to act. I've lived there and it doesn't bother me. I'd like to stay in the village if I can find a job to earn some money. I like it there. The four years spent in the village were good.

PAUL RETURNS TO THE CITY

In March 2003, Bruno visited the family to invite them to participate in the preparation of a seminar to be held in June, called 'Joining the families of children who live on the streets'. This was intended to assess the work done by the Courtyard of a Hundred Trades with the children and their families. They wanted Paul and his family to be interviewed for a video documentary about the steps taken to rebuild family ties. They accepted without hesitation. When Bruno came back with the director of the film, Joseph was not at home and did not take part in the filming. Paul's mother and grandmother participated, but said very little. Paul, never very talkative, chose to show his work rather than speak about it. He brought along his friends, and together they took Bruno and the film director on a tour of the garden and then to the place where they made bricks.

At the beginning of May 2003, Bruno and Claude went to Kobodogho to meet Paul to prepare for his contribution to the seminar, but Paul had left for Ouagadougou and was working in a restaurant in Goughin district. It took several days to find him. He was working in a restaurant owned by an Egyptian family, on the edge of Goughin market. The owner was happy to meet Claude, whom he seemed to consider a reliable character reference.

Later, Paul explained how the latest change came about:

It was at a time when the garden was a mess: the fence was broken and the sheep and goats could get in. The fence had been made with millet stalks, so there was nothing left to repair it with. I had to wait for the next harvest. I told my father that I wanted to go to Ouagadougou. He didn't say no because it wasn't the rainy season yet and my brother had just come back home. He was working hard to help the family and this gave me enough time to come to the city and find something to help my parents.

When I arrived in Ouagadougou, I had a place to stay with a friend behind the market in Goughin. I spent 20 days looking for accommodation. I paid for it within the month. I found this job at the Egyptian restaurant the day I arrived in Ouagadougou. All I did was go past and speak to them and they told me to come and work that evening.

At the beginning they gave me 7,500 FCFA a month. The second month I earned 10,000 FCFA, and the third month, 15,000 FCFA. The fourth month, the boss called me in to ask me how much he should pay me. I said I didn't know. The boss said he wanted to pay me 25,000 FCFA.

Paul was paid 25,000 FCFA on the second day of each month – close to the legal minimum wage in Burkina Faso – as well as 5,000 FCFA to pay for his room in the vicinity of the restaurant. He works at the restaurant every day from 2 p.m. to 3 a.m. He leaves his savings, sometimes 10,000 FCFA and sometimes 15,000 FCFA, with his uncle in the village. He goes back to the village to see his parents and his grandmother every third Sunday, which corresponds to the market day that draws the largest crowds.

After four years spent in the village, Paul's new departure for the city was no longer a case of an adolescent running away in search of adventure, but of an adult migrating to look for work. The reality of modern day rural life in Burkina is that life in the village is permanently connected to life in the city, either through work or other activities, or thanks to relatives who provide material support from the city. Today, living in the village also requires money: for sending children or younger siblings to school, for medical treatment, for transport, for the latest clothes. Because the village does not offer enough money-making opportunities, many choose life in the city.

In July 2004, Claude and members of the team paid a friendly visit to the restaurant where Paul worked. He was selling roast chickens, and the restaurant was doing a brisk trade. They were surprised to see that Paul was in charge of the cash register. This was a sign that the owner trusted him. Paul was proud to be able to offer them an extra free chicken.

Paul seemed stable in this job, except for one attempt to work for a competitor who made promises he did not keep. The Egyptian owner nevertheless took him back, but admitted that he had done so out of respect for Claude's friendship with Paul. Paul was thus once again living in Ouagadougou, but with a genuine 'position'.

Although Paul has gone to live in the city, he continues to identify himself as a villager and his plans are defined in the context of the village.

'HE WAS WALKING WITH DEATH'

Paul's family is happy with the changes they see in him. His grandmother had this to say:

> I'm happy with Paul. He has a job, he comes on Sundays and he gives me something for my tobacco. You helped Paul so much to be a man; I'll never forget you. Thanks to you, the boy didn't meet his end when he was living on the streets. He's cured, otherwise he'd have continued to walk the streets of the city and he'd have been killed. He was walking with death. Luckily, you intercepted him! His father should be happy with him because he never comes home empty-handed. Young people need money; we have to let them have that. What's important is that once they have money, they remember to give some to their family. We can't ask for any more from them than that. If a child decides to come and stay

with his parents, they can't say anything or complain. But if he leaves a good job to do so, then that's not good.

His father said:

Paul has changed. He doesn't have the same character as before. He has more money now than when he was in the village: he's able to look after himself, and make ends meet. He manages to hold down the job he wants and to make a little money. Whatever he is today is thanks to what he must have learned at school. Paul wasn't the first to apply for his current job. There were others who wanted to work there. Maybe it was due to their lack of education that the owner decided not to take them on. If Paul hadn't gone to school, the position wouldn't have been his for the taking.

PAUL TALKS ABOUT HIS FUTURE

It's difficult just to farm without trading. I came to Ouagadougou to look for the money to start trading.

Going to the market without anything to sell isn't good. If you sell, even if it's little by little, you'll become like the big shopkeepers. I want to sell new clothes in the village: hats, caps, Nike t-shirts, shorts, belts … I can buy them at Goughin market in Ouagadougou. I hope to start next Christmas. Once I start trading, I'll stop working at the restaurant. I can start by selling at the market in Kobodogho, as well as at the small markets in the surrounding villages on the other days. I'll buy myself a bicycle for that. When your market is a good one, you can make 3,000 or 4,000 FCFA. If you have something to sell at the market, you know when you get up every morning that's where you're going to go. All the young people want to trade.

As the market's not open every day, I'll also be able to farm. I'm not sure if I'll take up gardening again.

With agriculture, the problem is that you can't farm a lot if you don't have a donkey. We have a plough that my grandfather left us, but the donkey died. But if I can buy a donkey or an ox to pull the plough and work in the fields, it'll be easier. The more you grow, the less you need to buy.

Today, everybody's trying to get a job. I want to work in Kobodogho because it's my village and I want to help the old people farm.

Everything's a question of money: you need it for your health, you need it to eat and you need it to get married. I haven't started trading yet, so I have money but no profits. If I spend my money before I start trading, I could lose everything. If you work, it's so you can get married. But to get married, you have to have money. If you get married, you think you'll have children. That's why you make sure you can work.

If I have children, I want them to go to school to learn how to read and write. And I want them to farm. But if they go to school, they won't be able to farm as much as those that don't. And then one day, they'll go into trade like me. I want them to stay in the village first, so that they are part of the family. Later on, they can work out what they want to do and where they want to live. Children are more important than money. They are tomorrow's family. When we no longer have the strength to work, it's the children who'll take over from us. Even if you don't have money, you can still have children. I want at least four or five.

I want to look after my relatives during the rainy season and provide them with food. When they're old, the children will farm for them. I'll pay for them. My younger brothers can come and trade with me. They can come and help me, take things to sell and go around the market.

What's good is that I have work. If you don't have work, you don't know what you're going to do to earn money. Something else that's good is that I'm not far from the village: I go to see my family and I come back. I'm lucky that if I go back to live in the village, I'll always find work and people to show me how to do it.

EPILOGUE

In September 2007, Bruno Bambara and his wife went to the Egyptian restaurant where Paul had been working for the past four years. The restaurant was well situated, and employed 14 other people. Paul worked from 1 p.m. to 3 a.m. selling roast chickens, and still enjoyed a good relationship with the owner. With his monthly salary, he rented a room near the restaurant and paid for his electricity and clothes. He dressed stylishly, owned a mobile telephone and was saving money towards the clothing stall he had long dreamed of opening.

Paul regularly visited his family in the village with gifts of clothes and food. His father still farmed his field far away in the bush, but that year's harvest was hardly promising. Paul's younger brother was working as a mechanic in Ouagadougou, while his elder brother had returned to live in the village. His grandmother was still alive.

BURKINA FASO IN BRIEF

Geography[7]

Burkina Faso is a landlocked country in West Africa. It is bordered by Benin, Ghana, Côte d'Ivoire, Mali, Niger, and Togo. The northern provinces lie in the Sahel, the belt of semi-arid land with low rainfall that fringes the Sahara desert. During the dry season, permanent water sources are vital. Further south the rainfall is heavier, supporting the small-scale farming which provides a livelihood for most of the population. The rainy season in Burkina Faso usually begins in June and ends by October. It is warm throughout the year. In the hottest months, from March to May, temperatures rise to over 40° C. Most people in Burkina Faso are farmers who grow cash crops (peanuts, shea nuts, sesame, cotton), and food crops (sorghum, millet, maize, rice and vegetables). Industries include cotton lint, beverages, agricultural processing, soap, cigarettes, textiles and gold mining. The country's natural resources include manganese, limestone, marble and small deposits of gold, copper, nickel, bauxite, lead, phosphates, zinc and silver.

History[8]

As early as the fourteenth century, four Mossi kingdoms occupied the territory now known as Burkina Faso. Despite repeated attacks and attempted invasions from outside forces, they were never able to form a united political entity. In 1896, the French established a protectorate over the Mossi kingdom of Ouagadougou and placed the other three kingdoms, now weakened by dynastic quarrels, under their dominion. These territories were absorbed into French West Africa until the colony of Upper Volta was created in 1919. Upper Volta became an autonomous republic within the Franco-African community in 1958 and proclaimed its independence on 5 August 1960. A period of deep instability followed, and between 1966 and 1987 the country was rocked by no less than six military *coups d'état*. On 3 August 1984, the country took the name of Burkina Faso, 'the land of upright people'. In 1987, Captain Blaise Compaoré set the country on the road to democracy with a process that led to a democratic constitution in 1991. He was elected president in 1991 and re-elected in 1998, 2005 and 2010.

Key Figures[9] (statistics from 2009):

> Area: 274,200 square kilometres
> Capital: Ouagadougou
> Population: 15,746,232 inhabitants
> Principal languages: French (official language), Mooré, Dioula,
>   Gourmantché and Foulfouldé
> Currency: franc CFA (100 FCFA = 0.15 euros = US$0.20)
> Urban population: 20.4 per cent
> Agriculture: 92 per cent of the working population
> Fertility rate: 5.9 per cent
> Infant mortality: 84.5 per 1,000 live births
> Life expectancy at birth: 52.7 years
> Literacy over the age of 15: males 36.7 per cent, females 21.6
>   per cent
> School life expectancy: six years
> GDP per capita: US$1,124 (purchasing power parity US dollars)
> Public expenditure on education: 4.6 per cent of GDP
> Total external debt: US$1,840 million
> Debt service: 6 per cent of total exports

The Human Development Index[10] (HDI) is 0.389, which classes the country 177 out of 182 in the UNDP *World Report on Human Development 2009*. This is an average figure which hides great discrepancies, since the same report in 2006 shows that the HDI of the richest 20 per cent of the population is almost twice as high as that of the poorest 20 per cent.

NOTES

1. Thierry Dedieu, *Yacouba*, Paris: Seuil Jeunesse, 1994.
2. To protect the anonymity of Paul and his family, all the village names have been changed.
3. 100 FCFA (francs CFA) is worth approximately US$0.20.
4. Glue known as 'rubber solution', used to repair bicycle tyres. It has a hallucinatory effect.
5. Ministère de l'Action Sociale et de la Solidarité Nationale, *Programme National d'Action Educative en Milieu Ouvert*, Ouagadougou, Burkina Faso, 2002.
6. Lea Salmon-Marchat and Quentin Wodon, *Migration et enfants 'de la rue' au Burkina Faso et en Côte d'Ivoire*, Washington, DC: World Bank, 2007.
7. http://tinyurl.com/6law2ad
8. www.africa-onweb.com

9. *Encyclopédie de l'Etat du Monde, 2009*, Paris: Éditions La Découverte, 2009; United Nations Development Programme, *World Development Report 2009*, New York: UNPD, 2009.

10. The Human Development Index varies from 0 to 1 and brings together the figures for life expectancy, literacy and revenues, according to national averages obtained from international sources. It does not include important aspects of the quality of human development and thus should be treated with caution.

2
Gold Under the Bridge: The Story of Mercedita and her Family in the Philippines

Marilyn Ortega Gutierrez and Alasdair Wallace

Mercedita Villar Diaz-Mendez was involved with the International Movement ATD Fourth World in Manila over the course of 15 years. Marilyn Ortega Gutierrez first began taking part in ATD street libraries at the weekends when she was a student at the Philippine Normal University. After some years as a teacher, in 1999 she joined the ATD volunteer corps. This account of Mercedita's life focuses, in particular, on the experiences shared by Marilyn with whom she had a strong relationship.

All the information presented here concerning Mercedita's life was confirmed and approved by Mercedita herself and, where possible, her own words have been included.[1]

Marilyn first encountered Mercedita and her family in 1995, through a street library project in a very disadvantaged community that lived under a bridge in Manila. Marilyn explains:

> Every weekend, with other university students, I brought beautiful books, and pencils and crayons for drawing. I was amazed at how a child could read a book with full attention amidst all the noise and nuisances. I felt the thirst of these children for something beautiful, for anything that would bring their imagination to life. This is how I met Mercedita and her family for the first time. They were living along the canal under the bridge. I remember how scared I was every time I visited them. The path that led to their house was so narrow that I had to watch my steps not to fall into the canal.

THE BRIDGE

Quirino Avenue Bridge, located at the heart of the huge urban centre that is Manila, was home to Mercedita for much of her adult life.

Since 1989 ATD Fourth World has been in contact with more than 100 families living under this concrete bridge.

The bridge carries a busy road that connects to a main highway. Under the bridge is a heavily polluted canal with many small wooden shacks along its banks; some constructed on wooden stilts are actually standing in the canal. There is one public water point.

It appears that people first started living under the bridge in the early 1970s, in the period when a great number of families began migrating from their rural provinces to the cities. In the crowded, heavily populated city of Manila, the bridge provides living space for those who have little other choice. It serves as a roof for the houses under it, and the traffic lights on the busy road above provide a location for selling goods and begging. In official terms the community is known as an 'illegal squatter settlement', of which there are a great many in Manila.

Marilyn describes her first visit to the bridge:

I was walking underneath a concrete bridge, on a little path in between houses, beside a canal. It was dark, very hot and an acrid smell was seeping into my lungs. Above, cars and trucks were travelling fast. There were children at play, children with pails of water taking a bath. Mothers doing their washing and chatting with one another, men and women tirelessly pulling out nails from old wood which they hoped to sell afterwards. At one side of the bridge were several folding beds with adults and children lying asleep. On the avenue, taxi drivers were dodging between trucks and cars, honking their horns constantly. Men were standing in the middle of the road with wooden boxes full of cigarettes, candies, bottled water and newspapers for sale. Soon I heard a loud siren. It was the train. Someone grabbed my hand and led me aside. We stood, leaning on a house wall and waited for the train to pass. It was only a few centimetres away from us! Then, people started moving again, installing chairs, tables, basins, and even their pets outside. The next train will be in two hours.

Although Mercedita Villar Diaz-Mendez lived in many different locations, the community under the bridge could be described as an anchor point for her adult life. She continually returned to it after periods elsewhere, and she built friendships and strong community links there.

MERCEDITA'S CHILDHOOD AND EDUCATION

Mercedita Villar Diaz-Mendez was born on 5 July 1965, the youngest of six children. She grew up in the predominantly rural province of Camarines Norte in the Bicol region where her parents worked on a farm.

> What I remember most was that I worked a lot! I had a winnowing basket that I carried on my head, with vegetables that I had to sell around our village. At home, I would fetch water and clean the house.

Mercedita managed to finish elementary school, but it would not have been possible for her to continue to high school if she had stayed in the province because the costs were too high. If she had stayed in the household, her parents would have needed her to work. So when she was twelve years old she went to stay with her sister in Manila, where education was more accessible.

> My elder sister helped me get to high school but she and her husband had to work every day and I had to look after their children. I left my sister's place to find work. I had to grab any chance for work so I could get myself to school. I couldn't do one without the other.

Mercedita found a job working at night in a small store. Instead of being paid money, in return for this work she was able to attend school during the day. However, this arrangement proved too tiring.

> At school, I always felt sleepy. I could not concentrate on my lessons. I left my job and went back to Manila. There, I was hired as a housemaid by an old lady. She let me go to school for a while but then I had to stop again because there was too much work in such a big house.

Mercedita continued to find ways around the many barriers to gaining an education and, at the age of 16, she succeeded in finishing high school. However, she was never able to obtain the official papers to show her achievement:

> I didn't go to the graduation ceremony to get my certificate because I had no money to pay for the fees or the graduation dress.

EDUCATION IN THE PHILIPPINES

In comparison with other countries of similar economic development, the Philippines has relatively high adult literacy and school enrolment rates. However, as can be seen in the experiences of Mercedita herself and of her children, people living in poverty still face a great many barriers to entering and completing a school education. National data indicate that rates for participation in education are significantly lower for people living on low incomes. Associated costs, which parents are expected to pay – such as buying uniforms and stationery supplies, transport to and from school, and the lost earning capacity of the child – are all reasons for not attending school. For parents, these costs represent a real obstacle to education for their children.

It is clear that Mercedita and her children put a very high value on formal education, perceiving it as a way out of poverty. Yet, because of the difficulties they face in their daily lives, it is these families who require the most support if their children are ever going to be able to attend school regularly.

MERCEDITA'S MARRIAGES

In 1982, at the age of 17, Mercedita married and had two children: a daughter named Maritess, born in 1983, and a son named Juanito, born in 1986. However, after some four years together, she and her husband decided to separate. Mercedita and her two children moved back to her parents' home in Bicol and worked on the farm.

Two years later in Camarines Norte, Mercedita met a man named Roberto Diaz, also known as Juanio to his friends. They grew up in the same province; he was her *kababayan* (Tagalog for 'compatriot' or 'countryman'). They soon decided to move to Manila together. As a temporary arrangement, the two children, Maritess and Juanito, stayed behind with Mercedita's parents, with regular visits back and forth between Manila and the province.

Mercedita first started living under the bridge of Quirino Avenue when she and Juanio moved to Manila. He had lived under the bridge before and had relatives there with whom they could stay. While they were living under the bridge, Mercedita gave birth to a baby girl, who died at the age of seven months. A second daughter, named Roselina, was born in 1989. However, at the beginning of 1990, the family was again struck by tragedy when Juanio had a heart attack and died. Mercedita was devastated.

Soon after Juanio's funeral, Roselina, who was eight months old, became very ill. Mercedita found herself alone with no money and no means to get her daughter to a doctor:

> I had nothing in my pocket. I was running down the street, shouting for help, until a man saw me and grabbed my child from my arms. He stood in the middle of the road and flagged down a car which brought us to the hospital.

This man was Felix Mendez. When he met Mercedita he was living nearby and had been good friends with Juanio. While Roselina was in hospital, Felix showed great kindness to Mercedita and supported her both financially and emotionally. In 1991, he and Mercedita began to live together.

THE INFORMAL ECONOMY

Due to its complex and unregulated nature, it is extremely difficult to give an accurate estimate of the size and impact of the informal economy in the Philippines. However, it is certainly highly significant, both in terms of the number of people working within it and the contribution it makes to gross domestic product. A household survey carried out in the community under the bridge in 2006 found that the majority of people were self-employed and earning money through a very varied range of activities – none within the formal sector.

People like Felix show entrepreneurial spirit in finding and creating opportunities to earn money but, excluded from formal frameworks, they are subject to debilitating levels of instability and insecurity. They have no social security and therefore accrue no retirement pension, receive no holiday pay, and have no insurance against sickness or accidents. Although they have many informal systems of protection, they have no official safety nets, and are left extremely vulnerable to any shocks or crises that may occur. In terms of stability, they have no contract to ensure a regular wage, and there is a huge disparity in their earnings from day to day, with some days when they work long hours with no income at all.

Added to this insecurity – far from being supported – their efforts are neither recognised nor respected by 'formal society'. Very often the vendors who are trying to make a living are perceived as undesirable or unsightly; their activities are seen as a hazardous nuisance. As part of 'beautification' and traffic congestion projects, local authorities can clear the streets of literally thousands of unlicensed vendors who have set up small stalls along the roadside.

Despite all this, thousands of people like Felix continue to make the most of the opportunities open to them, in order to feed their families and improve their situations. However, they will never realise their potential unless they are offered support and respect.

The Community Life of the City

Although it is unstable, the diverse and dynamic informal economy in Manila offers many opportunities to earn a living, and the bridge itself provides potential customers in the form of motorists waiting at the traffic lights. Over a third of all the work undertaken by the residents under the bridge involves selling goods along the avenue.

Manila offers the family access to work and services which are unavailable to them in the provinces. Mercedita spoke of the importance of proximity to a market and a church but expressed most strongly the need for access to schooling for her children. One of them even received financial support from a charitable organisation.

Mercedita and her family continually returned to the bridge – a place they themselves denounced as unhealthy. Clearly, they found something at the bridge which they did not find anywhere else. Indeed, what looks no better than a slum from the outside shelters a community of people within which there is the hope, happiness, mutual understanding and solidarity that is vital to their survival and wellbeing. For Mercedita and her family, it is a place where they are accepted, where they have grown roots and developed friendships. They are part of a community where neighbours help each other, where they feel understood and accepted.

On several occasions when Mercedita had no home, she was able to live temporarily with neighbours, protecting her from living on the streets. Mercedita uses her own experience and knowhow to obtain aid for others from the municipal authorities. Neighbours mind each other's children so that the parents may go to work; they share money to pay for funerals.

This microsociety restores people's dignity and self-respect; it takes the place of the family left behind in the provinces.

The Dream of Life in the Provinces

None of the people under the bridge plans to live there permanently. They dream of having their own land where they do not have to be 'squatters', always at risk of eviction. Finding this dream impossible to fulfil in the city, they see hope in the provinces. At the very least, they see the provinces as a place where they may achieve stability, or where their children will have fresh air, rather than the polluted, heavy air under the bridge.

However, when they go to the provinces they find life difficult and often feel isolated and lonely. It is extremely hard for the children to go to school and there are very few opportunities for employment. Finally they are forced to retreat back to the city, where there is always the hope of gaining stable employment in the rapidly growing formal economy.

LIFE WITH FELIX

In his continual struggle to earn a living for the family, Felix found opportunities to work in a huge variety of activities across the informal sector, such as selling sweets, cigarettes or pancakes along the roadside on top of the bridge. At one point he had the idea of cooking and selling peanuts: 'Mercedita will cook them. Then I will sell them, one peso per pack. Not bad, is it?'

He managed to keep this small enterprise afloat until he was forced to stop when all the children were suddenly taken ill at the same time. So far, he and Mercedita had been managing to save a small amount of money each week from the profits, and were making plans for the future. But when the children became ill they were forced to spend all that they had saved on medical bills. They were left with nothing for buying the peanuts, and nothing to fall back on.

Not long after, Felix began earning a small income by spending all his time collecting and selling scrap wood. At one point he got an officially registered job, mixing cement and carrying sacks of sand for a construction firm, but this was only temporary. He managed to work in the local communities collecting and carrying water:

> Here I am, a *kargador* under the bridge. I fetch water for other people and get one peso for each container. I have to keep earning for my children; they will soon start school ...

Despite his constant efforts to find different ways of earning an income for his family, Felix was not able to find the stable employment that he dreamed of.

Back and Forth

For the next few years Mercedita's life was characterised by frequent moves back and forth between the city and the provinces in search of a better quality of life and a more stable future.

In 1991, Mercedita, Felix and Roselina, who was nearly two years old, went to live close to Felix's family in a rural area of Batangas, a province located in south-western Luzon. However, life was very difficult, with few opportunities for earning money. Mercedita explained:

> In that place, we were very far from many things! We were far from the market, from schools, from churches. There were only fields around us.

After a year, they moved back to the bridge and sold recycled wood. Rowena was born in 1992. They had to move again when the owner of the land they were living on wanted to turn it into a car park. The caretaker of that area gave them iron sheets and wood and they built a house close to the canal under the bridge. Their youngest daughter, Rosana, was born there in 1993.

In 1994, the family again went in search of greater stability and a better quality of life away from the city. This time they went further south to the large island of Mindoro where Felix had another relative. Felix got a job on a farm, but in 1995, during a visit to friends back at the bridge in Manila, he was hit by a taxi and hospitalised. Unable to work while he convalesced, he lost his job. Finding no more work in the area, the family again returned to Manila and the bridge. They had to live in a neighbour's house while their own house was restored.

Mercedita's two oldest children, Maritess and Juanito, had both been living with their grandparents in the province, keeping in regular contact with their mother and sisters in Manila with visits once or twice a month. Now the ageing grandparents could no longer look after them. Maritess had already moved from Bicol to live with Mercedita's sister in the province of Laguna, where she was able to go to high school. Ten-year-old Juanito now came to live with his mother and sisters under the bridge. However, he found it difficult to adjust and got into trouble with groups of gangs. Mercedita decided Juanito should live temporarily in a centre where he would receive education and support.

Throughout 1997 the family lived under the bridge and became very active in their community. Felix and Mercedita played a considerable role in co-organising a feeding programme to address the issue of malnutrition among the children under the bridge. It was planned and run in partnership with the parents as well as doctors, social workers, local officials and ATD Fourth World.

Parents like Mercedita and Felix were part of the decision-making process, and were responsible for buying and cooking the food. As part of her contribution, Mercedita would collect the money at the organisation's office every morning, then go to the market to buy the ingredients. The project was popular with the residents but was brought to an end after only three months because of a lack of funding.

In 1998, the family moved to the provinces again; this time they lived in Mercedita's parents' home:

> Felix took care of my father's farm until a strong typhoon came and destroyed all our crops. It was impossible to start again! The only way we thought of was to go back to the bridge.

In 1999, Felix found a job working on a sugar cane plantation, so the family again left the bridge and moved to the rural area of Batangas. The children were not able to attend school because they were too far away and did not have the papers they needed to enrol.

Three months later, Mercedita came to the ATD Fourth World office with tragic news:

> Felix has been murdered. We searched for him for several days and found him in the fields, almost decomposed. He was thrown like trash. He's a kind person. I don't remember him getting in trouble with anyone in Batangas. He was trying so hard to have a quiet life.

Mercedita filed for a police investigation, but no one was charged with the crime.

LIFE AS A WIDOW

After Felix's death, Mercedita discovered that she was pregnant. Unable to live amidst the memories of the death, worried for her family's safety and without the income from the plantation, Mercedita moved back to Manila, leaving her three daughters with her sister.

On her next visit to the bridge, Marilyn discovered that many of the neighbours had heard the news of Felix's death and wanted to pay tribute to him. It was agreed that they would dedicate some time to Felix during the 'seventeenth' gathering.[2] On the day they all gathered around the 'Stone of Life'. Someone read the words engraved on the stone, others took turns reading testimonies. A neighbour called Aracelli described Felix as a happy man and a doting father to his children. She said:

> My neighbour Felix was a kind man. I remember him often looking after my twins whenever I had to be with my husband to work on recycled wood. The commemorative stone was an important place for him. He would tell us, 'Go to the Stone of Life. There, you will not be alone.' I hope that he'll find peace and justice wherever he is now.

The Continual Threat of Eviction

In 1975, Presidential Decree 772 declared 'squatting' a criminal offence. It was used to convict and imprison squatters and, more commonly, led to a strategy of forced evictions. Between 1986 and 1991, around 100,000 families were evicted from their homes each year. Although the Decree was repealed in 1997, current policy focuses on removing the informal settlements through relocation programmes rather than on upgrading the settlements. Nevertheless, a 2008 report found that there were approximately 3.1 million urban poor households still living in informal settlements throughout the Philippines.[3]

Mercedita and her children all returned to live under the bridge. However, this time they had to rent a home. She managed to find a place under the bridge between two other shelters, with no windows and with the concrete road of the bridge serving as its roof. The house shook when cars and trucks passed overhead. Despite the difficult living conditions, Mercedita planned to stay under the bridge: 'Here my children and I are not alone. We have our friends and neighbours to help us.'

Her daughter Maritess was now 16 years of age and came to live with them, becoming a vital support for the family both in terms of income and in sharing responsibilities with Mercedita. A neighbour helped Maritess to get a job at a factory just above the bridge which made Christmas lights for export.

The electricity company that served the area discovered that many of the homes in the community were illegally connected and disconnected four electric meters; five to six families were connected to each meter. With no electric fans to circulate the air in their homes, the heat and humidity under the concrete bridge became intolerable, and the inhabitants were forced to eat and sleep outside, on top of the bridge. They spread out mats and folding beds on the pavements, often using sheets as makeshift tents to shield themselves from the dust and smoke of the passing vehicles.

The loss of electric lights meant that it was always very dark under the bridge, making it difficult to move around or carry out everyday tasks such as cooking and cleaning. It also increased the presence of rats, no longer deterred by the light, which led to a new problem for Mercedita:

> As we had no electricity, a rat came into the house and bit my leg while I was asleep. I went to the health centre and they gave me a prescription for medicines I can take even if I'm pregnant.

Many times, Mercedita and other families in her neighbourhood would go to the ATD Fourth World office seeking help in obtaining medicine. They would receive medical prescriptions from public health centres, but the prices were often beyond their means. The team would put them in touch with Caritas groups to obtain these medicines. If it was not possible, someone from the team would go with them to a pharmacy and buy the necessary medicine.

In February 2000, officials from the city council visited the community under the bridge to announce that there were plans to renovate the bridge and they would have to move elsewhere. The people living under the bridge had faced this threat in the past, but on this occasion they felt there was particular reason to be worried, as Mercedita explained:

> Last Friday, a journalist came and interviewed some of us. Then during the weekend, the Vice-President came. I was scared when I saw her! I think that she's really serious about making us leave the place. Otherwise, she would not have come. She asked if we would agree to be relocated and many of us somehow agreed, if the other place would really be better for us. We know that under the bridge is not a good place to live. Look at the piles of garbage blocking the canal: it stinks!

Since the mid 1960s, the permanent threat of demolition and forced evictions has stimulated the creation of residents' organisations, often referred to as People's Organisations (POs), throughout the many informal settlements in urban Philippines. The SMIT, Samahan ng mga Mararalitang taga-ilalim ng Tulay, meaning approximately 'Association of People in Poverty Under the Bridge', is one such residents' organisation. Several residents are voted in as

SMIT officers, who then act as community representatives in talks with outside officials, particularly with the local council, concerning demolition and relocation threats. The SMIT has no legal status but appears to include all sections of the community and gives them greater power than if each household were to speak alone.

On this occasion, the SMIT officers achieved a positive outcome through their talks with the city council and the demolition was postponed.

Mercedita described how she felt about the situation:

> Many of us would like to stay in Manila because of our children's education and our jobs. We will not move out unless we can all be sure to get relocation. We don't want to leave when others aren't sure of where they'll live. What scares me most is that when the day comes and the bridge cannot be repaired any more and we really have to leave, the government will still have no place for us. For now, we'll stay under the bridge. We will carry on with our lives.

THE FUTURE OF THE FAMILY

In the early part of 2000, Mercedita managed to find work doing the laundry for a family who lived in a house near the bridge. Although heavily pregnant, she continued to provide for her family as best she could. Yet, newly widowed, faced with severe financial difficulty, an uncertain housing situation and no electricity, Mercedita was unsure of her choices. With three daughters to take care of she was just managing to earn enough money to get by, but the new baby would make this precarious position difficult, if not impossible, to sustain.

> What can I do? I need to work for us to have something to eat. If I keep this baby how will I be able to work?

Mercedita came to the conclusion that she could not keep the baby and would offer her child a better future by giving it to a family with greater financial resources and stability. She made arrangements with the family she worked for to take custody of the newborn child.

In the Philippines, the child is considered as belonging to the community; it is not unusual to entrust the raising of a child to someone else. It is quite common for a child to be brought up by their grandparents, and it is also possible for a neighbour or a relative to help to raise a child. When this happens, the child keeps his own name and the biological family still sees him, sometimes daily. Often ties become close and the adoptive family is included in the extended biological family circle, or the adoptive mother will come and tell the birth mother how the child is getting on.

These different, informal ways of entrusting a child's upbringing to others are subtle and flexible, and cannot be compared to legal adoption. If a mother gives her child up for adoption at birth, the law stipulates that a social worker must be present. This was not the case when Mercedita's son was adopted.

At the beginning of May 2000, Mercedita gave birth to a baby boy whom she named Robertson. The adoptive family took Mercedita to the clinic and paid her medical bills, which she had no possibility of paying herself. They filled out all the official paperwork including the birth certificate, registered the baby in their own name and then took him home.

Two days later, Mercedita went to the ATD Fourth World office. Upset and somewhat confused, she explained what had happened:

> My son Robertson is now with a family who adopted him right after my delivery at the clinic near the bridge. They live near our place. When I came back home my three girls asked me about their brother. I explained to them why he was not home. Roselina couldn't accept that their brother lives with another family. She wants to take care of her brother. She said that she doesn't mind begging the whole day along the highway so that, at the end of the day, she could buy him some milk. What matters for her is that their brother stays with them. I feel that my children blame me. When I gave birth, I had nothing in my pocket but barely 20 pesos. That family helped me get out of the clinic. They paid for my bills, they took care of my son's papers and signed him under their name.

Mercedita was very distressed and now regretted her decision to give the baby away. She asked Marilyn and the ATD team to help her try and regain custody of Robertson. She wanted Marilyn to go with her to discuss it with the adoptive family. The team agreed that Marilyn and a colleague would go with Mercedita to meet the family, to act as witnesses and to provide emotional support. They were clear that they could not speak on Mercedita's behalf.

The following day they went with Mercedita to meet the adoptive parents. Glory, a neighbour and friend of Mercedita's, also went with them. The adoptive parents lived with their nine-year-old daughter in a house next to the nearby railway line. Their home was similar to those under the bridge, in that it was very small and cramped, but it was a two-parent household with a stable income, and therefore had the means to pay for electricity, food and schooling. Vicky, the adoptive mother, was in the house. Marilyn tells the story:

> Robertson was lying on a long wide wooden bench that served as his crib. Mercedita stared at her baby. She seemed to want to hold him but dared not do it in front of Vicky. The neighbours came out of their houses, eavesdropping, curious about what was going to happen. They had guessed why we came. Mercedita spoke. 'I came here with my friends. I know that you have already spent a lot of money to get me out of the clinic and I thank you. But my children keep asking me about their brother. They can't accept that he does not live with them …' She had not finished her sentence when Vicky started raising her voice, 'What are you trying to say, do you want to take him back? You come back tomorrow when my husband is here. He will make the decision!'

Despite their reluctance, the women decided that it was very important to return together the next day. Mr Daniel, the father, was waiting for Mercedita inside the house. Mercedita did not say a word. Mr Daniel's voice was firm and loud. He was not even looking at her when he said, 'You can't bring the child out of my house. Now that the child is with us, he has my last name, I will fight for him.'

Glory spoke to support her friend:

> It's clear that the baby will stay with you. I hope that this talk will not damage any relationship you and Mercedita could have had. I myself was an adopted child, born out of wedlock. My mother gave me for adoption to one of her friends. It was a complicated story but what's important is that my real mother and the one who adopted me have remained friends until now.

Mercedita returned home without her son. She wanted to continue fighting for her child by going to court. However, she was also afraid of the long process and did not have the means to pay for a lawyer.

Rosana, who was seven years old, said to Marilyn:

I told Roselina that our Mama couldn't do more to take our brother back. I tried to convince her that the baby is in good hands but she doesn't believe me. What else can we do? We have to be strong and accept what happened.

Marilyn realised how heartbreak could make a child grow up too soon.

Later, when she was talking to Marilyn, Roselina, who was eleven years old, explained why she felt so angry and unhappy:

When I learnt that my brother had been adopted, I already knew that it was impossible to take him back. I don't blame my Mama. I can't do that to her. What I cannot accept is that we seem to have lost another member of our family. Our father has just died. We could have had a new man in the family but we had to give him away.

Mercedita did not take the matter to court. It would be a long time before Marilyn heard the family speak of Robertson again.

DIFFICULTIES PILE UP

Very early one morning in June 2000, just a month after losing Robertson, Mercedita and Roselina again visited the ATD Fourth World house. Mercedita immediately said, 'Several policemen took Rosana and other children near the stoplight last night!'

The 'stoplight' is a busy crossroads just above the bridge, where traffic lights stop the cars every few minutes, allowing time for children and adults to go into the road, knocking on car windows, selling and begging. Mercedita did not hide the fact that her children begged from time to time, although she did not like it. This activity is illegal, and occasionally the authorities will step in.

She was playing along the bridge with her friend. They had just arrived home from the party of Pag-asa.[4] My neighbour saw everything. She said a car stopped in front of some kids playing along the avenue. Three men came out of the car, dressed in casual clothes. The kids didn't know that they were policemen. When these policemen told them to get in the car, other kids ran away but Rosana and her friend were scared and didn't manage. When the car left with the kids, she went running down under the bridge to tell me what happened. I went to the police headquarters but they wanted me to prove that she was not begging when they took her. My daughter was crying, still holding the teddy bear she got from the party.

Mercedita and Marilyn decided the best option was to ask the social worker at Pag-asa if she would go to the police station and testify that Rosana had been at the party and therefore had only just arrived at the traffic lights. Before hurrying off to speak with the social worker, Mercedita explained a further problem:

> Today is supposed to be my first day at work. With ten other mothers from our place, I was hired as a clothes trimmer in a garment factory. But how can I work today when I know that my daughter isn't safe? I asked my neighbours to explain the problem to the owner. I hope that he'll understand and let me start only tomorrow, or this afternoon if everything goes well for my daughter.

Later that evening, Mercedita called Marilyn to say that Rosana had been released from the police precinct. The social worker had gone there with her and talked with the policemen. They had scolded her for neglecting her child, letting her play along a bridge beside a main road, exposed and in danger.

The next day, Mercedita lost her job.

Street Children

At the time when Rosana and her friends were taken by the police, the Department of Social Welfare and Development (DSWD) had a particular policy drive in place to remove all 'street children' from the streets and into supervised care. However, the term 'street children' covers three quite diverse categories:

1. children who live with their parents but who spend time on the streets either playing, begging or selling items to help their family
2. children who are on the streets more than in their homes, perhaps spending up to 20 hours of the day on the streets away from their families
3. abandoned children who are permanently on the streets and rarely, if ever, see their parents.

The danger of bringing these groups under the one heading of 'street children' is that policies may be created which are suitable for one group but potentially damaging for others; Rosana was treated as an 'abandoned child', without allowing for the possibility that her mother was nearby.

Mercedita constantly voiced her concern that her children were in danger on the streets, and made many efforts to avoid it. However, with the very cramped, dark, badly ventilated conditions of their one-room home, it was not possible for her to keep them indoors for long periods.

Mercedita was now a single parent and could not afford to pay for childcare, so when she was trying to earn money to feed the family, there was no one to supervise her children. In this particular case, when she was forced to take time out to recover Rosana, she lost her job. The community operates an informal child care system where neighbours are always looking out for the safety of others' children, but this is not always possible or reliable.

Back to School

Despite the constant barrage of problems facing Mercedita, she continued to fight for her family, and succeeded in getting her daughters back into school. It had been some time since they had attended regularly so they all had to start in grade one, albeit in different classes.

> Yesterday I got some money from doing the washing and I bought bags and shoes for them. I got their uniforms from my neighbours whose children had worn them out. But I haven't yet managed to get them notebooks. They each need at least ten.

For some time the children appeared to be enjoying school and doing well, but, as the year went on, Roselina began truanting from school. One weekend Mercedita told Marilyn how worried she was:

> I don't know how to keep Roselina at school any more. She often goes with other children and begs. She said that she wanted to help me. She knows that we haven't paid our rent for a few months and the owner often asks me when I will pay. But it worries me whenever she goes near the stoplight. It's very dangerous! Sometimes she goes with her other sisters. I get so scared! Before, I did washing at my clients' houses, but now I prefer to do the washing here under the bridge. I'm afraid to leave my children alone, not knowing where they go when I am not around. The last time, my client scolded me because he saw that my mind was

not with my washing. The other day, a social worker came to ask if I know that Roselina often skips classes. She gets support from Pag-asa and they monitor if she goes to school regularly. Then the social worker told me that if I cannot look after them, there's the orphanage where they can be taken care of. It's really difficult when problems come all at the same time.

A further problem for Mercedita concerned her son, Juanito. When Juanito left the family home under the bridge, he lived on the street and started taking drugs. A social worker had placed him in a rehabilitation centre. But a few weeks earlier, Juanito, then 14 years old, left the centre where he had been for the last four years and came to live with his family under the bridge. With little space and already stretched resources, the family welcomed Juanito and managed as best they could; however, after some trouble with a neighbour, he ran away.

Mercedita also explained that she had felt it necessary to take Maritess out of her job at the Christmas lights factory because the owner had refused to register her officially as an employee, therefore denying her legal right to social security. Mercedita refused to accept this condition, and subsequently Maritess had moved to the province and was working as a maid. Once a month, she came and gave Mercedita some money for her sisters.

CRISIS POINT

In September 2000, Mercedita's precarious housing situation became critical. It had been five months since she could pay the rent of her house and the owner gave her two days in which to pay, otherwise he would have to sell the property to meet his own debts. Everyone tried to help: Marilyn and the ATD Fourth World team, friends and family. One organisation had a housing loan programme, but the application process took at least a month. Mercedita managed to borrow enough money from her friends to allow the family to stay in their house for two more weeks.

Mercedita's three daughters stopped going to school and instead spent all day begging at the traffic lights, in an effort to raise some money. In despair, Mercedita decided she must find a centre which would temporarily take in her children.

I feel it's better like this, so I can find a job. I can't go and look for one when I know my children are not safe. If they can be together in one place, then I can go and find a job. It hurts me to think that we will be separated. I thought of the orphanage because I know that the government can give them opportunities I may not be able to give them. They can go to school, something I wish for them. There, they can have a better place, unlike here under the bridge where they are exposed to many things, to a lot of troubles.

Putting children into an orphanage is not seen as abandoning them, but as seeking help. There, they have three meals a day, they are protected, have a roof over their heads, and go to school. As long as certain conditions are respected, such as visiting them at least once a month, the children are not eligible for adoption.

Within a week Mercedita had found places for her children in a nearby children's centre.

I had talked about this with them a long time ago. I told them this might happen but I assured them that I won't abandon them. I love them and I want to build a better future for them. My landlord was sorry for sending me out of his other house. His daughter has helped me get a job in Quezon City, making rags that others sell on the streets. I sleep there during the week. It's not bad but I hope to find a better one.

VANISHING DREAMS

For the three remaining months of 2000, Mercedita continued living and working in Quezon City during the week and was back under the bridge at the weekends. She visited her children at the centre as often as possible, and went on with her search for more stable employment and housing. On Christmas Day, she and her daughters joined the ATD Fourth World team and other families for a day of celebration. Before she left, she held Marilyn's hands and told her:

I wanted my kids to be in another place for Christmas. I wanted them to be happy today, that's why I brought them to your place. Thank you.

At the beginning of 2001, Mercedita was accepted for a job cleaning the park inside the North Cemetery. She was very happy with this news, particularly because she would be employed by the local government and would therefore have a formal contract and some kind of stability. She was required to purchase the work uniform before starting and did not have the money to do this. She asked Marilyn whether the ATD team could loan her the money. Not wanting to create possible problems in their relationship by getting Mercedita into debt with the team and, equally, not wanting to create a financial dependence by simply providing all the money, Marilyn offered to pay half of what was needed and for Mercedita to try and find the remainder elsewhere.

Mercedita spent several months working in the North Cemetery, living with various friends under and around the bridge. Then she telephoned to tell the ATD Fourth World team that she had a new cleaning job – still working for the local government but now at the Manila Zoo. She had also managed to rent a small room with electricity and water. It was near enough to the zoo for her to walk to work and save the money she usually had to spend for transport.

She invited the team for a free tour of the zoo one Sunday. Proud to welcome them, Mercedita told them:

> I am happy here. My colleagues are kind. They know about my three children in the orphanage and they understand me. The children are fine. I visit them during my days off. They have been to my new apartment, too. They are all back at school now.

In January 2003, however, Mercedita had new concerns over the future of her job. Although she had worked there for a year and a half, she was not yet on a permanent contract and if the current mayor of the city were to lose his position at the forthcoming elections, it was likely that Mercedita would be laid off. Inextricably linked to the stability of her income, the future of her children was uppermost in her mind.

> Every time I visit my children in the orphanage, the social workers ask me when I will get them out. If I take them out right now and then lose my job, where will we go? I don't want them to beg. I want them to finish school. I am just at the beginning of changing our life, building a foundation, a life where I won't worry whether we'll have something to eat tomorrow. But here I am, uncertain whether I can keep my job. I have a small place, better than under the bridge, with electricity and a small TV. But these things mean nothing without my kids. I pray nothing to God but to be with them one day, to be together as a family. It's the same dream that Felix had for us.

Mercedita continued to work at the zoo, trying desperately to gain a permanent contract. However, in July 2003 Roselina took the matter into her own hands and ran away from the orphanage to be with her mother. Not long after, Rosana also left the centre and joined her mother and sister.

Mercedita was delighted to be reunited with her children, but it was not without consequences, the most immediate being that they had to leave the room she had been renting. With three people living in the room near the zoo, the landlord had raised the rent, and this, coupled with the extra costs of feeding and looking after the two children, meant that Mercedita could no longer afford to live there. Added to this, the children's school was a long way from Mercedita's room which would make it difficult for them to continue to attend.

When a friend offered Mercedita a space to live by the bridge she decided to accept. Back at the bridge, Mercedita continued to work at the zoo, making the long journey there and back each day. However, she was never given a permanent position, and a few months later she was forced to stop working after contracting tuberculosis.

Tuberculosis kills over 32,000 people each year in the Philippines and disables thousands more.[5] Referred to as 'the disease of the poor', it is particularly prevalent in urban informal settlements, where the crowded housing conditions and bad ventilation encourage the spread of this contagious disease, and where malnutrition weakens the immune system.

Around the same time, Rowena also left the orphanage and rejoined her family. With no job and all three of her younger daughters back with her at the bridge, despite her illness, Mercedita found a new way to earn money for the family. She opened a 'sari sari' store, a shop that sells small, affordable portions of various general goods like coffee, sugar, cigarettes and sweets.

> With some money I got after leaving my job, I bought a small refrigerator and put up a sari-sari store in front of our house. My friend helps me to keep it and look after my three children. To own a sari-sari store has been one of my dreams!

In April 2005, families living under the bridge were evicted and their homes demolished as part of a 'beautification' development project for the city. Living beside the bridge but not under it, Mercedita escaped eviction but her illness continued to worsen. Her sister, who was living in the province, wanted Mercedita to join her there to get some rest and go to a hospital specialising in tuberculosis cases. However, she refused to leave the bridge because of her concern for her children's education. Although she received some assistance from a local organisation, Mercedita was forced to spend all her savings to pay for vital medication, leaving nothing on which to run the sari-sari store which ran out of goods.

In October 2006, a book chronicling Mercedita's life story was published in the Philippines by Anvil, and launched at the Philippine Normal University.[6]

A few days later, Mercedita died of tuberculosis. She was forty-one years old.

EPILOGUE

The team of ATD Fourth World continued to have a relationship with Mercedita's children. This was the news of them in August 2007.

At 18 years old, Roselina was living with her husband close to the community under the bridge. She found time to visit Rowena and Rosana and help in their studies if needed. Roselina was fulfilling her role as their older sister as she promised their mother she would.

Both Rosana and Rowena were living with Mercedita's sister in Metro Manila. Their aunt had regular work as a dressmaker in a small shop while her husband was a pedicab driver. They both had a regular source of income but were still supporting their own children, the youngest of whom was at university. They faced a constant challenge to cover the costs of their household commodities such as electricity and water and to provide for their extended family.

Rosana, then 14 years old, was a bright and disciplined student and had recently won a scholarship to a prestigious private school in Metro Manila. In return for the scholarship, Rosana spent her weekends with fellow students giving tutorial sessions in a public library for other children who had difficulty learning to read and write.

Rowena had a hard time accepting her mother's death and soon after began to rebel against her sisters and against the authority of her aunt. But with the understanding of her family, she settled down and, at 15 years old, was back in secondary school on a scholarship. 'I promised mama that I would finish my studies.'

Maritess was living with her husband in the family's native province of southern Luzon.

Juanito, on leaving the rehabilitation centre, went to live in Bulacan province where he learned to make and sell ice cream. In his early twenties, he was also back in southern Luzon and was looking for a job there after several months of trying his luck in the city without success.

Robertson, at seven years old, was still living with the family who adopted him. Once in a while, Roselina, who was living close to this family, had a chance to see him and spend time with him.

Mercedita's last words to Marilyn about her son were, 'He takes so much after my husband Felix!'

THE PHILIPPINES IN BRIEF

History[7]

There has not been a national cultural identity in the Philippines until recent times, due no doubt to the relative isolation of the populations living in the archipelago. The presence of Europeans in the Philippines dates from 1521, with the arrival of Ferdinand Magellan. The archipelago became part of the Spanish Empire in 1565. The end of the nineteenth century saw the beginning of a liberation movement that had the military support of the United States of America and led to Spanish defeat and sale of the Philippines to the Americans. In 1935, independence was proclaimed and the first president was elected. In 1942, the Japanese occupied the country, which regained its independence on 4 July 1946. Elected in 1965, President Ferdinand Marcos used opposition from Maoist guerrillas and Muslim separatists as a pretext to progressively impose a dictatorship in the 1970s. Under US pressure, elections were organised in February 1986, and Corazon Aquino was elected. In 2001, Gloria Macapagal-Arroyo became president and remained in power until the 2010 presidential elections won by Benigno Aquino III.

Geography

The Philippines is composed of an archipelago of 7,107 islands situated in the west of the Pacific Ocean, about 100 kilometres south-east of the Asian continent. The islands are divided into three groups: Luzon in the north, including the capital Manila, the Visayas in the centre and Mindanao in the south. Most of the islands are mountainous and of volcanic origin, covered in tropical forest. The country is buffeted by tropical storms and up to twenty typhoons annually. The climate is hot and humid, with an annual average temperature of around 26° C. There is a hot season from March to May, a rainy season from June to November, and a 'cool' season from December to February.

Key Figures (2009)[8]:

Area: 300,000 square kilometres
Capital: Manila
Population: 96,600,000 inhabitants
Principal languages: Filipino and English (official languages), some 80 local languages and many dialects
Currency: peso (100 pesos =1.55 euros = US$2.10)
Urban population: 48.9 per cent
Fertility rate: 3.23 births per woman
Infant mortality: 26 per 1,000 live births
Life expectancy at birth: 72.3 years
Literacy over the age of 15: males 92.5 per cent, females 92.7 per cent
School life expectancy: 11.5 years
GDP per capita: US$4,002 (purchasing power parity US dollars)
Public expenditure on education: 2 per cent of GDP
Total external debt: US$62,970 million
Debt service: 9.6 per cent of total exports

The Human Development Index[9] (HDI) is 0.638, placing the Philippines 97th out of 169 in the UNDP *Human Development Report 2010*.

NOTES

1. Quotations in this chapter are translations from the Filipino language, Tagalog. Names of people have been changed to preserve confidentiality.
2. Since the United Nations declared 17 October as the International Day for the Eradication of Poverty in 1993, ATD Fourth World in Manila gathers on the seventeenth of every month at Rizal Park where there is a commemorative 'Stone of Life' in honour of the poorest. This gathering, or forum, is a space for presentations and testimonies to be given, news and information to be shared and important issues to be discussed.
3. Philippine Partnership for the Development of Human Resources in Rural Areas, *Philippine Asset Reform Report Card*, Manila: PhilDHRR, 2008.
4. An NGO which runs community social welfare projects, primarily focused on children living on the streets.

5. World Health Organisation, *Global Tuberculosis Control 2010*, Geneva: WHO, 2010.

6. Marilyn Gutierrez, *Gold Under the Bridge: A Story of Life in the Slums*, Pasig City: Anvil Publishing, 2006.

7. http://en.wikipedia.org; *Encyclopédie de l'état du monde*, Paris: Éditions la Découverte, 2006.

8. *Encyclopédie de l'Etat du Monde*, 2009, Paris: Edition La Découverte, 2009; United Nations Development Programme, *World Development Report 2009*, New York: UNDP, 2009.

9. The Human Development Index varies from 0 to 1 and brings together the figures for life expectancy, literacy and revenues, according to national averages obtained from international sources. It does not include important aspects of the quality of human development and thus should be treated with caution.

3
Resist to Exist: The Story of Farid, Céline and Karim in France and Algeria

Floriane Caravatta

I can tell you that when you're homeless, you're nothing at all. You don't even exist on this earth. There are a lot of people who don't understand what it is to live on the streets, to sleep outside, to have problems, to drink, to do drugs, to go out and steal. Being homeless means being outside 24 hours a day with a bag on your shoulders. Sometimes I'd be sleeping peacefully, not bothering anybody, and be brutally woken up by the police or by people telling me, 'Get out of here!' And we're talking days and years, come rain or shine. It's awful, it tears you apart. It makes you nervous, it makes you wild. It drives you crazy. When you walk into an office to talk to somebody, it's impossible to talk to them calmly.

Farid was talking with Floriane from ATD Fourth World in the council flat which he had finally obtained with his wife Céline. When the formal interview was over, Farid said to her:

I've met with organisations, I've met loads of people. So why was I never offered a real place to live? Why was I never offered a real job? Because they didn't think I was responsible. You know, the key to success is someone taking an interest in you.

Farid and Céline Koffic have known the international movement ATD Fourth World for eight years and were very enthusiastic when they were asked to write their life story. Their lives illustrate many of the difficulties faced by households confronted with extreme poverty in France: immigration, family break-ups, insalubrious and overcrowded housing, inadequate schooling and health care, unemployment, life on the streets, petty crime and drugs, time spent in prison, admittance to psychiatric hospitals and children placed into care.

Nevertheless, in barely three years, this couple managed to obtain decent housing, secure employment, and to regain custody of their little boy, who had been placed into care by a Children's Court judge. They now live together not far from Farid's place of work, on a council estate on the outskirts of Paris.

Their amazing capacity to rebuild their lives and overcome extreme poverty in such a short time is very unusual, so it is all the more important to understand how it was possible. Farid keeps repeating, 'I'm very happy to be telling my story, to show people that there's always a way out.'

FARID'S STORY

Farid was born in Paris in 1971, the youngest of three children. His mother was from the Finistère region in the west of Brittany and his father from Constantine in Algeria. His mother died when he was nine years old. He has very few memories of her and no photos or mementos, but he remembers with pride how she did everything so that her children would want for nothing.

> We lived on the fourth floor of a building in Pigalle. There were French people, Algerians and Africans. It was an old building, overrun by cockroaches; there were holes in the wooden stairs and the walls, and bars missing from the banister. We had a small flat with only a kitchen and a living room. Four of us lived there and we all slept in the living room. When my father spent the night at the police station, we would sleep in his bed. The toilet was in the kitchen, separated only by a small door. My mother used to say to me, 'Push the walls to have more room'. We had 13 cats that lived on the landing, not in the flat. One day, a neighbour poisoned them and then my mother fell ill.

His father had a job as a security guard in a Paris bank near Pigalle. He wasn't a petty criminal, but he liked to gamble. He would also drink and get into fights. The police would often call Farid's mother and ask her to come and get him, even at two in the morning.

In spite of precarious living conditions and difficulty in making ends meet at the end of the month, the family remained close-knit and always managed to find a way to pay the rent. His parents had not come to live in the 18th arrondissement by chance. There was a great sense of solidarity in districts where there were many Algerians who had fled their country during the Algerian War of Independence. Farid's father arrived in this district in 1955 when he was barely 20 years old. Farid's mother had come to find work.

Farid had just turned nine when his mother was admitted to hospital with hepatitis. He recalls visiting her several times without realising the tragedy that was unfolding. His father was afraid they would be taken by the DDASS,[1] so they went to Algeria. Farid did not understand what was happening. He thought he was going on holiday with his sister and did not know that he would never see his mother again. It would be two years before their father visited and told them that their mother had died on 21 December 1981.

Life in Algeria

Farid and his ten-year-old sister arrived in Constantine unable to speak a word of Arabic, and were taken in by their paternal grandparents whom they did not know. In all, there were ten people living in a three-room flat. Farid said:

> We slept on blankets or sheepskins on the floor. My grandparents had their own bedroom. When we had an orange, five of us would share it. There was no bathtub and there were a lot of cockroaches. My grandfather must have worked in France; he spoke French perfectly and received a pension from France every three months. My grandmother didn't speak French; she could only say good morning and good evening.

Integration was difficult in the beginning. Farid had no news from his father or his older sister who had stayed in France, not even a parcel or a postcard at Christmas time, and he felt abandoned. He says:

> I didn't speak a word of Arabic when I arrived. I started by learning the swear words: all the boys on the council estate insulted me in Arabic, because I was an immigrant. Six months later I was fluent in Arabic and had lost all my French. I was part of a gang and I had to go along with them. But when I did, I'd get a good hiding from my grandfather.

He attended school for two years, but his results were disappointing because he did not write Arabic. He was then enrolled in a professional school for electricians and car mechanics. He would stay in the workshop instead of going to class, so he failed the academic subjects and did not get his diploma. But he did learn the trade.

The descent into hell

The neighbours often complained to his grandparents about Farid's behaviour, so he left their flat and went to live in the cellar, where he used his newly-acquired knowledge to connect the electricity.

> I had landed in a country I didn't know, where life was very different, and I was cut off from my parents. These were huge changes. Algeria was falling apart. I could see the years flying by and no sign of a return to France. I started dabbling in drugs and that's where it all started to go wrong: I fell into hell.

Life in Constantine was not easy. There were no jobs and no housing. Everything was on the black market: bread, coffee, tinned tomatoes, oil, couscous grain ... To survive, Farid turned to crime. He was still under age when he was first convicted of stealing and sent to prison in Algiers. Once released from prison, he tried to change the course of his life. He looked for a job without any success. He was driven to living off petty theft, sleeping in cars in winter and on the beach in summer. He wanted to go back to France, but it was complicated, because when you serve time in prison in Algeria it is difficult to get a passport.

> I managed to get a passport through a friend of my uncle's, a detective constable who lived in the same building. I still had fines to pay, but this friend interceded. Then the French Consulate refused to give me a visa because I was a French army deserter. I explained that I couldn't be a deserter, because they had sent me my call-up papers in France and I didn't live in France. I had to wait three months for my case to be sorted out.

He obtained his first visa in 1994, but had no money to pay for his ticket. His eldest sister had just arrived for a month's holiday and he thought she would help, but she left without him. Farid sank deeper and deeper into despair. To pay for his ticket, he sold cigarettes on the sly and stole to raise the money he needed. Then he requested a new visa.

In 1995, Farid took the boat from Annaba and arrived in Marseilles, before making his way to Paris. He was 24 years old.

Back in France

Farid was very happy to be back in France but he did not recognise the place he had left behind and could not find the friends he had known. He no longer spoke French and did not have a penny to his name.

He went to live in a suburb just outside Paris with his eldest sister, her husband and children. She helped him to obtain his identity card and social security cover, but all he wanted was to find his father again. In a bar his father used to frequent, Farid finally met an old acquaintance who told him that his father was ill and was working in the laundry of a hospice in Nanterre. Farid was badly affected by finding his father in that condition and kept turning to pills 'to forget'. His sister found out and a violent argument ensued, so he decided to leave her.

> I sold my ID card for 3,000 francs,[2] because I needed money to get to Nice where I had friends. I was 24 years old, I wanted to discover the world. I was alone and there was nobody to tell me what to do. I didn't want to ask anyone for food, but I wasn't above stealing to feed myself.

His father died a few months later in a state of extreme poverty. Farid had no mementos or photos of him. Soon after, he went to Germany to fulfil his military service. When he returned, he found himself in great difficulty as he had no training or experience in France. He fell into petty crime and was brought before the court where his sister worked as a clerk. He served two months in prison and when he was discharged he found himself homeless.

He spent the next five years living on the streets, in hostels or in trains, and surviving on his wits.

> When you're on the streets, you don't even have any words to say because you're thinking so much about other things, like how you're going to wash your trousers, for example. You have to find food at lunchtime, you have to find somewhere to sleep at night. You go days without eating. Nobody dies of hunger here in France: there are vans at the train stations. But how long should you queue up waiting for the van to come to get a bowl of soup? And that's just the start of your problems. You can't look for work because, for one thing, you have to be clean. If you turn up when you're tired, badly shaven or badly dressed, it

doesn't work. If you're looking for temp work and you give the address of a hotel, do you think they will take you on?

To survive, Farid stole wallets, and broke car windows to sleep inside. He found a way to empty parking meters to take the coins. He continued resorting to pills to keep going.

I was really in hell. Nobody treats you like a human being. When you're on the streets, you're not even an animal, you're nothing at all. But they don't know that it can happen to anyone overnight. It's easy enough to lose everything, but getting back on your feet sure takes time!

CÉLINE'S STORY

Céline was born on 24 September 1964 to a working-class family in Argenteuil. When she was seven years old, her family moved to Montreuil, east of Paris, to be closer to her maternal grandparents. They stayed there for 24 years. She was the middle child between two brothers. Her childhood was relatively trouble-free, but life on the estate was not easy. When she was 15, she was attacked in broad daylight by three men but, out of fear of reprisals, her family chose not to report the incident.

Céline adored her father and she was deeply affected when he was diagnosed with diabetes; he had to have three insulin injections a day and follow a strict diet. Her mother worked as a typist, then as a bookkeeper for a metal company, doing her best to cope with a sick husband, three children and her work, which was a long way from Montreuil.

Not really knowing what she wanted to do, Céline undertook a Certificat d'Aptitude Professionnelle (CAP)[3] in accounting. When she was 16 – still traumatised from the attack the year before – she became ill following a storm that terrified her. Suffering from hallucinations, she spent two months at Salpêtrière hospital. She believed that the drugs she was prescribed made her sleepy all the time and she did not attend the last year of her course. She was offered other training courses but always left before the end. However, she occasionally found casual work.

In 1992, her maternal grandmother was confined to bed and Céline took care of her until her death a year later. Céline was not in good health and the tranquillisers she had been prescribed had several side effects: weight gain, chronic fatigue and insomnia.

She stopped working to look after her father as his health had deteriorated. In 1995, while he was with his wife and daughter, he collapsed and died from a ruptured aneurysm.

Céline and her mother found life very hard after her father's death. She attempted suicide several times. Finally, she was recognised as being eligible for a disability allowance. She started to gamble the money she received and it was quickly squandered. Her mother and her social worker decided to place her under legal guardianship. Céline continued to gamble the little money she had and her mother told her to leave the flat they shared.

FARID AND CÉLINE TOGETHER

One night in 1997, Farid met a young woman in an emergency shelter. She was sitting on a bench, silent. She seemed so sad that Farid was intrigued and approached her. It was Céline, who had come to the shelter after leaving home. They spent a good part of the night talking to each other. Farid felt her pain straight away.

> I understand her: for 33 years she lived with her parents and overnight she ended up in a shelter for the homeless. How do you deal with that? When she told me her story, I promised myself that I'd save her.

From then on, they went from shelter to shelter together. When there was no room for them in emergency shelters, they slept in hotels or in railway carriages, sometimes being chased out in the middle of the night. Céline's legal guardian, Ms Leroy, paid her 76 euros a week, but Farid had no income. Farid said:

> It's hard to live on the streets as a couple. I already knew what it was like on the streets, but she didn't. You have to be tough. Céline was scared at being all alone, and then she met me. She saw that I only wanted what was good for her.
>
> We never argued. If you tell the Samu Social over the phone 'we are a couple', they won't even give you the time of day. They'll take a family with children, so you have to lie and say you have two kids with you, that they're crying, or that one of them's hurt, and they must come right away. You can even wait till two in the morning without knowing if the Samu Social van will come. But it's not their fault, the system is overloaded.

We spent so many nights outside, so many nights in the sleeping compartments in trains. The security guards with dogs would throw us out at one in the morning. I can tell you, you have to be tough to take it!

Some days we had nothing to eat, so we'd buy half a baguette and share it. It was really hard, especially at night. We'd steal batteries from Carrefour supermarket and sell them on in Barbès. That way, we could buy some bread and cheese.

Céline adds:

When you live on the streets, you have to pay for everything: to wash your clothes, you have to go to a launderette; and for a coffee, you have to go into a café.

Farid admits that he did not know how to ask for help, preferring to steal from shops so that he would not owe anything to anybody. He would take Céline along with him. They both ended up before the judge in court with Farid's sister as a clerk of the court. He said, 'It scared the hell out of me.'

One night when it was snowing heavily, they slept in a sleeping compartment in a train. The next morning, when they woke up, Céline's trousers and the seat were covered in blood. Céline thought she had miscarried but did not go to the hospital.

As she was under legal guardianship, Céline's situation was being followed by the Union Départementale des Associations Familiales (UDAF)[4] in Seine-Saint-Denis. In his efforts to improve their circumstances, Farid turned to them for help. Ms Leroy, Céline's legal guardian, was the first person to try and find solutions.

She saw this guy turn up without identity papers, without the RMI benefit,[5] with a scar and tattoos. I wasn't someone you could trust. Then she saw that I never left Céline.

Ms Leroy helped them through the administrative procedures to renew Céline's identity card. Staff members at the outreach shelter where the couple were staying helped Farid to obtain his identity card, which made it possible for him to apply for the RMI social security benefit. Once he had obtained this, Farid and Céline were able to rent a room in a cheap hotel. Despite this improvement, Farid was still very worried:

It was a place to rest, but how long can you stay in a hotel, just like that, without working, without anything? Do you think the RMI is enough for a person to live off? It's impossible to imagine being able to live your whole life like that.

Céline was still undergoing medical treatment and lived in fear that Farid would leave her. One night, he did not return because he was on a 'job'. Thinking he was not coming back, Céline swallowed a whole bottle of pills. The next morning, he found her almost unconscious and tried to make her drink some milk to make her vomit. He realised that he would really have to surround her with a great deal of care and support if he wanted to keep her. 'She has nobody and if I wasn't here, she would have committed suicide a long time ago.'

In March 1998, Farid was serving a one-month prison sentence after having been arrested by the police once again. Céline fell ill and, panicking, called her brother who took her to hospital, where she was found to be pregnant. In prison, Farid learnt that Céline was expecting his baby. As soon as he was released, he joined her at the hospital.

On 11 December 1998, Céline gave birth to a little boy they named Karim. Farid was there. He still lived on the streets, but came to the hospital every day to see Céline and their baby, and to shave and shower. He tried to be discreet to avoid revealing his situation. Céline stayed two weeks in the neo-natal ward.

Ms Leroy contacted several emergency centres in an effort to find temporary accommodation for the family when they left the hospital, but without success. A civil servant from the Aide Sociale à l'Enfance (ASE)[6] then phoned Céline to explain that her baby would be placed into care. She rushed from the hospital to find Farid, but when they got back the baby was no longer on the ward: he had just been taken into care. They left the hospital that evening, alone, not knowing where to go. Night fell and they slept in the street huddled against one another. The next day, they called the Samu Social who found them accommodation for two months in a young workers' hostel. Their child was apparently placed into care because they did not have work or a place to live, but also because of Céline's mental health.

Farid and Céline were then summoned to a Children's Court judge, who had jurisdiction to rule on cases involving homeless families. The judge explained to them that he was there to find a solution and not to take children away. He told them that step by step they would have to find housing, a job, show some stability, and visit their son regularly. Céline felt that the judge had given them hope that they would be able to get their child back. The parents were granted a weekly visit of one hour on ASE premises.

After spending two months in the young workers' hostel, they returned to a room in a cheap hotel. One night, Farid did not return because he wanted to bring Céline a small television. Céline thought he had left her and set fire to her room. The firemen took her to hospital where she was referred to the Ville Evrard psychiatric hospital.

In spite of everything, Farid and Céline both went each week to the ASE and did not miss a single visit; the hospital made sure that Céline attended the appointments. The visits took place in the presence of a family liaison officer and the foster mother.

Karim cried every time he saw his mother and it would take time for Farid to calm him. They were eventually granted the right to be alone with Karim during these weekly meetings. Soon they were even allowed to take their child out for short walks.

During this time, they maintained close ties with Ms Leroy and confirmed that they wanted to live together. Céline's doctor called Farid to say that her condition was improving and that she could be treated as an outpatient.

With help from an association, they found accommodation together in different places over the course of the next six months. Céline and Farid's main goal was still to regain custody of their child, but the road ahead seemed long. Farid would ask himself countless questions:

Why can't I have a family, play with my child, have a home or have a job? Why don't I have the right to be like everyone else?

Rebuilding a Life

Karim's birth transformed Céline and Farid. Céline had new energy and made new resolutions. Farid took several steps to find work.

There had to be a trigger, and for me the trigger was my child. I understood that I had to get it together, because if I didn't want my child to go down the same road as me, I would have to build him a new road.

The local centre for the integration of young people put Farid in touch with an association called Avenir, which offered him a six-month unpaid work experience placement with an organisation specialising in professional reintegration. Farid accepted, but after two weeks he stopped going to work. He was tempted to return to his previous activities. His training officer, Mr Marchand, called him to say that if he did not come back that afternoon, his contract would be terminated. Farid remembers telling himself: 'There I am, begging for work, and now my own trainer has to come and get me! What kind of a person am I?'

He went back to his training where he learned about different trades in the building industry. This work was the key to him breaking with his past, developing new habits such as getting up early in the morning and, little by little, establishing a normal daily schedule. What was vital, according to Farid, was the trust shown in him by Mr Marchand. Céline's support was also vital. 'We shared everything: the hard times, the surprises, the happy times. And that brings you closer together.'

Céline continued to go to the ASE to see Karim, but Farid could no longer attend because of his work schedule. They stayed on good terms with the foster family. They realised that they could talk to Karim's foster mother, that she was sensitive to the fact that it was hard for them to see their baby for only a few hours a week, and that Céline was deeply affected by the fact that Karim cried every time she took him in her arms.

Ms Leroy took steps to secure the couple a place in the Noisy-le-Grand Family Support Programme, managed by ATD Fourth World, to provide them with a safe environment as an anchor for their reintegration into society. Marie, the admissions manager at the Family Support Programme, went to meet them in March 2000.

When she arrived at the hotel where they were staying, Céline was busy writing the day's menus in the restaurant with the manager. She did this every day because the manager did not know how to write French. Marie could see that they had already made considerable progress. She handed them the application papers for housing within the Family Support Programme. Farid and Céline put in their application and, to their great surprise, three months later they were offered a flat. They finally saw their dreams coming true: to have a home for Karim and to regain the respect of their families.

THE CHÂTEAU DE FRANCE

On 21 June 2000, Farid and Célin arrived at the Château de France housing estate in Noisy-le-Grand. It was a small estate, with four blocks of flats and 46 houses. Through the Family Support Programme, ATD Fourth World rents out housing to very disadvantaged families and gives them support to reintegrate into society.

Farid and Céline were overjoyed. Marie helped them settle in and invited them for a meal. She took them to buy second-hand furniture thanks to a loan they had been granted. Farid recalls:

We couldn't sleep on the first night after we moved into the flat. I couldn't stop looking at the walls, measuring the space and looking at the kitchen. It was as if someone had said to me, 'Let's go and check out paradise.' I had never been in the position before of having work, having a home or getting a receipt for the rent.

A month after they arrived, Farid and Céline met with Christophe, the manager of the Family Support Programme, to draft a contract. This set out, on the one hand, their responsibilities as tenants (to pay the rent and annual insurance, to look after the flat and to be good neighbours) and, on the other, the responsibilities of the ATD Fourth World team at Noisy-le-Grand. Farid and Céline both expressed their desire to get Karim back, to make a home and to obtain stable housing and jobs. These elements were all noted down in the contract, point by point.

Then they talked about the support that the team would be able to give to Farid and Céline. A member of the team would help them approach the Agence Nationale Pour l'Emploi[7] (ANPE) and the organisation that paid out unemployment benefit. The social worker would ask for Céline's hospital file to be transferred to the Noisy-le-Grand medical centre so she could continue her medical treatment.

Alone in the small flat, Céline got very bored just waiting for Farid to come home and she wanted to take up some activities. Marie suggested that she should sign up at the multimedia library and join in the activities at the ATD Fourth World centre. Together they drew up a plan.

Céline was thrilled when Ms Leroy opened a bank account that she could manage by herself. She also hoped that the order of legal guardianship would be lifted in December as she wanted to prove she could look after herself. But the process would be a long one; first Céline would have to be examined by a medical expert and receive a favourable report.

Karim was now 18 months old – a handsome and very alert little boy. Farid and Céline went for an appointment with the judge to discuss custody, but the first hearing was cancelled because of a strike by court clerks. When they finally had an audience with the judge, he explained that they did not yet fulfil all the conditions to regain custody of Karim. He extended the placement order for two years, but added that this decision was provisional.

The ASE family liaison officer suggested to Céline that she should attend a mother-and-child centre in Saint-Denis to meet other mothers whose children had been taken into care. She soon stopped going: the journeys to and from the centre were long and expensive, her medication often left her exhausted, she did not feel welcome at the centre and was afraid of being criticised for her difficulties in dealing with her son.

At the end of September, Farid and Céline came to see Marie at the Family Support Programme, where they had to sign a new rental agreement: the amount of rent asked of them initially was very low and would increase gradually according to their income, until it reached a standard amount.

All the steps Céline was undertaking incurred substantial costs for transport that the couple could ill afford; Céline, in particular, was trying to save as much money as she could in order to pay the fares to go and see her son. Although Farid's work experience with a painter was going well, it was unpaid. Also, because they were now officially living together as a couple, Céline's adult disability benefit meant that Farid was no longer eligible for the RMI. Céline said:

> I feel sorry for him when he asks me if he can take some money to buy himself half a baguette. All he has for lunch is some bread and reheated lentils, and nothing else.

In November, Farid started work with a local company that he had found through a member of the ATD Fourth World team. With hindsight, Farid says:

> It was my first time really working in seven years. In the beginning it was hard to get up in the morning, to meet new people or to talk with them.

He was still taking pills, found it hard to obey orders and was constantly tempted to return to his old ways, but he attributes his success in persevering with work to his relationship with his foreman:

> For that first year, he taught me everything: to respect working hours, to be clean, when to get changed, what time to leave and when to clean up. When he wasn't there, I felt awful. With him, I worked on building sites as far away as Pont de Sèvres. They could send me anywhere and I didn't even worry about the work to be done, I only thought about the fact that I was working with him. He was the best in the company. He was my friend. This helped me to change my attitude and who I was hanging out with. I smartened my ideas up, so my family and my sisters could be proud of me.

Céline asked Marie to take her to an interview with an association that helps adults on disability benefit to find a job. The interview went well and she started on the personal action plan they had proposed.

Christmas was approaching and they were looking forward to Karim spending the whole of Christmas Day with them. A magnificent Christmas tree stood inside the flat, decorated with gold balls and coloured tinsel. A photographer marked their first family Christmas with a family portrait of Farid, Céline and Karim. On 25 December, four men, including Farid, dressed up as Father Christmas and walked up and down the streets of the estate, accompanied by small elves pushing a decorated wheelbarrow full of chocolates and presents for the youngest children.

In January 2001, the couple told Marie that they could not pay the instalment on the loan they had taken out to buy furniture, and asked to defer the payment for one month. Marie reminded them that they had set the repayment terms themselves and that they could not unilaterally change the contract. After some discussion, they reluctantly agreed to pay half the instalment and Céline came to pay the next day.

Céline had appointments for job interviews. This was vital as it was one of the conditions laid down for the couple to regain custody of Karim. Already she was starting to think of ways to go and visit her son outside working hours. However, she was not offered any of the jobs.

At the end of April, Céline's legal guardianship was finally lifted and Karim would be able to visit every second Saturday and stay on his own, without the family liaison officer. Encouraged by his wife, Farid progressively reduced his pill intake until he stopped altogether.

EMERGENCE OF AN ACTIVIST

In late January, the ATD Fourth World team invited Farid and Céline to take part in a discussion group about family support. The estate had been created 30 years before, thanks to the efforts of families in the Noisy-le-Grand emergency housing camp and Joseph Wresinski, the founder of ATD Fourth World. The purpose had always been to allow families living in hardship to get back on their feet and make a fresh start. Now they needed to rethink their family support projects in order to adapt them to today's world. All the residents of Château de France were invited to take part, as well as people from the wider neighbourhood. They needed a group of people to be the driving force of the group.

At first, Farid leapt at the opportunity and took part in the evening meetings with some 15 other people, but he did not feel comfortable. Ill at ease, he lost interest and stopped attending the discussion group, but Marie convinced him to give it a second chance. The group was working on a questionnaire, which would be given out to all the residents of the estate, and covered five themes: housing, life in the neighbourhood, family support, projects for children, and issues related to employment support.

Farid visited Marie to tell her that he had voted for the first time in his life at work to elect a representative in his company. Marie realised how much Farid and Céline needed to be recognised for who they were and also how much they needed friendship to keep moving forward and prevent them both from falling back into bad habits. She noted, too, how Farid seemed a different man from the one who had first arrived at the estate: he no longer looked so gaunt and the bags under his eyes had gone.

In May 2001, an open day was held at the ATD Fourth World centre to mark the 100th anniversary of a law pertaining to organisations. As part of the celebration, it was decided to bring in some giant sculptures based on Tapori children's stories.[8] These sculptures are kept in Switzerland, so arrangements had to be made to bring them to Noisy-le-Grand. Farid was invited to join the team in charge of this operation. He was nervous about leaving Céline alone for several days, and asked the ATD Fourth World team to support her while he was away.

Shortly before the open day, Farid helped the team to set up the sculptures and the sound system. He also helped a team member who picked up papers and other litter around the estate every Friday afternoon. Farid laughed every time he saw him pushing his wheelbarrow, followed by a pack of kids wearing gloves. Once the chore was finished, each child had the right to a glass of mint cordial. Farid helped out on the day itself, tidying up afterwards and putting protective coverings over the sculptures. When they had finished, an amplifier from the sound system was found to be missing. Farid's heart skipped a beat: 'I was really scared they would think it was me.' To his great relief, the equipment was soon found.

Many people had taken part, including a delegation from Switzerland. A People's University was held on the theme 'Coming together to take action'.[9] When Farid contributed to the discussion, he said:

> We have to fight to build a family, to have our children with us. If we don't have help from people who have been through extreme poverty and suffering, or who understand life, it can be hard.

In mid June, a People's University was organised at the European Economic and Social Committee in Brussels, based on the theme 'Parents as the first partners of their children's future: an objective for an inclusive Europe'. The various delegations, including that from Noisy-le-Grand, studied the question 'How should a family development project be supported?' During the preparation meeting in Noisy-le-Grand for this session, Farid explained what coming to live on the estate had meant to him:

> Having a place to live allows you to get a job. It helped me to think about what I was doing, to change who I was hanging out with. Marie encouraged me to take classes to improve my French, to take part in the theatre group and in the meetings. Those things didn't interest me before; I was ashamed and I was shy. Now that I have my own home, I listen, I learn, I take an interest, I participate. I want to go and meet people. I was given a second chance. Everyone deserves a second chance.

LOOKING FOR WORK

Continuing to look for stable employment, Céline found a paid four-month work-based training programme; first in a supermarket, then in a discount clothing shop, and finally in a minimart. Her performance was evaluated at the end of each work placement and her employers were satisfied with her work, but no job was offered to her. In October, the manager of the Family Support Programme offered her a job cleaning the ATD Fourth World centre's communal premises under a special one-year contract for the long-term unemployed. The support given by the team and the centre's secretary was crucial in helping Céline to get back into the routine of working.

> In the beginning, it was hard. Often, I didn't show up and they had to come and get me at home. Sometimes I would come in late and ask if I could still start work. They said I could but made it clear that I'd have to finish later. I hadn't worked alone for a long time. As time went on, it got easier.

Farid's contract ended, but his manager promised to help him find work and let him use an office and a telephone for his job search. One month later, Farid was offered an 18-month contract as a handyman in a low-income housing organisation.

In February 2002, Marie left for West Africa. The team went to the airport with some of the families from the estate to say goodbye. It was important for Farid and Céline to be there and to show her how much she meant to them. Farid said:

> It was something special with Marie. Whenever I needed to pour my heart out, I'd go and see Marie and she'd always listen to me. Meeting Marie changed everything. She taught me to accept people, to speak properly and to behave like a human being. She'd let me rant and rave, but she didn't let it impress her.

Since Céline had started working at the adult education centre, she seemed to be blossoming. She wanted to continue working as a cleaner, and contacted ten hospitals in the area; she did not receive a single acknowledgement.

In April, a new family moved onto the estate. Farid recognised them straight away since they had once stayed in the same shelter. Céline was a great support to her new neighbour, Melanie. The fact that this mother trusted her to look after her baby boosted Céline's confidence that she was capable of looking after her own son. Farid, on the other hand, found relations with his new neighbours difficult, particularly with the young people on the estate. On more than one occasion he had to step in when there were fights. With the noise, the burglaries, the fights, the stones thrown through windows and people knocking on the door at all hours of the day and night, Farid felt he had to lay down the law: 'I told them that my flat was not a nightclub or a bar, and if I had to open my door after 11 p.m., it would be with a knife in my hand!'

Despite this, Farid and Céline would discover a real sense of solidarity on the estate. They were generous enough to lend money, give out food and cigarettes, and even feed a neighbour's dogs.

WINNING BACK THEIR RIGHTS

Two years after their arrival on the estate, Farid and Céline met with Christophe to review their action plan. They had achieved all the objectives they had initially set: they were both working, their rent was paid, they had tax declarations and were debt-free. A project to find housing off the estate and outside of the Family Support Programme could now be envisaged.

Summer arrived. As Farid and Céline had never been away on a holiday together, the ATD team suggested that they should have a three-day holiday on a community farm in Normandy. The family liaison officer agreed that Karim could go with them and suggested that he should sleep at his parents' flat at least twice before leaving.

At the end of August, all three of them set out for the farm with two other families and members of the ATD Fourth World team. Karim was fascinated by everything. Farid took charge of the games of petanque and helped to prepare a couscous meal. Then, in the evenings, he played chess by a log fire while Céline sat by Karim's bed until he fell asleep.

By the end of September, a request they had made earlier to have Karim circumcised was finally approved by the judge. In October, during the school holidays, they made an appointment at a clinic and asked Christophe to drive them there. Farid's sister organised a party, invited friends and prepared a special meal, with music and gifts. With the consent of the family liaison officer, Karim stayed with them for the week so that Céline could look after him. Despite saying that she was unsure how to keep Karim entertained for a whole week, she was confident enough to organise activities for him. At the same time, they finally gained the right to have Karim stay with them for the whole weekend.

In November 2002, they were offered a larger flat on a low-income housing estate on the outskirts of Paris, closer to Farid's place of work. A family welfare officer helped them with all the administrative procedures, including applying for a loan from the family benefits office to buy a fridge and a cooker. Céline sent all the necessary notifications of the change of address by herself, but she called the social worker every day.

> In the beginning, it was difficult to get myself organised. I didn't have a job any more and I didn't have Karim. Sometimes there wasn't much to eat. Our new social worker sometimes wrote a letter for us to get food vouchers from the CCAS.[10] But one day she wasn't there when I arrived. I spoke to someone else but she didn't give me anything. Sometimes the MPDH[11] didn't pay me my benefits when they were supposed to. I waited six months to be able to buy a bed for Karim, and even then it was only half a bed: the bed had a drawer and the family benefits office didn't want to pay for the drawer. We had to buy that ourselves.

The new estate posed its own problems: it was very noisy, children kept ringing the doorbell and the frequent electricity failures combined with the lift breaking down meant they had to climb six flights of stairs to reach their flat, sometimes in the dark.

Life was not as hard for Farid because he was happy in his job. It now only took him an hour to get to work, taking two buses and two metros.

> I'm a handyman. I look after all the building maintenance on a council estate. It's a rough area: there are young people with knives and weapons. Sometimes accidents happen and sometimes there is vandalism, but I know how to handle the kids. I have appointments with the tenants, who are our clients. It's thanks to them that we get paid, so you have to respect them. I feel I get recognition from my company, from my area manager and from my boss. What I like about my work is that it helps people, especially the elderly. My manager caught me leaving early three times, so he talked to me about it and since then I've stuck with it and I toe the line.

Eighteen months later, his employer offered him a permanent contract, but he had to pass some tests.

> I had to calculate surface areas in square metres. I must've got none out of twenty. I was shaking and panicking. I kept telling

myself, 'For once I've found a company that's willing to hold on to me. I'm not going to end up unemployed!' So I told them, 'Listen, I really need this job. I want to make it. Can't you just turn a blind eye to the maths?' And, in the end, they took me on.

Although his salary was considerably lower, because he was no longer eligible for the benefits that were paid to compensate for the lack of job security, he now had a decent job.

I feel accepted on the estate where I work. My boss knows that I am an activist with ATD Fourth World, and that I help some people on this estate. I do a lot of work with the people who live here and I don't want to leave. My boss offered me the chance to move to a different estate and I refused. I'm in a working-class area, I'm paid a performance-based bonus, my public transport costs are reimbursed, I get five weeks' paid annual leave and every year I get an extra month's salary as a bonus.

In April 2003, Céline was offered a job as a gardener through an employment reintegration association, starting the following week. It was a godsend as they were soon to have their next meeting with the Children's Court judge and they would be able to show him that they had fulfilled all the conditions that had been set to regain their parental rights.

The long-awaited interview went well, and the Children's Court judge granted full custody of Karim to his parents. The little boy was not very happy with this decision so the judge took time to explain everything to him.

Looking back, Farid says that the judge helped them a great deal by finding the right words to explain the reasons for placing Karim into the care of the local authorities, by setting them a series of objectives to meet, and by encouraging them each time they made progress.

In August 2003, Karim came back to live with his parents. Farid and Céline have maintained a very good relationship with his foster mother and Karim always sees her during the school holidays. She is still his second mum: sometimes he calls her 'Mummy', sometimes 'Aunty'.

Céline loved her gardening job but, after one year, her reintegration contract expired and she found herself unemployed once more. Four months later, she was contacted about a job as a cleaner for a company working at Charles de Gaulle airport. After a one-month trial period, she was offered a part-time job on a permanent contract. She had to clean 24 offices every day, working as a team with a woman with whom she got on well. Now that she was taking Karim to school, Céline met other mothers and made friends.

Farid makes sure that his son works well at school and remains very worried about anything that might lead to Karim being taken away:

> I'm cool, but I don't want him to get caught up in anything. The school could report us to social services, and then they'd look into our past and see what happened.

SHARING THEIR STORY

In early March 2005, Farid agreed to take part in a commission led by the then president of Emmaus France, which was writing a report at the request of the Minister for Solidarity, Health and the Family. The aim of the commission was to determine how to tackle the problems faced by families living in poverty more effectively. The starting point was the experiences of these families.

Six main points emerged from these discussions:

1. Access to housing is essential and must be the starting point for any support.
2. Actions must be part of an overall plan.
3. Better coordination was needed within the ASE.
4. Families must be given time to rebuild themselves.
5. Families must be empowered to become responsible for their own development.
6. Mutual help between families must be encouraged.

Farid says:

> The only thing that allows you to move forward is to meet someone who takes your case seriously. Without housing, you don't exist. You're running around like a maniac, looking for somewhere you can wash, somewhere you can make your own meals. When you get up, you're still tired. Having the key to your own door is an incredible thing! Once I was given a key and could prove I'd paid my rent, I noticed that when I knocked on a door, it opened for me. I was always freshly shaven, my clothes were clean, my eyes were wide open and my mind well rested:

everything was as it should be. Now I could go looking for work and live with my wife.

An article featuring Céline and Farid's story, 'Our marathon struggle to get a roof over our heads', was published in *Résistances*, a newspaper produced by ATD Fourth World in collaboration with Amnesty International France and Secours Catholique. Throughout October, 1.5 million free copies were distributed.

April 2006 saw the fiftieth anniversary of ATD Fourth World. Over 300 people from People's Universities in France, Belgium and Switzerland came together to mark the day. With others, Farid prepared a joint presentation on people's experiences within the Family Support Programme at Noisy-le-Grand. He explained:

When a family arrives on the estate, it is in pieces; there's not one healthy family here. More often than not, they're tired of telling their story to people who just aren't interested. After all that, they need time to rebuild the confidence to express themselves. Some of the families really have something to say. The first thing to do is to listen to what the families have been through – not to say or do things for them, because there are good things in what they say and, from there, they can start again. If you tell them what to do, they won't get very far.

He went on to list his four main rules in life:

1. Believe in people.
2. Give them another chance.
3. Accept them as they are.
4. Always keep hope alive – it's never too late.

In conclusion, he said, ' I see so much extreme poverty where I work. It means a lot to people when you take an interest in them.'

EPILOGUE

In September 2006, Farid and Céline took part in a film about family support made by ATD Fourth World. It had now been four years since they had left the estate, and they could step back from their experience and talk about it in front of the cameras. They retraced their progress and restated their desire to support other families.

Céline continued to work four hours a day as a cleaner at Charles de Gaulle airport. She had told her boss that she wanted to get a full-time job and to stop receiving disability benefit. She took a great interest in trade union negotiations concerning the improvement of working conditions and salary increases.

In June 2007, the couple was allocated accommodation by the low-income housing organisation on the estate where Farid worked. The estate manager encouraged Farid to take on more responsibilities by becoming a building caretaker.

Céline and Farid wrote their life story with the help of Floriane from ATD Fourth World. It was sometimes painful as it brought back bad memories, but the effort was worthwhile. They conclude their story by saying:

> We want Karim to be successful in life and in his studies. We want him to be happy but, above all, we don't want him to go through the same experiences as us.

FRANCO-ALGERIAN RELATIONS IN BRIEF

Colonisation and the Franco-Algerian War

In 1830, the French colonised the territories which correspond to present-day Algeria. By 1914, there were 750,000 French settlers in the country in a population of 5 million.

On 8 May 1945, popular demonstrations for independence were violently put down by the French army in what became known as the Sétif massacre. An Algerian Assembly was created in 1947, whose Governor General was still appointed by the French. With the creation of the National Liberation Front (FLN) by Ahmed Ben Bella, violent attacks broke out in the early morning hours of 1 November 1954 and marked the beginning of eight years of the Algerian War of Independence. Upon the proclamation of Algerian independence on 5 July 1962, 1 million expatriate French people returned to France.

The term 'Algerian War' was not used officially by French authorities until 1998. Casualties were heavy, and the war has left lasting scars on both French and Algerian society. On the French side, approximately 23,500 soldiers and 2,800 civilians were killed and 3,200 people were reported missing. Estimations of losses vary widely for the Algerians: 200,000 according to General de Gaulle, 1.5 million according to the FLN and 250,000–400,000 according to several historians. After the ceasefire, 60,000–70,000 Harkis (pro-French Algerians serving in the French army) were killed.

Algerian Immigration to France

The first phase of Algerian immigration to France began in 1905; by 1912, between 4,000 and 5,000 Algerians were arriving every year. During the First World War, 80,000 Algerians took part in the war effort. Between 1946 and 1962, the population explosion in Algeria and growing poverty brought unskilled workers who were no longer needed by the French economy. As a result, in 1964 France imposed quotas on the number of Algerian immigrants allowed to enter the country and, in December 1968, a Franco-Algerian agreement defined the status of Algerian nationals in France. They received preferential treatment compared to other nationalities. Subsequently modified, today this status is close to the general regime applied to all immigrants. In 1975, 20 per cent of immigrants to France were Algerian. Several unsuccessful campaigns were led by the French government to encourage Algerian workers to return to their country. In 2006, the Institut national de la statistique et des études économiques (INSEE) estimated that, during 2004–05, 675,000 Algerians were living in France.

NOTES

1. DDASS: The Direction départementale des Affaires Sanitaires et Sociales is the French Social Services.
2. Three thousand French francs translates to approximately 460 euros or US$665; 1 euro equalled US$1.45 as of June 2011.
3. The Certificat d'Aptitude Professionnelle is a vocational training certificate.
4. The Union Départementale des Associations Familiales is a public family support organisation.
5. The Revenu Minimum d'Insertion (RMI) is a basic social benefit.
6. The Aide Sociale à l'Enfance is a child welfare services agency.
7. The Agence Nationale Pour l'Emploi is a national employment agency.
8. Tapori is a worldwide network of children whose motto is: 'We want all children to have the same chances.' Through newsletters, mini-books and activities, children learn of the efforts of children in other countries to fight against exclusion.
9. People's Universities were established by ATD Fourth World in 1972 to provide a forum for dialogue between people living in persistent poverty and people from wider society where each participant's knowledge is recognised and enriched by the knowledge and experience of others. They usually meet once a month to discuss a specific subject and are held in several countries across Europe.
10. The Centre Communal d'Action Sociale (CCAS) is a municipal social action centre.
11. The Maison Départementale des Personnes Handicappées (MPDH) is a public centre for the disabled.

4
Staying Together Through Thick and Thin: The Story of the Rojas Paucar Family in Peru

Rosario Macedo de Ugarte and Marco Aurelio Ugarte Ochoa

This account was written by the Rojas Paucar family together with Rosario Macedo de Ugarte and Marco Aurelio Ugarte. Rosario and Marco founded ATD Fourth World Peru with some friends in 1991. They met the Rojas Paucar family in 1992 through activities led by the movement in El Mirador, a poor neighbourhood in Cusco. They built up a relationship of mutual trust with them over a period of more than twelve years.

When they were asked to take part in this project, the Rojas Paucar family's agreement was based on one condition: 'As long as it brings poverty to an end, so that in the future no family lives as we have lived.' For this family, it is not a question of 'alleviating poverty' or 'reducing poverty in 10 or 20 years', but of 'bringing poverty to an end so that other families do not have to suffer it'. This sentence stayed in the authors' minds all through the writing of the story.

The Rojas Paucar family consists of Alicia Paucar, Benigno Rojas, and their four children – Margarita, Laura, Miguel and Fernando – all born in Cusco, a city located in the southern mountains of Peru. Despite the constant difficulties the family encountered, they still had the strength to move ahead. This story is about these strengths. Extreme poverty will only ever be truly eradicated when those who are trying to combat it base their actions on the strengths of those who experience poverty every day.

THE EARLY YEARS

The Childhood and Youth of Benigno Rojas
Benigno Rojas was born in 1951 in the province of La Convención in the department of Cusco. He is the oldest of eight children. His

parents were farmers, but they did not own the plot of land they worked in the area of P'ispitayoq.

At the end of the 1950s, Benigno's father was unjustly accused of theft and served a six-year prison sentence. The family had to leave their home and land. Benigno's mother moved to Cusco to be near her husband and Benigno joined her there later. He described their lives in Cusco when he was eight years old:

> My mum rented a room opposite the jail. We went together to Huancabamba to the potato fields. My mum carried sacks of potatoes as if she were a man. I did too, as much as I could. We went down to Cusco with the sacks to sell potatoes, beans and root vegetables. Mum sold some and we kept some to eat. Sometimes she prepared food to sell in the central market. But my dad wasn't idle. He worked in the jail. He made wooden combs, spoons, lots of things. He was a really good craftsman. Mum used to go to the jail on visiting days. He gave her what he had done and she sold it. That's how we used to live from day to day. At that time I used to sell blocks of ice near the San Pedro market for ten cents, which was just enough for a loaf of bread.

Benigno also worked in a brick factory and as a servant in a private home. He alternated these jobs with his first years at school.

While in jail, Benigno's father sold everything the family owned on the property in P'ispitayoq. Benigno said that the buyers took advantage of his father's situation to pay less than the full value. Despite this, when his father came out of jail there was enough money for him to buy cattle in the province of Anta and take them to the slaughterhouses of Cusco. The trip took between four and six days on foot. Benigno helped his father, but it was hard work for a child.

At the start of the 1960s, one of Benigno's uncles, who was a foreman on a ranch in Paltaibamba in the province of La Convención, offered his father some land to rent in this area. His father accepted and once again started farming. The new land had to be slashed and burnt, then sown. Benigno and his brothers helped their father with this work.

On 24 June 1969 – called 'Day of the Indian', later changed to 'Peasant's Day' – the Agrarian Reform law of Juan Velasco Alvarado's government came into force; this compelled landowners to give up the land they had let out to tenants. The land was then handed over to the peasants as agricultural cooperatives. Thanks to that law, Benigno's parents came to own the land they were farming in Paltaibamba, where they were still living 40 years later.

Benigno finished primary school but he could not continue his schooling because Paltaibamba was too far from the nearest high school. So at 16 he left home and went to Cusco, where he found a job in a garage. With the help of an uncle, he studied until the third year of high school, doing the last two years at night school.

At the request of his father, Benigno then went back to Paltaibamba to help on the land. The relationship between father and son had always been difficult, so his father decided that Benigno should join the army to 'become someone in life'. In 1972, after two years, Benigno left the army. For the first time in his life he had identity papers so he went to Lima to try to join the Republican Guard. This dream came to an end when his documents were stolen on his arrival in the capital.

He went back to Cusco to work as a builder's labourer. There he met his first partner, and together they went to live in Yoruba, where they had a son. For eight years they lived by peddling small hardware goods, until his partner left him, taking their child and all they had earned during that time. This setback was a great shock to Benigno and he even considered committing suicide. He then worked first in Paltaibamba as a farmhand, then in Urubamba on a building site, and once again in Cusco, in 1984, as a builder's labourer. That was when he met Alicia Paucar, his current partner.

The Childhood and Youth of Alicia Paucar

Alicia Paucar was born in 1961 in the province of Anta, in the department of Cusco. She is the youngest of three daughters.

Her childhood was marked by frequent changes. Shortly after her birth her parents separated and her mother went to live in Lima with a new partner, taking Alicia with her. From this time on she was separated from her sisters, who had gone to live with their aunts. After four years, at her father's request, Alicia was sent to live with one of his aunts at Iscuchaca, in the province of Anta; she was put to work in the household. Father and daughter now lived in the same city and saw each other occasionally, but never lived under the same roof.

Alicia's mother died in Lima in 1968. Alicia had never seen her again.

In 1969 Alicia was sent to her grandmother's in Cusco, along with her elder sister Rosa. It was an unhappy time, as her grandmother did not show her any affection. She had to work hard all week, preparing sweets and ice cream to be sold in the markets on Sundays. Her grandmother enrolled her in school but never bought her school stationery or new clothes.

When she was twelve years old, Alicia ran away from her grandmother's home. A woman took her in to look after an elderly lady. After a year her grandmother forced her to come back home, only for Alicia to run away again soon after. This time she went to Quillabamba to join her sister Rosa. Rosa had also run away from their grandmother's home and was now married. The sisters worked together selling fruit in the market. In 1975, their father died after a long illness. The sisters moved to Cusco and continued to work at the market. Rosa did all she could so that Alicia, who was then aged 14, could continue her schooling.

Rosa was involved in a fight and was sent to jail for 20 months; her husband left her. Alicia visited her sister twice a week. Rosa knitted pullovers and baby clothes and gave them to her sister to sell in the streets and markets. Alicia carried on studying at the same time, and managed to finish primary school.

She also started to sell coffee from four till seven in the morning near San Pedro railway station; in 1976 she met her first partner, Ruben Pastor, there. Alicia was 15 years old. The couple lived together for seven years and had three daughters. The last, Margarita, was born in 1982. When Ruben left, he took the two elder daughters with him, leaving Alicia with Margarita, who was still being breastfed.

She went back to selling vegetables, fruit and cheese to earn a living. In 1984 she met Benigno Rojas. He remembers, 'I met Alicia. She sure caught me with her little cheeses from Anta!'

About her other two daughters, Alicia said:

I never see my daughters. Their father married another woman and he and his wife kept me away from them. How I would love to see them! But I'm afraid that she'll reject me and say, 'What do you want? Do you think you're my mother?' They are close to their stepmother, that's why I don't go.

Recalling her childhood, Alicia said:

I don't know what it is to have a mother's or father's love. I don't want to see my children suffer as I suffered when I was a child.

FAMILY LIFE

Benigno and Alicia spent the first years of their life together in the neighbouring provinces of La Convención and Cusco. They knew the area well and had relatives and friends there.

During this period they sold clothes that they bought in Tacna (on the border with Chile) or in Desaguadero (on the border with Bolivia).

Between 1985 and 1989, they moved house three times within the same Zarzuela neighbourhood. Benigno and Alicia became members of the district association of San Camilo, a new neighbourhood in Cusco, and bought a 200 square metre plot in which they invested a large part of the capital they used for their trade. When the district association encountered grave financial problems, Benigno had a serious fight with the association directors and the family had to leave the district, losing everything – their land and their capital. The couple had to find somewhere else to live. They settled in the El Mirador district on the top of a hill in Cusco.

Life in El Mirador

This neighbourhood is very steep with much seepage from underground water. Eucalyptus trees have been planted to stabilise the ground. The first inhabitants in El Mirador, who bought the land, divided it into 90 lots. Some of the landowners left El Mirador in 1984 after a landslide, fearing a second one. So as not to lose their property, they placed it in the care of watchmen or let it out for a very low rent. Mr Gutierrez, a friend of Benigno's, suggested that the family could live on his land and watch over it. In exchange for rent, Benigno had to join in the *faenas* – community work that the district association organised every Sunday.

Life for the Rojas Paucar family became more difficult in El Mirador during the 1990s because Benigno could not find regular work. He said:

> There wasn't much work and there was a lot of competition. We got by as best we could. Even if the two of us didn't eat, we always made sure that the children did, whether it was only some bread, potatoes or *mote* [boiled corn]. It was hard because people didn't know us much in El Mirador. There weren't many shops, only one or two. My wife got bread, sugar and pasta on credit from one shop and then another. But the debts ran up and after a while no one would give us credit any more.

One night in January 1993, El Mirador experienced another landslide and many houses were swept away. The El Mirador Association was then given financial assistance to channel the Urcupunku stream that formed the boundary of the neighbourhood. To carry out the work, the Board of Directors first chose men from among the members' families and only occasionally gave work to a watchman or a tenant. They never employed Benigno as they considered him to be unreliable.

It was at this time that Benigno first came to ATD Fourth World to ask if they were hiring people to work on channelling the stream. He said, 'They won't give me work. Look at my hands. These are a workman's hands!' The despair at being excluded from this work could be seen in his face. When the ATD Fourth World members explained that they had no work to offer him and that they fought to eradicate poverty in the world, he replied, 'Great, I'm poor! How are you going to help me?' They told him that ATD Fourth World did not give handouts, but by working together they could make society recognise his rights.

The family relied mostly on the sale of vegetables that Alicia peddled in the central San Pedro market. She laid out three to five sols[1] to buy vegetables every day, and tried to make two or three sols profit. She also sold *anticuchos*, typical Peruvian food made with slices of meat and ox heart grilled on a skewer, and *chicha blanca* (a type of corn beer).

The Rojas Paucar's house was directly opposite the small building provided for ATD Fourth World by the El Mirador Association. However, it took a long time to establish contact with Alicia as she always left home very early in the morning. When she came home at midday, she responded to members' greetings but did not stay to talk. She met them courteously when they went to her home to ask permission for the children to take part in an activity, but remained outside and kept her door closed.

In 1995, the Rojas Paucar family was evicted from their home. Benigno had been drinking *chicha* with his friends and boasting that nothing could stop him buying the land they were living on. When the owner heard this, he made them leave. The family found another room for rent at 15 sols per month in the same neighbourhood. There was no electricity or toilet, and the landlady insisted that the rent was paid on time every month. The family could not manage this and after a few months they had to look for another home.

Benigno knew a family in the neighbourhood of San Juan who were looking for someone to look after their house, which was under construction. Behind the house there was a small, one room lean-to with a sloping roof. It had no toilet, no electricity, and no water. The whole family moved in. In exchange for living in this accommodation, Benigno had to take part in the Sunday communal jobs with the San Juan Housing Association. The family spent two years there.

At the beginning of 1998, the family moved back again to the El Mirador neighbourhood. The district had changed while they were away. The problem of landslides had been solved thanks to a foreign non-governmental organisation. A storage tank had been built so that each house now had water; a transformer had been installed to supply electricity for the whole neighbourhood. Electricity consumption was divided equally between the owners, tenants, and watchmen each month. This put the poorest families at a disadvantage as they generally used less electricity.

The neighbourhood also looked better. The lower area, which used to be a garbage dump, had been turned into a garden thanks to the collective work carried out by the inhabitants. In addition, the urban transport companies had set up two minibus stops at the top and bottom of El Mirador.

As the neighbourhood improved, rents increased. Coupled with the cost of electricity, this created great difficulties for many tenant families. At the same time, those owners who had left the neighbourhood years earlier started coming back, which meant that many watchmen and tenants had to leave. Despite all the obstacles, the Rojas Paucar family managed to stay in El Mirador and to maintain their social relationships.

Benigno made a number of trips to the province of La Convención to earn money as a labourer, staying for several months. Despite their efforts, the family still could not achieve even a minimum of economic security. Benigno explained:

It's hard not to have money to buy food. There are five or six of us at home. If we have money, we buy bread for each person because that's what we eat in the morning with a hot drink. For lunch we make vegetable soup or a rice or pasta dish. When we can, we buy chicken or meat bones to make it thicker. If there is any left over, we save it for dinner. Alicia and I prefer the children at least to eat. We've got out of the habit of having dinner. But just for that, we need at least seven sols. If we haven't got that much, we can always try asking for credit in one of the local shops. If we have nothing else, we eat potatoes, we nearly always have some potatoes at home.

Laura said:

> If Mum didn't have anything, she borrowed from her friend Olga, even if it was just a potato with a bit of sauce. She always gave us something; she tried to make sure that we didn't go without. She preferred to go hungry so as to give us food.

Even if Benigno could not find work as a builder's labourer, he contributed in various ways to the family upkeep. As a child he had accompanied his mother to Huancabamba, a three-hour trek from El Mirador. Now he returned there periodically for two or three days at a time and brought back potatoes and other vegetables. Some years he worked with the peasants in share-farming, which means he supplied the seeds, and at harvest time he shared the crop equally with the owner of the land.

Margarita commented:

> My father found work from time to time. Sometimes, someone would say to him, 'How about coming to help me in my field?' If he couldn't bring home any money he would come back with some food from the country. That's how he helped us. We used what he brought home and at least that was something we didn't have to buy.

MARGARITA'S STORY

Margarita's first contact with ATD Fourth World Peru was in early 1992 when she was 10 years old. She took part in the holiday workshops programme organised by ATD Fourth World, in agreement with the El Mirador District Association. The children in El Mirador call them Tapori, a word meaning friendship between the world's children. Through Tapori, they learn how children in other countries fight against exclusion in their daily lives. Laura, who was five, kept interrupting her older sister's work saying that she wanted to learn to sew too. Margarita would bring her sister to the activities, then sometimes go back to help her mother with the housework. She did the washing so her hands were scarred and lined from water and her clothes were damp.

When she talked about the Tapori activities Margarita said:

> We learnt how to draw, read and be sociable, and I loved that. I liked it best when they came and said, 'We're going to do some acting and dancing', because that's what I liked the most ... I liked it when they came to fetch us. They taught me. They saw how we lived and gave us support.

At lunchtime there was a break in the workshop activities for the children to go home. Some would come back after ten minutes saying they had finished, despite the fact that they had had nothing to eat. Some of them would burn paper so that the neighbours, seeing the smoke, would think they were cooking and not look down on them. A child rarely asked to share another child's bread, even if they had not eaten all day.

In 1988, at the age of six, Margarita started at El Rosario, a state school for children with limited financial resources. It was the school Alicia had attended. At this time the cost of schooling was minimal for the family, as only Margarita was at school.

Margarita began working in the cemetery of La Almudena along with many other children from the poorest families in the district. She could earn two or three sols on weekdays, and up to ten sols on Saturdays and Sundays, her best days.

> Some of the children from El Mirador asked me 'Do you want to come and sell water in the cemetery?' I said 'Yes', because I liked being with the others. I sold water for flowers and for washing the gravestones all day Saturday and Sunday. From Monday to Friday, I went to school in the morning, and at two o'clock, after lunch, I changed out of my school uniform into old clothes, and took my little bucket down to the cemetery to sell water. I sold water for about three or four years. One day, a lady asked me 'Don't you want to sell flowers?' I said 'Yes, I do', because it brought in more money. I spent nearly two years selling flowers. Sometimes, when people came for a funeral, I would also slip away for a short while to look after their cars.

Financially, Margarita contributed a great deal to the family. In 1997, she stopped selling flowers in the cemetery and began to work on the buses in Cusco. Generally, men or boys did this type of work. Margarita was one of the city's first *voceadoras* – people employed by the bus drivers to attract passengers by calling out the destination and route. She talked about how this new work began:

> As I sold *chicha blanca* and other things at the bus stop, I got to know the Inti drivers and *voceadoras* and I started selling tickets for them. One day I asked a bus owner, who I trusted, 'Can't you give me some work?' So he said to me, 'All right, you can come with me on Sunday.' He took me on trial on Sunday and that's how I started to work. As I'm always laughing, I attracted people. It went well, and the owner said, 'That's fine. You can work with me every day.' I spent five years in that job and that's where I met my first son's father. When there weren't any buses, I went to sell *anticuchos* as I didn't like sitting at home doing nothing.
>
> My mother had had an accident a while before, and there was nothing in the house to eat because my father had started to drink. He was disheartened, I don't know why, I really don't. I can't understand it. I was paid a set wage of ten sols and then there were side benefits. I gave the ten sols to my mother. My wages went to her to pay the rent and the electricity or so that she could cook something and buy food. The rest I kept for my clothes. There were a lot of expenses but we tried to manage, by supporting each other, my dad, mum and me.
>
> When he knew I had exams, my father would say, 'My girl, get up early and study. You learn better in the mornings, so that way you'll be well prepared for your exams.' So I got up at five in the morning and studied until six. Then I had to make breakfast before going to school as I was the eldest and I had to look after my younger brothers and sisters.

In 1997, Margarita was about to give up her studies because there was no money and, at the age of 15, she was too old to be accepted in high school. Her godmother took her in and enrolled her in a night school for a year. But in 1998 she had to abandon the course.

> When I was working on the buses, I tried to study. I got through to the second year of high school, but I had to repeat. Sometimes I couldn't sit the exams because it wasn't easy to study in the bus, and I didn't have enough time. I couldn't pay for all the stationery: I was always missing an exercise book or I couldn't afford a textbook … But I wanted to be someone. I wanted to have something to show for myself. My dream didn't come true.

Margarita's first child, Juan, was born in 1999, when she was just 17 years old. She described what happened in the hospital:

> I had a Caesarean and had to spend 15 days in hospital. I didn't have any money to pay the hospital fees or the medicine. We owed 500 sols. My mother went to see the social worker to ask for a reduction. She said that we had to pay 250 sols but we didn't even have that … Then the nurse arrived and said, 'If you don't pay, we'll keep the baby. Why are you going to take the child if you can't raise him? If you haven't even got enough to get him out of the hospital, you won't have enough to buy food, you're not going to be able to breastfeed him or bring him up.' Then she said to me, 'Let him stay here. We'll give him to someone who can adopt him and offer him a better life.' My mother and I started to cry, and I said, 'Go and borrow money from anyone you can find. Start by pawning my TV first of all.' But she only got 70 sols for it, which wasn't enough. My mother went everywhere to try and get help. Then we went to ATD Fourth World as they had already supported us in the past. I got out of hospital with my son, and since then I've kept him with me, for always.

Margarita could not live with the young man she had fallen in love with, and to bring up her son she needed to find a better-paid job. Through an unofficial employment agency, a woman offered her a job in a restaurant in Juliaca, in the Department of Puno. Margarita accepted the job and left her son in her mother's care. Once there, she realised that she had been tricked, and spent the next two years suffering exploitation and abuse.

One day during that time, Margarita phoned the ATD Fourth World office to tell them she wanted to speak to her mother the next day at four o'clock in the afternoon. Alicia was there at four o'clock. She asked her daughter where she was but Margarita only said that she would send her a regular amount of money via a bank transfer. Alicia replied, 'I don't want your money. I want you to come home, because I miss you.'

Mother and daughter spoke on the phone once or twice a month, until Margarita managed to leave Juliaca, thanks to a man whom she called *el caballero*, 'the gentleman':

> That man got me out of there, out of that nightmare. The gentleman was a *charla*, a fortune-teller. He said to me, 'Girl, I'm going to get you out of here. But you're going to work with me

and my wife. You're going to wash our clothes and help us load up our equipment. I'll pay you and we'll go to Cusco then Lima, Ayacucho and Abancay.' And that's what we did. Sometimes I was the one who told fortunes. They put a veil over my eyes and I had to answer their questions. The gentleman taught me how to do it.

One day he said to me, 'I think we should go and talk to your mother. We'll tell her where I got you out of, where you are and who you're with.' The gentleman told my mother everything, and gave her some money saying, 'Take it, it's your daughter's money, she earned it.' When he left he said to me, 'If you go back to Juliaca I'll come and get you and drag you back as if you were my daughter. I don't want you to go back to that place.' So I swore to him and promised that I wouldn't go back.

Back in Cusco, Margarita found work once again as a *voceadora* on a minibus. But there was greater competition and she could only work one or two days a week, so she started peddling acrylic boards for school children. She met a young man, Oscar Ruis, who was also selling boards. Shortly after, they decided to live together.

When I was eight months pregnant with my second child, we started to sell pens and card games. I would sell them in the morning, and in the afternoon I sold 'Cañonazo' chocolates. Oscar sold these things with me and we managed to make enough to live on. In fact, we did quite well. We were both trying to get a better life. I'm happy living with him. Sometimes we fight but that's normal. We love each other a lot, and we work well together.

LAURA'S STORY

When Laura was six, she was already going with Margarita to the cemetery to sell water. However, she was not as successful in this work as her sister. Laura was first enrolled in the same primary school in 1993. The enrolment fees for the two girls were 20 sols and the school stationery cost about 40 sols. This represented a large financial burden for the family. Laura said:

My parents always tried to make sure we didn't go without, so that we could study. They wanted us to attend every day, and to finish school so that other people wouldn't look down on us. They used to say, 'You have to continue your studies. You have to do better than us, otherwise you are going to struggle just like we have.' It was my mother who took charge of the enrolments. She would try to put money aside. She always got the school stationery on credit. There was so much that she couldn't get it all at once because we never had enough money. Whenever she could, she would put one or two sols aside and she paid it off little by little. Each month she had to take the money we owed to the shopkeepers otherwise they came to our home to get it and the following year they wouldn't give her credit any more.

Laura finished primary school in 1997 and Alicia looked for a high school. El Mirador belonged to an area where the high school had excellent results, but parents had to give a sizeable amount of money at the time of enrolment, as well as contributions during the year to pay for equipment. A member of ATD Fourth World was a teacher in a school with less stringent financial requirements in the centre of town. In agreement with Laura's parents, she initiated procedures for Laura to be accepted at this high school.

Benigno arranged to meet with the school's Board of Directors and the Parents' Association, accompanied by a member of ATD Fourth World. He wanted to tell them that it was impossible for him to pay his daughter's full enrolment fee at once, and to ask them to let him pay in instalments. However, he fell and fractured a rib after leaving a *chichería*, and could not attend the meeting. He stayed at home in bed for several days. Nevertheless, on the last day that Laura could be enrolled, he managed to get up and, together with Alicia, walked the seven kilometres to the school because they did not have any money for transport. As he said, 'Each step I took, I felt a sharp pain in the ribs. The pain was unbearable.' He finally managed to enrol Laura. His face lights up whenever he talks about this achievement.

Laura's attendance at this school represented a heavy financial investment for the family. For example, Alicia remembered having to buy a blue cardigan that was part of the school uniform. She said, 'For Laura's uniform, I bought a cardigan on credit which I paid off over two years. Thankfully, it lasted the five years she was at school.'

In 1999, there was a change of government and a new education plan was adopted. The new methodology encouraged working in groups, for which more school supplies were necessary. Laura often felt excluded because the other students said, 'No, you can't come with us, Laura. You never have what we need, and when we have to buy something, you never have any money.'

Laura remembered:

For computer class, they always asked us for floppy disks. My mother knew this so she tried to put money aside on Saturdays to buy them. But during the week they also wanted money for photocopies. As I went to school without any money, when a teacher handed them out, I would ask him, 'Can I have one, please? I'll pay you tomorrow.' Some teachers accepted, but they only gave you one chance. If you didn't pay them the next lesson, they wouldn't give you any more. There were days when my mother didn't have the money, so the teacher didn't give me any the next time. I felt sad because I saw that my classmates could pay for everything we needed. I always felt jealous when I saw that the others had more than me, but I had to put up with it as I knew my mother couldn't give me any money.

Nobody else in my class had the same problems, or at any rate if they did they weren't game to tell me. You only talk about those things with a person you trust or an older person, not somebody your own age. If you do say something to somebody, and then you have a fight, you're always scared they'll tell people. That's why you're more likely to talk to an adult, and even then not often. You're ashamed to talk about your problems to somebody who has things that you can't have or won't ever be able to have. But just because you don't have as much as the others doesn't mean they're better than you.

Laura often received the teachers' support but there were hard times as well. For instance, her neighbourhood was not paved and one day she arrived at school with dirty shoes. In front of her classmates, a teacher stepped on her shoes, saying, 'These shoes are so dirty that it doesn't matter if we dirty them even more. That will teach you to come to school with dirty shoes!'

For physical education classes, students had to wear a top, shorts and training shoes. As Laura could not buy all this, she was excluded from these lessons. When she insisted on taking part, the teacher told her that she could come to class without the training shoes and with just a top and shorts. The teacher sincerely thought that he had found a satisfactory solution but he did not realise how humiliating it was for Laura to be the only girl in the class barefoot.

In September 2002, Alicia was knocked down by a hit-and-run driver. Laura and Miguel had to take it in turns to look after her. She did not want them to miss school but some days she was in so much pain that she could not get out of bed on her own. Laura missed school so much that they threatened to expel her, without even trying to find out why she was not attending. After many discussions with the teachers, they finally decided to give her one last chance with a conditional enrolment: Laura could stay at school to finish her last year of secondary education, but if she missed one more day she would be expelled.

With the threat of expulsion hanging over her, Laura's last year of school was distressing. Yet, in December 2003, she successfully completed high school. She achieved this through her own efforts, willpower and courage, and also the continual support she received from her parents and several of the school's teachers and directors.

Laura's story also brought about a change in the school's policy. As they had given Laura an extra chance, the directors and teachers had to do the same for other students: they decided they would take their background into consideration and try to learn why they did not attend school regularly or misbehaved.

In 2004, after finishing high school, Laura looked for a job that corresponded to her level of education. Her baptismal godfather took her on as a clothes salesperson in his shop. She worked from Monday to Sunday twelve hours a day for a monthly wage of 150 sols. The day Margarita went into labour with her second child, Laura had to accompany her to hospital. When she returned to work, her godfather's wife told her that she was fired. Laura had asked one of her friends to let them know she would be absent but the woman denied having received the message.

A few months later, somebody offered Laura a job in a restaurant near Machu Picchu. This was a job without set hours and it was poorly paid, especially considering the very high cost of living in this tourist area. Laura spent two months there, returning home with only 100 sols.

MIGUEL'S STORY

Benigno passed on to Miguel the value of work. Miguel would go down to the cemetery from time to time with friends to guard cars. On several occasions during the school holidays he accompanied his godmother, a trader who sold goods in the region's markets. But, best of all, he would go with his father to grow potatoes. Benigno spoke about these times with great tenderness:

Miguel was my workmate. He made me happy. He'd say, 'Come on Dad! Let's go to La Puna to see how the potatoes are coming on.' He encouraged me. Everyone liked him. He was always ready to help. What he liked was to have a good snack. They eat well in the country because the work is hard. They'd say, 'Come on lad, eat some more!' but he'd answer, 'No, Ma'am. You've already served me enough.' He went everywhere with me. He got milk for the work he did, and he was happy with that ...

Miguel finished primary school in 2000 and started at the same high school as Laura in 2001. From a very young age, Miguel had taken part with his sisters in ATD Fourth World activities in El Mirador. Like the other children, he had been able to read books, draw, paint and try other artistic activities. He especially enjoyed drawing and painting, and he drew very well. He also learnt to get on with other children. All of this experience helped him at school. Alicia said:

Miguel is very clever and very active at school. He said to me, 'You know, Mum, my classmates like me. I help them, and they respect me.' He's always said that he gets on well with them. He's got a school friend there who often comes to the house to get help for his work. He gets Miguel to explain it to him. As Miguel can draw well and his friends can't, they come to the house and say, 'Come on Miguel, draw it for me!' So he does.

Miguel, who was twelve, was a source of pride for his family. He often came to the ATD Fourth World office to do his homework. Following the attack on the World Trade Center in New York on 11 September 2001, ATD Fourth World members decided to organise a peace march on 20 November, the anniversary of the signature of the Convention on the Rights of the Child. When he heard about the march, Miguel offered to write a letter to the President of Peru saying what violence meant to children. The letter was addressed to the Prefect of Cusco, Carlos Tovar, the President's representative. Miguel's initiative led other children to write letters to various local figures. All the public and private schools were invited to this march. Hundreds of students of all ages took part.

At the end of the march, as a sign of their rejection of violence, the children were invited to throw their toy guns into rubbish bins. In exchange, they received sweets donated by city shopkeepers. Carlos Tovar attended, and Miguel read out his letter and presented it to him. He ended his message by saying:

Peace is very important for both children and adults. That is why, together, we must fight against war; when there is war, many children and adults die and families suffer. The guilty ones are not those who go to fight, but those who lead the war. After killing someone, those who fight feel very badly. I therefore send this message on behalf of children and adults so that they no longer fight with their brothers and friends. If you want to apologise to a friend after a fight, maybe he'll reject you, maybe he'll forgive you, but inside you both, there'll always be a deep wound – the pain of having fought. We're all brothers and sisters and we mustn't fight any more.

Such words struck a chord in a country marked by 20 years of terrorist activities from 1980 to 2000, between the army and the Maoist Shining Path guerrillas, which left tens of thousands of victims.

Impressed by the content of this message, and by Miguel's personality, Carlos Tovar asked him to accept the position of 'Child Prefect of Cusco'. This gesture was backed by Dr Silvio Campana, Ombudsman, who was also present at the peace march. Alicia recalled:

I was very excited about it. One day my son comes home and says to me, 'Mum, I've been chosen as Child Prefect.' I couldn't believe it. They sent me a letter saying, 'Madam, please come to the school.' I went with my husband and my grandson. When we arrived we were surprised to see they had prepared a whole ceremony in honour of my son, in front of all of the teachers and other students. Then they gave him a medal! We were asked to attend another meeting the next day in the Council. There the Prefect swore him in and gave him his sash. They interviewed me and I didn't know what to say. I got all emotional seeing my son like that, and I started to cry. Everyone was saying to me, 'Madam, how lucky you are to have a son like yours.' From the Council we went to the Prefecture and there, in front of everyone, they gave him an office and a secretary. I am really proud that my son has become a Child Prefect.

Miguel's duties as Child Prefect consisted in taking care of requests related to children. For example, he received a request to look for support to send a girl with cancer from the Department of Cusco to a hospital in Lima. Her parents were poor and could not meet the costs of treatment. Miguel asked an airline company to provide free travel for the child, her mother and a nurse. The company agreed and the girl travelled to Lima. Miguel's position ended eight months later when Carlos Tovar stepped down as Prefect of Cusco, but this experience continued to affect his life; he was admired by his schoolmates. In El Mirador, the children were happy and proud that he was a Child Prefect, and said that if they could help him in his mission then they would gladly do so.

In 2004, Miguel was in the fourth year of high school. He had two years of school left. His health problems started that year with a toothache. As there was no money for treatment, the tooth was not extracted; this led to a local infection, which, in turn, spread to a generalised infection. Miguel first went to a state hospital, but they refused to treat him. ATD Fourth World members spoke with three associations that work in the area of health care. Together they found a way to support the family and Miguel was admitted to one of their health centres where he was treated for three months.

However, Miguel's health worsened after he returned home and this time he was admitted to a state hospital. On several occasions, regardless of Miguel's situation, the hospital threatened to stop treating him if the bills were not paid. One day a doctor said to Alicia, 'Listen, *Señora*, if you want your son to survive, hurry up and find some money, otherwise, he's going to die.' In fact, Miguel suffers from chronic renal failure and must have haemodialysis three times a week, until he can have a kidney transplant. When Alicia asked to be exempted from the hospitalisation costs, an official replied, 'Is that why you have children? So as not to give them what they need later on?'

Alicia tried everything, but for several months nobody informed her that Miguel was entitled to treatment under the Integral Health System (SIS), a health care programme for disadvantaged families, which the Peruvian government had just set up. Finally, with support, she managed to complete the procedures for Miguel to be eligible for the SIS. In Cusco, only the Workers' Social Security Hospital has the equipment to perform haemodialysis. Those who do not have an insurance policy with them must pay for the treatment. However, in Lima, the SIS has agreements with various health centres that offer this treatment. The director of the SIS in Cusco authorised Miguel's transfer to the capital. There he was to receive haemodialysis free of charge until November 2005, when legally he would be considered an adult. After this date, another solution would have to be found for him to carry on benefiting from this service. With the cost of haemodialysis at US$70 dollars, Miguel's treatment amounts to a total of US$840 a month.

THE ISSUES FACING FAMILIES LIVING IN POVERTY IN PERU

Health: The Sword of Damocles

The Rojas Paucar family, like many very poor families in El Mirador, resort mainly to traditional medicine. Alicia gave one such example:

> My husband's parents have a plot of land in the valley, in Chaullay above Quillabamba. They grow coffee there. He went there in March 1996 and spent almost three months working the land. He was to do the harvest but he fell sick. He got *mal de tierra* because he had not made the offering to Pachamamá, Mother Earth, before starting work. So she got him. This sickness shrank his feet and he could hardly walk. He came home because he was in so much pain. In Cusco he got worse and spent two months in bed ... My neighbours told me that I couldn't leave him like that and if I didn't do something soon, the *soq'a* [an evil spirit who can enter a person's body and cause sickness] would stay in him forever and never let him get better. That's why they said I should go to a healer. The healer asked me to prepare a *cuy*, a guinea pig, and a *mesa* [ritual elements for Andean ceremonies] to see what was wrong with him. As it was the *soq'a*, the healer moved the *cuy* all over his body and he was cured.

When an illness gets worse, families are obliged to go to a health centre or a hospital. But they do so warily. They are afraid of being criticised and humiliated by the inevitable reproaches about their 'lack of hygiene'. Unable to explain, made to feel guilty, and faced with the shame of being treated in such a way, they avoid health centres as much as possible.

When they give birth, many poor families, especially those who live in the country or come from the country, use a *partera*, a midwife, who attends the family's home in the husband's presence. Often, the husband does not want a male doctor to attend to his wife, an attitude that is common to Andean culture.

Alicia grew up in the city; while rural traditions were still important in her life, she did not follow them at all times. She always went to the Antonio Lorena Hospital del Cusco, known as the 'poor people's hospital', for her children's birth. A consultation there costs around three sols, whereas in other places for those with scarce resources, it can be five or six sols.

When Fernando was born, Alicia decided not to have any more children. She said:

> When I was pregnant with Fernando, I said to my husband, 'I'm going to have this baby but then I'll have my tubes tied. I don't want to have any more children.' He agreed, but he didn't really accept it. He said to me, 'You've had that operation so you can go off with another man and abandon your children.'

This kind of prejudice, frequent among men, is hard to change and can lead to violence in the home. In the Andean culture, children are a form of wealth. One of the worst insults for a woman is to be called a *mula* – a mule, a sterile animal. For a man, *uspha*, which means 'ash', something that has no use, is a powerful insult.

From 2002, the Alejandro Toledo government implemented measures to support low-income mothers, but healthcare is not free of charge in Peru. Even public hospitals and medical centres pass on a part of the hospital and medicine costs to the extremely poor. Although this is a minimal cost, it can be difficult and even impossible for very poor families to find the money. Then there is a lack of basic materials in the public health centres, which means that patients must bring their own gauze and cotton wool.

As long as there are financial obstacles to medical care, families with scant resources will always live in the fear of seeing the precarious balance in their lives totally disrupted by health problems.

The Struggle for Education

Whenever Benigno and Alicia talk about education, they always say how much they wanted their children to go to school. Alicia did her utmost to pay all the costs of her children's schooling. Benigno was always concerned that his children should learn something new and take on a role of leadership. He encouraged them to learn poems, write speeches and take part in various activities.

Alicia said, 'We've always had problems because sometimes there wasn't any money. I had to do everything I could to enrol them, as my husband didn't help me … It's been hard every year to enrol them. I had to explain everything to my children.'

As they could not buy all the books they needed, Miguel, Laura and other children from El Mirador often came to the ATD Fourth

World office in the centre of Cusco on their way home from school. There was always a teacher who could help them.

Like the Rojas Paucar family, most families in El Mirador strongly believe their children's education is the way out of their current situation. In the words of one parent, 'I want my children to study so that they don't suffer like I have suffered.' Another said, 'It's only by studying that they'll get somewhere in life.' However, sometimes families have to make a choice between paying the enrolment fees so they can send their children to school or buying food to feed them. For them, the dream of sending their children to school is over.

The Family's Position in the Neighbourhood

The Rojas Paucar family has a very small circle of close friends among the neighbouring families. Alicia said that Olga was her only friend.

Olga's family is one of the better-off families in El Mirador. She knows all about everyone in the district through her shop and small family bakery, where Alicia buys her flour. Olga respects Alicia and is aware of her efforts to feed her children and provide them with a good education. Such is the level of trust between these two women that when Alicia wants to save money for the rent or to buy a book for one of the children, she gives the money for safekeeping to Olga. 'I give my money to her because she already has money, so I know she won't steal mine.'

Benigno considered his participation in the *faenas* as a sign of recognition by the El Mirador community. Alicia did not see it in the same way. She noted that although everyone had to take part in community work, when a landowner did not participate, he was excused. However, when a watchman did not show up, one of the El Mirador Association directors went to his home and told him to take part.

Nevertheless, there were times when Benigno and Alicia did feel they mattered and were recognised. Such an occasion was in March 2000 when Rosa, Alicia's sister, died. Rosa used to come and stay with her sister and she died one Sunday in her sister's home. The coroner on duty should have come, but only the police arrived, so permission to remove the body could not be given. After Benigno requested the intervention of an ATD Fourth World member, permission for burial was finally granted.

At that time the family lived in San Juan, but most of their friends were in El Mirador. So Benigno and Alicia asked to use the community function room there for the wake. To start with, the neighbourhood association president denied them permission. This was very distressing for Benigno as he had expected to be treated as a friend. Fortunately, another member of the Board of Directors spoke up for him. Several years earlier he had entrusted Benigno with organising a religious celebration. He declared that Benigno had worked on behalf of the community, that he was a former tenant, and that he could not be denied the use of the community function room. He gave him the key and told him he could bring Rosa's body for the wake. Many El Mirador neighbours came, bringing candles and sugar for the tea. There were many there the next day to accompany Rosa's body to the cemetery.

This event was very important for Alicia, because it concerned her sister. It was also significant for Benigno, who could hold his head high in front of his neighbours despite being out of work at that time.

As is the case for many poor families, the relationships with the children's godparents play a very important role in the life of the Rojas Paucar family. In Peruvian society, especially in rural areas and poor urban districts, the relationship between godchildren and godparents is very strong. The godparent becomes a member of the family. He not only has spiritual duties, but must also assume certain other responsibilities for his godchild, such as contributing to his education, or offering support to the family when health problems arise. Having a godparent who can help during hard times is an essential element in the strategy for survival or improvement.

Ties similar to those with godparents can also be established with benefactors at the time of the child's first haircut, the *chukcha rutukuy* ceremony. According to Andean tradition, a child's hair is not cut until he is at least three years old. This ceremony is the equivalent of a christening. On the chosen day, the child's hair is braided into little plaits tied with coloured ribbon. Relatives, friends and benefactors are invited. When the ceremony begins, the father or a respected person in the family, sometimes a grandparent, reminds everyone of the reason for the gathering and thanks them for their presence. Scissors decorated with coloured ribbon are placed in a basket covered with a bright cloth. Red and white carnation petals are scattered over the four corners. The scissors pass from hand to hand, starting with the benefactors. Each person cuts off a plait which corresponds in length and thickness to the gift that they put in the basket; in rural areas, the child traditionally receives a certain number of head of cattle, which constitutes his future capital. The ceremony has now moved to the cities, where it is both a form of cultural resistance and a mechanism against poverty.

The crux of Andean culture is reciprocity, and at the heart of this is *Ayni,* giving in order to receive. As the people of the Andes say, 'Everything in life is *ayni.*' For instance, if one person helps another person for a few days to build his home, the person he has helped will return the favour, for the same number of days. Every day, *ayni* is present in the activities of both adults and children.

Community Life: A Source of Identity, Pride and Fraternity

In 1993, a party was organised in El Mirador for Mother's Day. Alicia had not yet taken part in any events organised by ATD Fourth World. After going to the house several times, an organiser finally managed to speak with her. Alicia said that she would come and asked if she should bring anything. The organiser said it was not necessary but she would be grateful if everyone could help serve the drinks. On the day of the party, Alicia was the first mother to arrive. As promised, she helped serve the drinks. When the mother of another child brought a small bag of make-up to add a bit of colour to the girls' cheeks and lips, Alicia helped, and they shared this moment laughing and joking.

Ten years later, talking about taking part in ATD Fourth World activities, she said:

> What I remember most is getting together with other people. I've always enjoyed taking part because sometimes it lets me forget about my worries and it gives me a breath of fresh air. They would come along and say, 'How are you today. Alicia? Where's your smile today?' I've always felt good with them. It was like being with family because I treated them as if they were my brothers and sisters. They've always supported me whenever they could. They always explained and said things to my children like, 'Miguel, you have to do this; Laura, you have to study.'

Alicia also joined the civil parades in which ATD Fourth World and other associations take part, such as the celebration of the *Inti Raymi*, the Sun Festival on 24 June, or the parade held every 17 October for the International Day for the Eradication of Poverty. For families who struggle against the shame and humiliation of extreme poverty day after day, these parades give them the opportunity to take part publicly as active members of a group, proud to be engaged in a fight for solidarity and justice.

In April 1998, Benigno spoke at a regional seminar organised by ATD Fourth World. He took an active part in the event, jotting down notes in a notebook that he kept with him at all times. He spoke freely and also listened to the experiences of others for whom the fight against poverty is a priority. At the end of the meeting, he said that listening to others had helped him to think, 'so as to get out of this scourge which is like a disease'.

That same year, he filed for a passport to travel to France to participate as the Peruvian delegate in a working session for the fortieth anniversary of the International Movement ATD Fourth World. First he had to obtain an identity card. Then, when he applied for a passport, the official said, 'Why should you be able to travel to France while I, head of immigration, can't travel?' 'I don't know about that, sir,' Benigno replied, 'but I have to go to France as I have been invited as the delegate of the Peruvian families and my participation is important.'

For a week, he was part of discussions with delegates from all walks of life, from Africa, Asia, Europe and America. He reflected afterwards:

> I didn't think poverty existed in France because I saw a lot of cars. I also thought that the poor people were just like us, *cholitos* [a derogatory term used to refer to people of mixed race, who are constantly discriminated against]. Then there was a white woman who looked like a real gringo [a derogatory term used in Latin America to refer, in particular, to people from the USA]. First I thought she worked for ATD Fourth World. Then I found out that she was a poor family delegate as well. They took us to visit places and in the street we saw very poor people, especially in Paris. We also saw places full of caravans where people live without electricity, water or anything. Some sleep in cars and I was surprised to hear that they cook in them too. I can't imagine how so many people can fit in a car.

Back in Peru, Benigno passionately shared his experience with other families, some in Cusco, some from the rural community of Kuyo Grande, 50 kilometres from Cusco, and yet others from the Bolivian association Friends of ATD Fourth World. He did so in his own words, in Spanish in Cusco and Quechua in Kuyo Grande. People listened and understood him. Benigno helped the ATD Fourth World family members in Peru and Bolivia to become aware that poverty is a universal phenomenon.

When Benigno took part in ATD Fourth World public activities, such as the civil parades of 24 June, he was always part of the host team and served *ponche*, a hot drink made out of fruit, almonds and milk, to the passers-by, saying, 'We're from ATD Fourth World, and we share.' He did so very naturally and, for many people, he was their first point of contact with the movement. On the next day, when he was thanked for having looked after people in such a special way, his face shone with happiness.

The Family's Priorities: Setting Goals and Reaching Them

The Rojas Paucar family has had times of suffering and moments of happiness.

During an interview, Margarita pointed out that moments of both joy and pain formed part of the same reality:

> On our feast days, sometimes on our birthdays too, we would go to Sacsayhuamán, an archaeological park and picnic area a few kilometres from Cusco, and we'd cook a nice meal. We would dress up and take the bus there. My mother and father played with us and looked after us. Every birthday, we had a nice meal. Then we'd go to the cinema, or to see a street show, something to enjoy. Those are the best times I've had with my family. There were good days when we were really happy.
>
> But there's been so much hardship. I don't know why those things happened to us. Sometimes we went hungry because there wasn't any work for my mother or me. At times we earned one or two sols. What were we supposed to do with that? Nothing. Sometimes, with my sister Laura, we went to collect twigs to cook the food. We ate boiled corn, a plain dish, and tried to keep each other's spirits up … We only had two beds, a small stove, a table and a small cupboard, nothing more. And a black and white television. We were ashamed. When we went to visit our friends we saw how nice their homes were but when our friends asked 'When can we visit you?' we didn't say anything, because we couldn't bring our friends to an empty house. A few years later, when my mum bought some furniture, she said to us happily, 'Now you can bring your friends back to do your homework and play together.' We were very happy. It was wonderful.

On another occasion, following a family argument, Benigno left home for a short time. Reconciliation was hard, but nevertheless they managed it. He explained it like this:

I said to Alicia, 'For how long are we going to refuse to talk to each other? What about the children?' She looked at me and didn't say a word. In the afternoon, she came back very calm. Leaving the house, she said to me, 'So people won't gossip, we're going to walk in the street hand in hand. I know that they're going to tell tales but are you going to believe them?' I said, 'No. I'm not bothered about gossip.' She said to me, 'Listen, why don't we go and eat some chicken?' As I had some money from work, we went out to eat, and that's how we've stayed together.

This incident illustrates the words of Joseph Wresinski:

> The family … is a person's only refuge when all else fails; it is the only place where a person might still feel a welcome; it is the only place where one can still be 'somebody'. A person finds identity in the family. The children, the spouse or the companion constitute a person's last refuge of freedom.[2]

In the same way, when Margarita gained her independence and set up her own home, she still provided support and affection for her family. When there were fights between Alicia and Benigno, both sought refuge in Margarita's house. Benigno said with real feeling, 'When I'm sad I visit Margarita, and she never lets me leave without giving me something, even if it's only a glass of water.'

At first glance, the Rojas Paucar family's experiences with regard to work, health, the home and relationships look like a series of failures. The truth is more complex. It is not a question of denying the family's difficulties, but of highlighting their successes in the two areas that Benigno and Alicia have always considered to be the most important: their children's schooling and keeping the family together.

Margarita was only able to study until the second year of high school, Laura finished high school and so will Miguel if his illness permits it. Both have progressed further than their parents.

The threat of splitting up hangs over all families trapped in extreme poverty, and parents and children are all aware of moments of tension in the family. But they have managed to stay together and when a particularly serious situation has arisen, they have always united to tackle it head on. Neither Benigno nor Alicia had this experience with their own parents.

Benigno, Alicia and their four children do not consider that they have ever escaped poverty. They always say that their lives continue to be very difficult. As Benigno said:

> What really hurts is poverty, which affects us a lot as a family. We're shaken by it and I'm really looking for ways to get out of it and get my children out of it as well. That's my struggle. It's a very difficult thing and although I'm trying to get out of it, I can't. I'm faced with too many problems.
>
> That's what I am really sad about. I want my children to continue on a better path. But I'm always trying to get out of this poverty. I would really like to have some form of support, God willing, like Miguel going to a school of his choice, a faster course because I won't be able to afford him going to university.

Yet in conclusion to their story, Alicia and Benigno talked about their hopes for the future. For Benigno, a better life would be:

> always having work, providing my family with good food and being together with them at home; having a better environment so my children have a better experience at school; being in contact with people like ATD Fourth World, where the kids have more experience, are well prepared and have a wider outlook for their education.

Alicia added:

> I want my children to have a stable job and to be somebody in life. I want to carry on helping them as much as I can. I'm happy when my son Miguel says to me, 'I'm going to be a doctor.' Laura also said to me, 'Mum, I'm going to study to become a tourist guide.' We're always supporting my daughter thinking that she'll carry on studying and perhaps go to university. If only God will let me live longer to help my daughter.
>
> I always feel proud that my children are studying. I've always had this urge to see them progress because of my own personal experience. I didn't receive any support from my dad or my mum. That's why I have to give my children something more. If only they can continue and finish school and be someone. I've always wanted to see my children do well in life, even if it's just one of them. I tell my children that they have to learn to value what they have. The children make me cry and suffer … I remember

everything that I went through as a child and say to them, 'My mum and my dad couldn't encourage me, send me to school or give me any support. I give you everything. Learn to value what you have.'

I'll be at their sides if God lets me live longer. He'll take me away whenever he wants. If one day they have children, I want them to fight as well, like I am fighting for them.

PERU IN BRIEF

Geography

Peru is situated in the intertropical zone between the equator and latitude 18° south. Bordered by five countries, it is divided into three major regions:

- A narrow, arid band 3,070 kilometres long on the Pacific coast, home to most of Peru's cities and industries. Temperatures are very hot all year, the summer months being from December to March. Lima has a microclimate characterised by a thick fog known as 'la garua' from June to October.
- A central mountainous region reaching above 6,000 metres altitude and a vast plateau, the Altiplano. The climate here is inverted, meaning the seasons are the same as in the northern hemisphere.
- In the east, the wooded plains and hills of the Amazonian Basin. Temperatures here are also hot or very hot but, unlike the coastal zone, humidity is high.

History[3]

There were six successive civilisations during the pre-Columbian period from −1000 BC to AD 1531. The most famous was the Inca Kingdom of Cusco, which extended from the north of Ecuador to the east of Chile. In 1531, the Spanish conquistadors landed in the north of Peru. From 1542 to 1821, three different territories were established, governed by a viceroy, the last including Peru, Argentina, Bolivia, Paraguay and Uruguay. Eleven million Incas were decimated during this period. On 8 July 1821 Peru declared its independence, but it was only recognised by Spain in December 1879. In 1933, the first constitution gave voting rights to literate citizens, a very low percentage of the adult population. *Coups d'état*, dictatorships and territorial conflicts between Peru and its neighbours followed. Since

1980, there has been much bloodshed from Shining Path terrorist activities. Alan Garcia Pérez, the country's leader from 1985 to 1990, was re-elected President in 2006. He was replaced in 2011 by former army officer Ollanta Humala.

Key Figures[4] (statistics from 2009):

Area: 1,285,220 square kilometres
Capital: Lima
Population: 29,500,000 inhabitants
Principal languages: Spanish (official language), Quechua, Aymara
Currency: nuevo sol (1 nuevo sol = 0.25 euros = US$0.33)
Urban population: 76.9 per cent
Fertility rate: 2.4
Infant mortality: 22 per 1,000 live births
Life expectancy at birth: 73.7 years
Literacy over the age of 15: males 96.4 per cent, females 89.4 per cent
School life expectancy: 13.8 years
GDP: US$8,424 per capita (purchasing power parity US dollars)
Public expenditure on education: 2.7 per cent of GDP
Total external debt: US$30,040 million
Debt service: 25 per cent of total exports

The Human Development Index[5] (HDI) is 0.723, placing Peru 63rd out of 169 in the UNDP *World Report on Human Development 2010*. The HDI varies greatly between different ethnic groups within the country.

NOTES

1. In June 2011, 1 Peruvian sol equalled US$0.33.
2. Gilles Anouil, *The Poor are the Church: A Conversation with Fr. Joseph Wresinski*, Mystic CT: Twenty-Third Publications, 2002, p. 9.
3. http://fr.wikipedia.org; http://abc-latina.com
4. United Nations Development Programme, *Human Development Report 2010*, New York: UNDP, 2010.
5. The Human Development Index varies from 0 to 1 and brings together the figures for life expectancy, literacy and revenues, according to national averages obtained from international sources. It does not include important aspects of the quality of human development and thus should be treated with caution.

Part Two

Introduction:
Human Rights and Responsibilities:
The Foundations for Living Together

Xavier Godinot

Sixty years after the General Assembly of the United Nations adopted the Universal Declaration of Human Rights, it is widely accepted that having rights that allow a person or group to exercise their responsibilities is one of the foundations for living together.

> The idea that our freedom and rights entail in exchange certain responsibilities towards others, our neighbours, the human race as a whole and all living beings, is an ethical principle that makes good sense and is recognised by all civilisations.[1]

This principle is applicable to both individuals and governments and societies. But 'while all human beings have equal claim to their human rights, their responsibilities are proportional to the means at their disposal'.[2]

The more assets, knowledge, power and freedom people have, the more capable they are of fulfilling their responsibilities and the more they should have to answer for their actions. Conversely, extreme poverty is characterised by a deprivation of basic capabilities, according to Sen, or a persistent accumulation of hardships, the view of Joseph Wresinski, and 'severely compromises people's chances of regaining their rights and reassuming their responsibilities in the foreseeable future'.[3]

Interpreting the four life stories presented in part one does, however, raise an important methodological problem: how can it be acceptable to compare and draw lessons from stories that take place on four different continents and in extremely different cultures?

THE BASIC FORMS OF POVERTY

The *Voices of the Poor*, which was conducted with the support of the World Bank, involved the participation of 60,000 poor people in 50 countries that are either emerging, developing, or in transition. In that study, Deepa Narayan wrote:

> As we moved more deeply into analyses of poor people's experiences of poverty, we were struck repeatedly by the paradox of the location and social group specificity of poverty, and yet the commonality of the human experience of poverty across countries. From Georgia to Brazil, from Nigeria to the Philippines, similar underlying themes emerged: hunger, deprivation, powerlessness, violation of dignity, social isolation, resilience, resourcefulness, solidarity, state corruption, rudeness of service providers and gender inequity. The manifestation of these problems varied significantly, but we often found ourselves saying, 'we have read this before.' Sometimes even the words and images poor people evoked in describing their realities were uncannily similar, despite very different contexts.[4]

In exploring the genealogy of the notion of poverty used in all human societies, Majid Rahnema states that it is always linked to a number of material conditions such as hunger and impecuniousness on the one hand, and to multiple or even opposite meanings on the other, depending on the region and the times. More precisely, he states that:

> The social perception of poverty follows an architecture that is based on four types of factors: a) the facts or material conditions that are part of any perception of reality; b) the perception the subject has of himself and his condition; c) how others see the poor person and his condition; d) the cultural, social, political, economic and technological conditions that influence and determine the first three sets of factors in a given time and place.[5]

So the fact that a person lives on the streets comes under the first type of factor, the material conditions. But living on the streets in France, in Burkina Faso or in the Philippines does not necessarily mean the same thing. The significance of such a fact only becomes apparent when you take three other elements into account: what the person living on the streets says about it; what the people who know this person or see how he lives say about it; and in the context of which country and what times it is happening. This analytical grid allows us to avoid interpretations which take only one factor into account while disregarding the others.

Following several comparative research programmes conducted on poverty in European countries over a ten year period, Serge Paugam endeavoured to elaborate and test an analytical framework for comparing the different types of interdependent relationships between the groups labelled as poor (in the sense of a specific social status) and the society of which they are a part and on which they depend for survival.[6]

His analysis of basic forms of poverty sheds light on our understanding of the life stories presented in part one. He distinguishes three basic forms of poverty:

- **Integrated poverty** describes a configuration in which a large number of people are referred to as 'poor'. Because they form an extensive social group, they are not highly stigmatised. Family, neighbourhood and village solidarity protect them from social exclusion. This group is a survival of a mainly peasant economy where wage-earning held only a small place and is more likely in traditional communities than in industrialised societies. The poverty of southern European countries still resembles this type, because each of them has economically under-developed regions.

- **Marginal poverty** characterises societies in which those we call 'poor' constitute a small fringe of the population. These poor are often considered to be ill-adapted to the modern world, are highly stigmatised and receive close attention from social welfare institutions. During the 30-year period of prosperity following the Second World War, both France and the United States experienced this type of poverty, which is played down and often denied; some consider Switzerland and the Scandinavian countries are still experiencing it today.

- **Disqualifying poverty** characterises societies within which those we call 'poor' are ever-increasing in number and, for the most part, rejected from the productive sphere. Disqualifying poverty is clearly distinguishable from integrated or marginal poverty because it does not stem from a state of deep-rooted extreme poverty that reproduces itself from generation to generation, but rather from a process that can affect fringes of the population which were, until now, well integrated in the job market. In these groups, poverty is perceived as a social decline following several setbacks. Disqualifying poverty develops in post-industrial societies that are faced with a strong increase in casual work and unemployment, generating collective anxiety. These societies are constantly looking for new solutions in the areas of social protection and intervention. This situation can be seen in the United Kingdom and in France, where over half the population now fears that it will be affected by exclusion.

This analysis allows us to situate the stories of Farid, Céline and Karim in a country – France – where disqualifying poverty dominates. The other three stories are situated in countries where integrated poverty dominates. But this analysis presents clear limitations: since it was developed in Europe, it does not allow us to see subtle distinctions in the specific forms of relations between poor communities and societies in the Philippines, Burkina Faso or Peru. There is insufficient research to allow us to analyse these specific forms. But the idea that there exists a national psyche that is unique to each country allows us to conduct a more in-depth analysis.

THE ROLE OF NATIONAL PSYCHE

Serge Paugam has demonstrated that the representations of poverty and extreme poverty are not definitive, but vary according to both the cultural heritage of a country and its social and economic situation. In Europe, where there is a shortage of available jobs, people are becoming more aware of the fact that poor people are not to blame when they cannot find work. Each country maintains a specific social relation to poverty – one that is tied to its history and its institutions, and which constitutes its national psyche. Though the latter is not unchanging, it endures.[7]

This national psyche differs substantially in the four countries featuring in the life stories. In France, fear of unemployment and hardship is much higher than in most other European countries: in 2007, 48 per cent of French people thought that they could one day find themselves homeless.[8] This allows us a glimpse of 'a society that is fragmented and rigid, and haunted by the fear of a drop in status' and that has been filled with 'extraordinary anxiety for the last 20 years', according to economist Eric Maurin.[9]

In the other three countries, the issue of poverty perception is twofold, since the countries themselves are often referred to as poor, as is a large part of their population. The globalisation that is currently under way carries with it a conception of wealth, poverty and modernity that is largely dictated by the west. Some people virulently denounce the 'Westernisation' of the world that is marked by global uniformity rather than a respect for diversity.[10] In this context, the effects of the 'poor' label that is imposed on certain people and countries are highly stigmatising, since they imply incompetence, an absence of talent and a lack of character or culture. Being recognised as poor and recognising oneself as poor is part of the tragedy of being poor.

THE COLONIAL HERITAGE

For some of the elite in the south, the fact that their countries are called poor in the West constitutes a symbolic and political violence that prolongs a history of domination spanning half a millennium. In the Philippines, the arrival of Ferdinand Magellan in 1521 marked the beginning of a long period of segregation of the archipelago's inhabitants by the new settlers. The Spanish coloniser named the archipelago 'Philippines' in honour of the Infante of Spain, the future Philip II of Spain. In Peru, the arrival of the Spanish Conquistadores in 1532 led to the break-up of the Inca Empire, which had 12 million inhabitants in 1525 and fewer than 2 million by 1586. This was the result of death by diseases imported from Europe, of the 'pacification' practised by the colonisers and of widespread forced labour in the mines and in the *encomiendas* – those indigenous lands which were handed over, along with their inhabitants, to Spanish people. The Philippines and Peru remained part of the Spanish Empire from the sixteenth to the nineteenth century.

According to African historians, Africa – like Latin America – had reached a high level of political, social and cultural development before the slave trade and colonisation by the European powers began the decline of the continent.[11] The transatlantic slave trade started there in the 1500s and in 1850 it was in full swing in the four Mossi kingdoms that occupy modern-day Burkina Faso, where at least six slave markets also supplied the trans-Saharan trade.[12]

Over the centuries, the Philippines, Peru and Burkina Faso were deeply marked by their history; this forms part of their national psyche. Wangari Maathai, the Kenyan environmentalist and political activist awarded the Nobel Peace Prize in 2004, states:

Historically, our people have been persuaded to believe that, because they are poor, they lack not only capital, but also knowledge and skills to address their challenges. Instead they are conditioned to believe that solutions to their problems must come from 'outside'.[13]

'We are not poor, but rather impoverished and deluded',[14] wrote Aminata Traore, a former Minister for Culture in Mali. In this context, colonised peoples have devised numerous methods of cultural resistance in order to preserve the values and customs that are still alive today, because 'cultures possess a vital quality that enables us, even a thousand years later, to rediscover elements that are exploitable for the lives of individuals and communities'.[15]

POVERTY OF NATIONS

Of course, colonial heritage alone is not enough to explain the current situation of these countries. Economist Jeffrey Sachs clearly demonstrates that it is the result of a complex set of historical, political and geographical factors.[16]

After their independence, some countries made disastrous political decisions and found themselves in the grip of dictators who were sometimes backed by the west. This was the case for the Philippines, which was under the dictatorship of Ferdinand Marcos between 1972 and 1986. Peru lived under the dictatorships of Manuel Odria between 1948 and 1956 and Velasco Alvarado and Morales Bermudez between 1968 and 1980.

The 'betrayal of the African elite', who sometimes enrich themselves outrageously to the detriment of the populations of their countries, has been denounced many times, including by the Africans.[17] Sachs also notes that in the last quarter of the twentieth century, the economic policies for development imposed on poor countries by rich countries have had devastating effects. This point is treated in greater detail in Chapter 6.

According to Sachs, the impoverishment of sub-Saharan Africa from 1960 to 2000, as well as that of some other countries, is due to specific causes.

Burkina Faso is one of the 'least advanced' countries in the world, with a Human Development Index (HDI) that placed it 161 out of 169 in 2010, while Peru and the Philippines are middle-income countries, ranked 63 and 97 respectively.[18] France comes fourteenth in this listing.

Widespread corruption in the public and private sectors, although often blamed, does not in itself explain the discrepancies in these rankings. According to the index produced by Transparency International in 2007, public and private sector corruption is less widespread in Burkina Faso than it is in the Philippines, a country which is more developed economically. In this index, which goes from the least corrupt to the most corrupt, France is ranked 25, Peru 78, Burkina Faso 98 and the Philippines 134.[19]

Rather, Sachs points to other specific difficulties to explain a lack of human development in certain regions: diseases such as malaria, climates that are prone to drought in areas where it is difficult to irrigate, an absence of energy resources such as coal, gas or oil and no access to the sea. Burkina Faso is indeed faced with all these difficulties.

It should be added that more and more African intellectuals consider their peers partly responsible for the current situation in Africa:

> Instead of carrying out a courageous and objective analysis of black people's condition ..., too many African high-ranking individuals and intellectuals take refuge in a culture of blame. To their own detriment, they forget that blaming the White man does not make the Black man strong.[20]

In Chapters 5 and 6 we seek to establish what we can learn from the four life stories that make up the part one of this book.

In Chapter 5, 'Basic Ties and Fundamental Rights', we analyse the life stories in the context in which they took place, in order to understand the realities of life and lack of choices in which these people are trapped, the strategies they implement and the factors that contribute to the success or failure of these strategies. We will show that, in developing countries as well as in those considered to be developed, maintaining and strengthening the basic ties of the most weakened people and groups is a necessary condition to allow them to gain access to their fundamental rights.

Chapter 6, 'Democracy, Globalisation and Extreme Poverty', will situate the plan for a society free of extreme poverty within the major debates of our times, which are marked by the confidence of some people in the new possibilities offered by science and technology, and the radical scepticism of others when it comes to world-changing ideologies. The risks and opportunities that globalisation holds for the most disadvantaged are examined, along with the recent works of three economists on this subject.

Through contributions by Joseph Wresinski, whose new vision brought about new practices, we will analyse which social movements contribute to the fight against extreme poverty.

NOTES

1. Pierre Calame (ed.), *Pour une governance mondiale efficace, légitime et démocratique*, Paris: Éditions Charles Léopold Mayer, 2003, p. 40.
2. Ibid., p. 42.
3. Joseph Wresinski, *Chronic Poverty and Lack of Basic Security: The Wresinski Report of the Economic and Social Council of France*, Paris: Fourth World Publications, 1994, p. 1.
4. Deepa Narayan, *Voices of the Poor: Can Anyone Hear Us*, Oxford: Oxford University Press for the World Bank, 2000, pp. 3–4.
5. Majid Rahnema, *Quand la misère chasse la pauvreté*, Paris: Fayard/Actes Sud, 2003, pp. 121, 124.
6. Serge Paugam, *Les formes élémentaires de la pauvreté*, Paris: Presses Universitaires de France, 2005.
7. Serge Paugam and Marion Selz, 'La perception de la pauvreté en Europe depuis le milieu des années 1970', *Economie et Statistique*, Vol. 383–384–385 (December 2005).
8. *La Vie*, 22 November 2007.
9. Eric Maurin, *Le ghetto français. Enquête sur le séparatisme social*, Paris: Éditions Seuil/La République des idées, 2004, pp. 83, 85.
10. Serge Latouche, *The Westernisation of the World: Significance, Scope and Limits of the Drive Towards Global Uniformity*, Cambridge: Polity Press, 1996.
11. See Joseph Ki-Zerbo, *Histoire de l'Afrique noire, d'hier à demain*, Paris: Hatier, 1978; Cheikh Anta Diop, *Nations nègres et culture: de l'antiquité nègre égyptienne aux problèmes culturels de l'Afrique noire d'aujourd'hui*, Paris: Présence africaine, 1954.
12. Maurice Bazemo and Sidi Traore, *Rapport national sur l'esclavage et la traite négrière (Burkina-Faso)*, 2004.
13. Wangari Maathai, Nobel Lecture, Oslo, 10 December 2004.
14. Aminata Traoré, *Le viol de l'imaginaire*, Paris; Actes Sud/Fayard, 2002, pp. 38–9.
15. Joseph Ki-Zerbo, *A quand l'Afrique? Entretien avec René Holenstein*, Paris: Éditions de l'Aube, 2004, pp. 162–3.
16. Jeffrey Sachs, *The End of Poverty: Economic Possibilities For Our Time*, New York, The Penguin Press, 2005.
17. See also works by Aminata Traoré, *L'Etau, l'Afrique dans un monde sans frontières*, Paris: Actes Sud, 1999, and *Le viol de l'imaginaire*, Paris: Actes Sud/Fayard, 2002.
18. The HDI is a composite index established by the UNDP using indicators based on health, nutrition and education. See www.undp.org.
19. Transparency International, *Corruption Perceptions Index 2010*, Berlin: Transparency International, 2010.
20. 'Poids de l'histoire sur la race noire et pastorale de l'Eglise d'Afrique', document drafted by Father Barthélémy Adoukonou, Secretary General of the Episcopal Conference of Francophone West Africa (CERAO), presented at the 13th Plenary Assembly of the Symposium of the Episcopal conferences of Africa and Madagascar (SCEAM) in Dakar, in October 2003.

5
Basic Ties and Fundamental Rights

*Xavier Godinot, Patricia Heyberger,
Claude Heyberger, Rosario Macedo de Ugarte
and Marco Aurelio Ugarte Ochoa*

In the light of the four stories in Part One, what does 'overcoming extreme poverty' mean in each of the countries concerned? What strengths did the individuals and their families draw on in their attempt to escape extreme poverty – that is, a combination of material poverty and social exclusion? What were the obstacles that impeded their progress or paralysed them? We will endeavour to confirm the following hypothesis:

> In order to overcome extreme poverty, an individual or group must be able to rely on basic ties that will allow them to gain access to their fundamental rights. Without these basic ties, access to these fundamental rights is impossible.

In the name of the equal dignity of all human beings, the Universal Declaration of Human Rights of 1948 recognises that each person has a certain number of economic, social, civil, political and cultural rights. Each nation and international institution must endeavour to ensure these are accessible to all citizens. For these rights to become legally binding, states must sign international pacts that invite them to implement these measures. In 1966, during the Cold War, countries were asked to ratify two separate covenants – one relating to civil and political rights, which was not signed by China; the other relating to economic, social and cultural rights, which was not signed by the United States. The notion of fundamental rights seeks to overcome this opposition by guaranteeing each person rights in terms of employment, housing, health protection, justice, education, training, culture, and family and child protection.[1]

Based on work by Serge Paugam, this analysis will take into account several types of fundamental social ties that connect individuals to society and which social exclusion can seriously impair or destroy.[2]

- *Family ties* which bind individuals to their nuclear or extended families and contribute to shaping their identity from birth.
- *Community ties* which characterise the socialisation process that takes place outside the family, during which people learn to manage their relationships with neighbours, local communities, religious, sporting or cultural institutions, and so on. Here, they also experience mutual aid and solidarity.
- *Ties formed by organic participation* in education and the working environment where each individual learns a social position that is likely to give him both basic protection and a feeling of usefulness.
- *Citizenship ties* based on the principle of belonging to a nation which recognises that its members have certain rights and responsibilities and must allow them to be fully-fledged citizens.

FAMILY AND COMMUNITY TIES

Unsurprisingly, the importance of family is apparent throughout the four life stories. In various opinion polls carried out among the populations of 34 European countries over more than 20 years, family has always come first in the list of 'areas of life that are deemed very important', often far ahead of work, friends and leisure activities.[3] Starting life as a couple and establishing a family require support from a favourable family and social environment – basic ties – as well as effective access to a number of fundamental rights. The family is the basic social unit and is an essential source of roots, ties, transmitted values, security and affection. It plays a central role in defining a person's identity.

Whatever form they take, all families manage their relationships within a system of interdependence with their neighbours and various external contributors: religious, sporting or cultural groups, schools, social services, medical staff, neighbourhood leaders, and so on. The family must be considered within the context of its relations with the social fabric that surrounds it.

Basic Ties Threatened by Extreme Poverty

The four life stories show the extent to which people from very disadvantaged backgrounds – children, young people or adults – contribute to the life of their family, be it the family they were born into, a foster family or the one they have created. They do not uphold a certain idea of the family based on morals or social conventions, but rather their own tangible family whose natural bonds have often been mutilated and reconstituted under conditions imposed by extreme poverty. Each day is lived with the desire to stay together, to maintain the ties with one's children and provide them with a good education, but this aspiration must be constantly rebuilt due to a lack of money and food, separation from one's partner, illness and death.

Hardship and poverty are a threat to the bonds which unite a couple. In the European Union during the 1990s, the probability of living without a partner or of being separated was, in all countries, much higher for people who were in a precarious situation in the labour market.[4] The stories that take place in Peru and the Philippines reveal young men and women faced with extremely difficult living conditions, eager for affection and security, who set up home together as teenagers, joining together two lives of poverty. Married too young and living in a situation of extreme hardship, they separate after a few years of living together, the mother often keeping the children, whereas in Burkina Faso children nearly always stay with their father. These people are sometimes extremely depressed by this failure, but subsequently start another relationship and have more children.

What is even more serious is that extreme poverty threatens the bond between parents and children, as is illustrated in the four life stories and confirmed by two recent studies which included contributions from 15 countries.[5]

> The parent-child bond is sacred: we know how to destroy it, we know how to assess and predict the worst in a poor family, but we do not know how to replace this bond, even when the father is in prison or when the parents have nothing. We are not gods. We can control many things, but we cannot take the place of the bonds that make up a human being. And the parent-child bond is one such element ... Supporting the parents should be a priority when they are poor and excluded from society at every level.[6]

If this bond is deeply damaged or destroyed during childhood, individuals can prove to be resilient and develop a sense of their identity by drawing on their own intellectual and physical resources and those offered by their family circle.[7] But some can also permanently lack the resources necessary for shaping their identity and so remain vulnerable all their lives. To come to terms with a past filled with intense suffering or to fill a void of deep emotional deprivation, adults can require a great deal of time and support, which are often unattainable in an environment of extreme poverty.

María Teresa González, a woman from a very disadvantaged family in Guatemala, explains:

> If my husband drinks, it's because life is too hard. All of this stems from his childhood. He remembers all of his suffering and that is why he can't give up drinking. It's because of all his childhood memories. I think that when he stops drinking he sinks back into despair. He can't manage to give his children what he wants to make their childhood happier than his own. When he drinks, he forgets about his life of poverty and all the things that hurt him.[8]

Although family and social ties are constantly endangered by extreme poverty, the four family accounts do, however, reveal that preserving the family unit is a crucial aspiration for adults and children alike. That does not mean that these families remain united forever. The myriad difficulties and accidents of life lead many of them to separate. But despite these break-ups, the wish to build a close-knit family is ever-present and is an ideal in their lives.

Family and Community Solidarity

One preconceived idea we hold is that people living in extreme poverty are isolated and have few connections with the world around them. The four life stories tell us otherwise.

In the Philippines, Mercedita and her partner constantly turned to family and neighbourhood solidarity to ensure that their family stayed together and their children went to school. Analysing their movements between Manila and the provinces shows that when they left for the provinces they always chose places where there was a relative of at least one of the two partners. Their returns to Manila were always motivated by opportunities that were lacking in the provinces and by what little security was provided by the solidarity of the families living under the bridge.

Similarly, belonging to a neighbourhood is essential to the daily life of the Rojas Paucar family in Peru. It is something they value because they have built relationships there that they are not sure they could rebuild elsewhere and because, ultimately, they feel they are a part of the community. The network formed by the children's godfathers and godmothers is also crucial to the survival of the family.

Is it appropriate then to claim that these two families are excluded? The answer is yes, because, in terms of economic and social integration, their ties are mostly with people from the same environment and offer scarcely any possibilities for overcoming poverty. The situation of both families is marked by frequent periods without work, an urban environment, and non-ownership of the means of production – three criteria used in economics and sociology to identify the urban underclass. Frequent unemployment is precisely what sets this class apart from the working class or the proletariat.[9] This underclass lives in an environment that is scarred by social exclusion, an environment that dominant society considers 'repellent', but we can clearly see that it is also a 'refuge' for its members, according to sociologist Paul Vercauteren.[10]

In the life story from France, Farid and Céline went to live in the residential Family Support Programme in Noisy-le-Grand, where they established many relationships with their neighbours. The ties they created helped them to overcome their isolation and to find their place within the community – a path that is essential to overcoming extreme poverty and one that is not possible through strictly individual-centred social action.

In Burkina Faso, Paul's parents are in a highly precarious material situation but it cannot be said that they consider themselves, or are considered, to be on the fringe of the economic, social, customary and religious life of their village. Professor Amade Badini from the University of Ouagadougou explains a traditional Mossi environment:

> Poverty is not measured in terms of material belongings or money: the determining factor lies in the feeling of belonging to the group. Mossi culture teaches us that being rich means having people around you with whom to share. It is almost the antithesis of what is meant by rich in the 'modern' system. What is more, a person in need will not go and seek help 'from the rich' as we define them nowadays, but rather from 'someone who is likely to give him something', meaning: someone close, an uncle, an aunt, even if they are not wealthy. In our regions, indicators are essentially social or relational: we are poor when we have no relationships.[11]

Majid Rahnema cites some examples that demonstrate a similar reality in other traditional African societies such as the Bornu, and he states that, in most traditional societies, 'destitution' and 'extreme poverty' are terms used to describe exclusion from the group rather than a lack of material possessions.[12]

Every job Paul found in the village resulted from his family and community ties. So for Paul, family solidarity came from wider afield than just his nuclear family. This dependence is not only economic; it also affects education, health and all other areas of life. For as long as he can remain in this state of interdependence, he will not be completely destitute. This reality seems no different to the Andean tradition of reciprocity that is still alive in Peru today. This reciprocity, which consists of giving in order to receive, is called *ayni*, and provides the entire structure for social life. It is a sign of social exclusion when someone is no longer able to practise *ayni* or is no longer solicited by others for favours.

Family Stability and Social Mobility

According to S.M. Miller, family and emotional instability have a greater influence than economic insecurity on the origins of poverty and its persistence from one generation to the next, and only those people who have the benefit of family stability stand a chance of breaking out of the cycle of poverty.[13] This is one of the principal conclusions of his analysis of social mobility in the lower levels of American society in the 1960s. Within this society he distinguished four types of poverty based on an economic security indicator that took into account income origin, level and stability, and on a family stability indicator that encompassed a variety of elements such as marital stability, alcoholism, and so on. The more negative these two indicators were at the same time, the harder it was to overcome poverty.

Thierry Torche, who never knew his parents and lived on the streets in France for ten years, wrote:

> Of all the people I know who live on the streets, many didn't have parents, and others had problems with their mother or their father. You have to go back to childhood.[14]

A survey among 1,160 adults living in shelters for the homeless in France, conducted in 2000, confirms the impact of traumas suffered during childhood. Among them, one person in five had been placed in a foster home or an institution, 28 per cent said they had been ill-treated, and 17 per cent of women claimed to have been victims of sexual abuse.[15] Those who had lacked paternal or maternal affection maintained a strong desire to find a substitute presence and source of recognition in their surroundings, in a community that would take the place of the family.

This theory is supported by the upward social mobility of Farid and Céline in France, and of Paul in Burkina Faso, since all three had known family stability and affection in their childhood, even though Farid had suffered the trauma of being transferred to his grandparents in Algeria. In Peru, however, the Rojas Paucar parents' fierce struggle to stay together and guarantee their children's education can be understood from this perspective: both parents knew from experience that the family unity and affection they had never had during their own childhood were necessary conditions for their children's advancement.

In Burkina Faso, ATD Fourth World workers observe that children who have maintained an attachment to a mother figure – someone with whom they feel a maternal emotional bond – find it much easier to re-establish periods of stability in their families in spite of the time they have spent on the streets. This 'mum' can be a biological mother, a grandmother, or a woman to whom the child was entrusted from a very young age because the biological mother had died or was unable to fulfil her role.

In the Philippines, if Rosanna and Rowena are now able to successfully continue their studies, it is first of all thanks to the strong and loving relationship they had with their mother, and her ability to make them understand the value of a good education. As their mother had hoped, it is reasonable to think that their education will one day allow them to escape from poverty.

The Importance of Re-establishing Basic Ties

What strengths did Paul, in Burkina Faso, and Farid and Céline, in France, rely on to overcome extreme poverty? The study shows that, even in their completely different contexts, re-establishing basic ties was essential for them to gain access to their fundamental rights. Paul and Farid fled the poverty of their family environment in search of new opportunities, only to find themselves on the streets, cast into extreme poverty. In spite of the values they had learnt from their families, they turned to petty crime, and the line between what was allowed and what was not became blurred. Paul escaped from this vicious circle by renewing ties with his family and his village, while Farid did so by building a new family with Céline. For several years, they both benefited from the support of experienced teams of professionals who wanted them to succeed.

Paul's path involved renewing ties with his family and village, a strategy which was initiated and supported by the ATD Fourth World team. Attending the streetlight library made him realise that in town he felt as if he was just 'passing through', whereas back in the village he felt at home, and it was possible for him to return there. This feeling of belonging to his family was stronger than any feeling of belonging to a gang on the streets, which proves that the notions of education and integration had been successfully inculcated by the family and the village community. With support over several years, Paul renewed his basic ties with his family.

Linking Basic Ties with Achieving Fundamental Rights

Farid's path out of extreme poverty was marked by his decision to build a new family with Céline, and by the support they found in the Paris region to make these plans viable. He set himself a personal challenge: to save Céline and to save himself at the same time, because the mutual recognition that living as a couple can bring is a tremendous defence against the risk of becoming long-term homeless, or in other words 'mad from exclusion, mad from poverty, mad from alcohol'.[16]

The birth of their child gave the parents a new-found energy and sparked off new resolutions: Farid put an end to his delinquent behaviour, drew on the values he had learnt from his grandfather and undertook a vocational training course. Céline's support was valuable in helping him persevere.

The couple was given accommodation in a residential Family Support Programme, and this was truly the support they needed to overcome extreme poverty because they became part of a small human community, the Noisy-le-Grand Family Support Programme, where the fight against poverty and access to fundamental rights had been developed as a pilot project for learning to live in the community.[17] Drawing on their own strengths and the support of this community allowed them to set in motion a virtuous circle of access to other fundamental rights, allowing the parents to regain custody of their child.

Although the existence of basic social ties is a necessary condition for gaining access to one's rights, this condition alone is not sufficient; it must be accompanied by opportunities for finding housing, work, education, health services, and so on. Their link to ATD Fourth World, like other organisations in France, allowed them to access housing and support for families in danger of being split up. Financial support from public authorities is essential to guaranteeing that this service lasts well into the future.

In the national contexts of Burkina Faso, the Philippines and Peru, civil society organisations do not have the resources to be able to offer such a service and public authorities do not have the means to support it.

Strengthening Family and Community Ties

Even when its members do not live together, the family – whatever its configuration – fulfils essential functions in terms of affiliation, identification, education, protection and imparting a sense of responsibility. Depending on whether it has the abilities and resources necessary to fulfil its functions, the family may or may not be a factor of development. Very often, the most vulnerable families cannot fulfil their responsibilities, because they do not have access to their fundamental rights. In the opinion of the Director of the United Nations Division for Social Policy and Development:

> Families all over the world remain the most vital force in the battle to eradicate poverty ... The irony is that, often, the centrality of the family has escaped the attention of policymakers ... [they] are only beginning to realise that programmes to eradicate poverty and to provide basic services must recognise and support the ongoing efforts that families already make.[18]

When Paul lived on the streets, he spent time in a shelter in Ouagadougou, which like others of its kind, should try to rekindle ties between children and their families. But, in Burkina Faso, very few shelters are able to follow up with the family, so children end up disheartened and lose hope of ever re-establishing family ties. In Burkina Faso, and in most other 'least developed countries', most shelters are backed by the private sector and international organisations; no such facilities are financed exclusively by the state.[19] Yet this country has ratified the Convention on the Rights of the Child and its government has adopted a National Plan of Action for Children and set up a committee charged with monitoring and evaluating the plan's application. In this area as in many others, political intentions come up against a lack of resources which limits the state's ability to intervene as it grapples with a set of private initiatives that do not comply with the guidelines set out in their national action plans.

In spite of the security that family and community can provide, and in spite of the solidarity mechanisms that allow people to survive, community ties are not an unconditional guarantee against extreme poverty. The marks of social exclusion become apparent when an individual who is deeply affected by extreme poverty is considered disqualified and is no long solicited by others for favours. The story of the Rojas Paucar family shows how difficult it is to participate in what draws the community together, when life is so filled with hardship. Their vulnerability, their reputation and the marks of extreme poverty which they bear, all hinder their participation in community activities. The deterioration in their ties with the community increases their insecurity and makes them even more vulnerable. The more hardship a family is faced with, the more its participation becomes uncertain and unpredictable, even though its participation becomes all the more necessary in order to generate opportunities and possibilities for renewing its strength.

Participation of the poorest families, who tend to benefit only sparingly from community solidarity, requires support both from people who are very close to them and from the wider community to avoid them being permanently excluded from the community to which they belong. Reaching the poorest in the community and building partnerships with them as part of programmes aimed at combating poverty requires a close-working relationship, time and the ambition to pool together the forces that exist within the community in order to support them. With the help of the most disadvantaged, what is needed is to develop a plan for the whole community and to create the consensus necessary for putting it into practice.[20]

Solidarity even extends beyond family relations and can lead to very disadvantaged people taking great risks for those more disadvantaged than themselves. In the Philippines, following the death of her partner Felix, Mercedita was taken in by her neighbours under a bridge in Manila. In Cusco, the Rojas Paucar parents took in Josefa and her newborn for two years, since they were otherwise homeless. Josefa looked after the children when the parents were absent. North of Paris, even though their lease forbade it, Farid and Céline housed Hichem for four years because he was homeless and an illegal immigrant. These informal strategies for combating poverty, when resources or services are lacking, provide support and security that are within people's control.

When social welfare systems are non-existent or ineffective, community solidarity is the best defence against extreme poverty.

TIES FORMED BY ORGANIC PARTICIPATION

Education and Transmission of Values

In supporting Paul and other youths and families in Burkina Faso, the ATD Fourth World team have always refused to consider the parents and the village environment as being without resources, even though the frugality of rural life is striking. But often, the first opinions expressed by the parents have been: 'With you, our child has more opportunities ahead of him.' Thus these populations, who have passed on to their children the knowledge of living and working together, have come to consider themselves as destitute in the eyes of their children.

There are a number of possible explanations for this shift in attitude. Ibrahim Zougmoré[21] of the Ministry for Health in Burkina Faso states:

> The first element that weakens their position is diminished economic power. Nowadays, parents' ability to make their children listen to them depends on their economic power. Each child has many new needs to satisfy, and when parents cannot meet these needs they are aware that they are in a weak position … A child who goes to school hears things that the parents have never heard. Communication and modernisation have given children a level of comprehension which surpasses that of their parents.

Cohesion among the adults that surround the parents is not as strong as it used to be. Professor Badini states:

> Previously, the extended family could be called upon to defuse internal crises within the nuclear family. For example, an uncle could take over from the father if the latter was not properly fulfilling his role. The extended family was involved in bringing up all of the children, and thus it represented a broad system of values for the children and support for the parents. Today, however, society has become more individualistic, even in the most isolated of villages. This individualism has weakened the traditional family model which underpinned education and solidarity.[22]

The traditional education that transmitted the values needed for rural life is no longer the natural point of reference in the family. It is challenged by the young people who no longer accept its constraints as normal, since they have been exposed to the model of success that is conveyed by those who come from the city. Ibrahim Zougmoré says:

> In traditional education, unilateral communication, ie one-way communication from parent to child, was favoured over bilateral communication. There was not really any such thing as bilateral communication: a father would call his child, give advice or instructions, and the child had to comply. Since the child was not allowed to raise his voice to his parents, he generally obeyed. Today, communication has inevitably become bilateral.[23]

This analysis of the factors that are weakening families in Burkina Faso is valid in other contexts, including industrialised countries.

Reconciling Community Education and School Education

For centuries, the cohesion of communities in traditional societies has conditioned their capacity to deal with calamities and to seek out more security. One of the vital elements of this cohesion, still visible today in the Andean traditions of *ayni* and *faena*, lies in the organisation of relationships and activities through which everyone joins forces to fight against need. Sharing, extending hospitality and limiting needs, together with the individual acceptance of poverty as advocated by many spiritual doctrines, constitute certain bulwarks against falling into extreme poverty.[24] This method of functioning presupposes that the people concerned have assimilated the rules and behavioural codes for living together. The question arises whether the modern schooling system contributes to this assimilation. Today, family and community education are completed by school education. The latter can however provoke strong resistance if it comes into conflict with the values promoted by the former, which makes it problematic to implement the right to education for all.

Education in the Family

The first type of education received comes from parents, family and the community. Paul's story paints the portrait of a youth shaped by the teachings of his family and community. The education received within the family gave him the perseverance he needed to remain in the village doing work based on a totally different system of relations from the paid work model he had been exposed to in the city. If his employer trusts his honesty today, it is also thanks to the education he received in the village. The fact that he needs no prompting to share his earnings, to take part in traditional ceremonies and to feel partly responsible for the future of his younger brothers show the impression his education left on him.

In Paul's story we also discover that emigration forms part of the education of young people in Burkina Faso. Professor Badini, from the University of Ouagadougou, states:

> Emigration, in itself, is one of the elements of traditional education. It corresponds to the child's level of social, intellectual and physical maturity, which should be confirmed by his leaving. As long as a person has not left his environment, it is not sure that he can appreciate it, value it and contribute to its transformation … He brings back knowledge that he would not have found in the village, but which will be of value to the village. The traditional environment is not a block; it evolves by integrating the successive and more or less conscious contributions from those who have left and returned. Emigration has an extremely important social and cultural impact. The Mossi people say that it is important to leave, because 'it is not the oldest who knows the elephant, but he who has travelled.' This is why families encourage their children to leave before coming back to settle in the village. Changes in the villages have come about as a result of the migration of previous generations. Today, they continue due to those who have been to school.[25]

The Rojas Paucar family story reveals several characteristics of family education; for instance, a mother will teach her eldest daughter to make and sell *anticuchos*, while an eldest son will help his father to grow potatoes. Later, the children will share the knowledge they have inherited from their family with one another. The fact that the parents take care to participate in the *faenas* that are part of the Andean traditional culture, stems from an education that emphasises sharing and working for the good of the whole community rather than individual remuneration.

Schooling: Caught between Material Hardship and Social Tensions

In Paul's life story, we discover a context in which schooling is far from widespread, exemplified by Paul's younger brothers not going to school when they had reached the required age. Paul retained some knowledge from his time at school but this is not the case for all the children: many of them forget everything they have learnt in school because they never use it.

According to the UNICEF statistics for Burkina Faso, between 2000 and 2009 only 49 per cent of boys and 44 per cent of girls of primary school age actually attended classes. Between 2000 and 2004, the rate of youth literacy was 47 per cent, while for women it was 33 per cent.[26] Schools must cope with a lack of resources, such as teaching materials and teachers. It is not uncommon for there to be only one reading or arithmetic book for 15 students, since families cannot afford to pay and neither can the state. In primary schools in the city, there can be an average of 84 children per teacher in classes that use a multi-shift approach, with a group of 30–40 children in the morning and another in the afternoon.

Several theories can be put forward to explain why some children who have the opportunity of being educated give up school. Firstly, the schedule at school is not always compatible with that of very poor communities where children have to work for part of the day to earn enough to eat. Secondly, knowledge acquired at school is very far removed from the everyday reality of children from rural environments; when they have trouble absorbing this knowledge, they become discouraged.

Teachers are often posted to provinces far from their homes and have little affinity with their pupils' parents. There are some 20 major ethnic groups in Burkina Faso and some 40 other ethnic minorities, so the teachers do not always come from the same traditional culture and their language and ways of life can differ from those of the region to which they have been assigned. Finally, schools are vulnerable because resources are limited and the status of teachers is insecure.

Parents observe that going to school takes their children away from traditional food-producing activities but, much as this might pose problems for them, do not renounce the idea of a school education for their children. In Burkina Faso, as in Peru, parents hope that a school education will provide their children with the means to emigrate, since this is the only way they can see of supporting the community. Those attending secondary school appear not to have gained more work opportunities or vocational training. Young people remain confined to their insecure jobs, which do not really improve the family's living conditions and do not foster community development.

The Rojas Paucar family's story paints the picture of a context in which schooling is more widespread, since the father himself went to school and each child in the family will have a chance to continue their studies a little longer than those who went before.

Yet, as is the case for other low-income families in Peru, obstacles remain; the first and foremost of these are economic.

The Peruvian constitution, dating from 1993, states that education is free, but this is not universally applied because the budget allocated to education is insufficient.[27] Enrolment fees alone may cost 40 or 60 sols a year, a sum that can take the poorest families 20–30 days to earn. In addition, textbooks, exercise books, stationery and uniforms must be bought – usually on credit.

Nevertheless, the greatest difficulties are frequently human relationships. As in the life stories, although many teachers offer support, children from a very poor background often face being humiliated by the attitude of other teachers. Very disadvantaged people are often thought incapable of projecting themselves into the future. The sacrifices that adults and children agree to make so that the latter can continue to attend school prove that this is not always true. What is important is to find out where, and how, families living in extreme poverty invest their efforts, and help them by supporting their vision of the future this reveals. If schooling is perceived as a chance for their children to have a future, it is also a burden that regularly threatens the family's ability to meet their other obligations. Access to a school education forces them to make impossible choices between health and school, the rent and school, food and school.

In the Philippines constitution, adopted in 1987, the state undertakes:

> to establish and maintain a system of free primary and secondary public education ... and to establish and maintain a system of scholarship grants, student loan programs, subsidies, and other incentives which shall be available to deserving students in both public and private schools, especially to the underprivileged.

Mercedita's daughters, Rosanna and Rowena, were able to benefit from these grants when the family situation was stable enough, but demands on students and their families are high in terms of results and attendance and the chaotic life of the most underprivileged often leads to grants and aid being lost or suspended. Families who live in illegal squats and are forced to move back and forth because of demolitions and rehousing often lack the administrative documents they need to transfer their children to a new school. If a child is unable to prove that they have completed a school year and show the marks they obtained, they must repeat the year. Many children thus end up in a class of younger children, and this is a major reason for teenagers giving up school.

The enrolment rate in schools is much higher in Peru and the Philippines than it is in Burkina Faso, which seems to suggest that in these countries there is not the same resistance to schooling because the educational content is better adapted to their circumstances. In 2009, 94 per cent of boys and 95 per cent of girls were enrolled in primary school in Peru, and 75 per cent for both sexes in secondary children. Figures for the Philippines were 91 per cent for boys and 93 per cent for girls in primary education and 55 per cent and 56 per cent respectively in secondary education.[28]

However, Professor Lynch Gamero, a former Minister for Education in Peru, observes that the quality of the education is very low. Many students repeat the school year, leading to the estimate that only 30 per cent of children are in the right year for their age. Each year, 1,200–1,400 hours of teaching should be dispensed in state schools, but the actual number is, in fact, only 500. In rural areas this figure even drops to 250 hours – the equivalent of one day of school per week.[29] It is difficult to introduce new teaching methods as these are sometimes blocked by political and economic choices imposed by the authorities that control funding.

This is also the case in the Philippines where the shortage of teachers and classrooms and the very poor quality of school textbooks are a burning issue that gets a lot of media attention at the beginning of every school year. Many complain that the level of education has dropped considerably over the last few years, as has government spending on education, which fell from 4 per cent of the state budget in 1998 to 2.6 per cent in 2010.[30]

In Burkina Faso, as in a number of other African countries, the solution implemented to speed up the development of schooling and finance more teachers was to reduce the time spent in teacher training and lower the level of qualifications necessary to become a teacher. This justifies their low wages, based on the false argument that salaries are based not on the work done but, rather, on the time spent studying to get the job. Professor Badini feels that:

> By pauperising teachers and schools, we are lowering the expectations placed in the schools. Few people want a career in teaching, and those who can afford to do so send their children elsewhere, to private schools or overseas.

In Burkina Faso, as in other West African countries, there is a growing number of schools created by private individuals, and of satellite schools, where children are taught in the national language in the first years, before learning French.

Education: Looking Back and Looking Forward

In the late 1990s, several great authors very harshly criticised the school system that colonisers had implemented in their country, as they considered it to be 'an instrument of cultural defoliation', 'a school for uprooting [people]', a 'process of depersonalisation' and 'an instrument of humiliation'. Whereas in Europe school has been a means of creating an identity and a national conscience, in colonised countries it has been an instrument for imitating the identity and national conscience of European countries and has been a contributing factor in the disintegration of identity and culture in the colonised countries.[31]

More recently, Mamadou N'Doye, former Minister for Education in Senegal and General Secretary of the Association for the Development of Education in Africa, wrote:

> Serving colonial domination, in Africa school set itself against the continued internal development of societies by disqualifying, from the very start and even today, all of African culture – values, practical knowledge and languages – as it was considered to be in contradiction with the aims of civilisation and progress. This has caused a dichotomy, resulting in a sort of primary identification where what is African inevitably belongs to tradition, the past and magic, and what is from the West is associated with modernity, rationality and science.[32]

In October 2000 the Customary Chief of Manega in Burkina Faso stated:

> Those children of ours who went to 'the white man's school' do not want to use their knowledge to improve their parents' living conditions, so they go off to the city. Once there, they spurn manual labour in favour of desk jobs, which I might add they do not get. These situations lead to extreme poverty. That is what I mean when I say that our extreme poverty is modern.[33]

Professor Badini adds:

> The modern day system of education in our country seems to be the antithesis of the traditional education system. It centres on

school, and the values that it encourages are mostly individual ones, if not to say individualist. These values are based on competition, on the pre-eminence of the individual as opposed to the group, and they emphasise individual success rather than an individual's contribution to the success of the group. And yet, to me, it is precisely this last point that characterises the aims of traditional education. So over the last few years we have witnessed a social resistance to school, which has led to children leaving school. It is not school education as a principle that is being challenged, but rather its content and its purpose.[34]

The notion of the right to education must not be limited to the right to a school education or to vocational training, as is confirmed by a study which investigated the subject. Conducted in Burkina Faso over several years, the study was based on contributions from representatives of public institutions and local NGOs, from village and neighbourhood communities, teachers, students, parents of students in both formal and informal education settings, as well as parents of children not in school.[35] Almost unanimously, participants declared themselves to be attached to the idea that children of all ages should be able to benefit from the right to an education, which includes the right to be educated by their parents and family, by their community and finally by the state, through a complete and adapted school system or through informal education.

The main idea that comes out of this study is that education begins within the family from a very young age, with help from the extended family, and it continues within the community. Education received inside and outside of school complements the education received from the family and the community. There is no fundamental contradiction between family and community education and the education received in school. They can be based on the same core values overall, in spite of the misunderstandings that stem from the adjustments that must be made in order to reconcile positively tradition and modernity.

Professor Badini believes that school could play a major role in reducing the contradictions between tradition and modernity.

Given their republican aims, schools could remedy this split, provided that traditional education is not systematically denigrated. To some extent, school is the only place where the desire for an integrated lifestyle and the constraints of modern life can be reconciled, so that people may be less torn between the two. It is possible, in our countries, to develop education systems that are based on combining the different forms of knowledge – because we do not want to lock ourselves up in tradition like in a ghetto – to allow the traditional body of knowledge to evolve and take into account the new issues that face all societies. It is not certain that this would carry a higher cost for the international financial institutions that currently support our States and promote a type of schooling that we disparage.[36]

A major expectation of people is for their schools to stimulate a sense of their identity and develop their capacities as individuals and as a group. Schools could encourage teachers, parents and children to define for themselves the values by which they want to live and to arrive at their own definitions of wealth and poverty, rather than accept those being dictated by others.

On a broader level, access to schooling remains a struggle for the families living in extreme poverty all over the world. In Europe[37] and North America[38] as in Asia and elsewhere, families living in situations of extreme hardship all denounce how difficult, or even impossible, it is for their children to attend a school from which they might emerge truly educated. Completely free education would be a positive contribution, but the strategies put in place to ensure that school objectives match the aspirations and specific needs of people living in difficult conditions often seem highly insufficient where social tensions are concerned.

In France, the report on primary schooling submitted by the Haut Conseil de l'Education (High Level Council on Education) in late August 2007 criticised the fact that primary schools seem to be resigned to early academic failure and their results have been stagnating for ten years. The difficulties faced are material in nature, but also concern social tensions and teaching methods. Some sociologists remind us that students, especially those who struggle the most, are still subjected to humiliation,[39] and the Director of Education, Claude Pair, stresses the difficulty and the need for teachers to consider parents from the poorest walks of life not simply as problems, but as partners who also have knowledge and experiences to contribute.[40]

The Right to Education for All

The objective of 'education for all' was first formulated in March 1990, and then reaffirmed by the General Assembly of the United Nations in September 2000 as part of the Millennium Development

Goals. One of its targets is a 50 per cent reduction in adult illiteracy by 2015. The second Millennium Goal for Development aims to ensure that all children – boys and girls – are given the opportunity to complete a full cycle of primary education. To achieve this, it seems necessary to promote a truly free education for all. But that is not enough: school supplies should also be taken into consideration, as well as providing balanced meals in educational facilities and affordable transport for those children who live in remote areas.

It is also important to ensure that the content of the education for all concept is adapted to each country. 'We are not so much trying to speed up the education "train" but, rather, change the direction of its tracks,' states Joseph Ki Zerbo.[41] In this sense, the point is not to deliver a standard level of school education to as many as possible, but to extend and broaden the education that is given by communities. The results would be seen not only in an increase in the number of children in school, but also in the detailed evaluation of the progress made in relations between the people and all those involved in the education system. Intense dialogue between educational institutions, teachers and populations is required for success in adjusting the content and pace of teaching.

The attitude of teachers is of fundamental importance. During their training, they must be able to learn about the world of extreme poverty in order to understand that if a child arrives in their classroom and is not as clean as the teacher would like them to be, it may be because the child does not have access to water at home. If the child has not done their homework, it might be because they do not have electricity at home or because they had to work to help their family. If the child has missed a day, they may not have had enough to eat for several days or a member of their family may be ill. Without this concrete understanding of extreme poverty, teachers will have trouble keeping the door to their classrooms open to children from families in the most difficult situations, and will not find it easy to support and encourage them in their schooling.

Opportunities for education aimed at young people and adults who did not get the chance to attend primary school should not be pushed into the background. The right to lifelong learning must be implemented in centres offering literacy classes, non-formal education, vocational training and training in the craft industries. In countries such as Burkina Faso, Peru and the Philippines, and in the so-called 'sensitive' areas of France, young people and adults seek training that is rarely available to them. It is also important to draw more on the knowledge and skills of the populations to integrate these into the education process. The education given by communities and families aims not only to increase knowledge, but also to impart a sense of identity, and of how to behave in the social group – something that is a vital foundation for both individuals and the group. Teaching people how to live together should be at the core of any teaching or development initiative.

Employment and Basic Services

The four stories told in part one describe parents, youths and children struggling for their own daily survival and that of their families. They are forced into the most precarious jobs on the edge of the formal job market and the informal economy or, as a last resort, into activities such as begging, theft and prostitution. These activities only allow access to temporary and often unfit housing and result in children working from a young age, as illustrated in the life stories from Burkina Faso, Peru and the Philippines.

The employment history of subjects in the life stories, such as Benigno Rojas, confirms a valid observation regarding the most insecure labour markets in many countries in both the north and the south: the impoverishment of small-wage earners over the course of their working lives as a result of the progressive wearing down of their capacity to work due to the hardship of working from a young age and in extremely physical activities. In contrast with more qualified employees, who progress in a better protected labour market and can build a career and increase their earning potential, many unqualified workers become poorer during their working lives. Indeed, their health inexorably deteriorates, and this is due as much to the difficult and dangerous working conditions of the precarious jobs they hold as it is to the long periods of unemployment that sap their morale and can lead to addictive habits.[42]

When basic needs cannot be met under normal conditions, there is a strong temptation to resort to unlawful activities that clearly put one at risk of being excluded from the community. In Burkina Faso, many of the young people met by the ATD Fourth World team, were unable to renew lasting ties with their communities due to their sometimes unlawful activities and their resulting bad reputation. In France, illegal means to earn money is often widespread, if temporary, among young people from disadvantaged urban areas.[43] Many of these youths eventually leave such acts behind them and conform to social conventions, particularly when the time comes to start a family, as is confirmed by Farid's change of attitude following the birth of his son, Karim.

Work and Employment as a Means to Reinforce Basic Ties

Sharing is another way of guaranteeing a secure existence. It seems that children who grow up in the village communities of Burkina Faso learn to assimilate this in their approach to life. Finding ways to support their family and community is an integral part of their conception of social success. ATD Fourth World teams in Ouagadougou have encountered this concern in almost all of the children and youths living on the streets, even those who had been there for a long time. Paul confirms this at every stage of his life, every time he earns any money. This sharing is one of his reasons and objectives for working. Similarly in the Peru life story, at every step, Margarita's work represented an important and almost constant financial support for the Rojas Paucar family: she contributed to paying for the studies of her younger brothers and sister and she continues to do so today even though she now has her own family.

Access to Housing and Decent Employment

The course of Mercedita's life in the Philippines illustrates that the people with the worst living conditions, those who have no legal right to occupy land, are often subjected to outright mass evictions without being offered any alternative housing. UN-HABITAT, the United Nations Human Settlements Programme, has identified forced mass eviction cases in a number of countries and is trying to find alternative solutions.[44] In the Philippines, housing assistance programmes that grant low-cost loans for land acquisition and construction can constitute alternatives to the simple removal of populations. But these programmes tend to benefit a middle class of elite squatters and exclude the poorest squatters and tenants, not to mention those living on the streets.[45] Access to housing and a stable job are two determining factors for escaping extreme poverty, and the stories of Farid in France and Paul in Burkina Faso serve to illustrate this.

The difficulties Farid faced in finding emergency accommodation when he was on the streets, and later in finding a flat together with Céline, must be viewed in the national context. The number of homeless people in France is estimated at 133,000 and nearly 3 million in sub-standard housing.[46] Yet the government spends 1 million euros per day on providing people with emergency housing and keeping families in residential hotels, often in substandard conditions, because emergency response costs more than long-term solutions. One million households are registered on the waiting lists for low-rent public housing.[47] Approximately 65 per cent of people seeking public housing earn at least one third less than the minimum income to be eligible for standard low-rent public housing.[48]

A connection can be made between substandard housing and the increase in the amount of temporary work and in the number of poor workers, whose incomes are too low to allow them to overcome poverty. Céline and Farid's story very clearly illustrates the interdependence and indivisibility of fundamental rights. They managed to overcome poverty because, within a short period of time, they gained access to housing, integration into a community and then employment.

In Burkina Faso, Paul's employment history greatly differs from that of his parents. The latter make their living by farming, which provides the bulk of their security; their other activities are extremely modest and sporadic. For Paul, income streams outside of farming have become essential: crops are less lucrative, needs have changed, and farming alone cannot meet these needs.

Paul does not seem to feel that he learned important skills from the family farming business. This type of work does not correspond to the jobs of today which are the reference for young people like him – mechanic, cabinetmaker, welder or sales person, for instance. These are jobs they see performed in the city or at the village market.

It is all the more difficult for young people like Paul to think of farming as a profession, since their parents' generation continue to cultivate using very modest traditional methods that produce barely enough food for the family and bring in very little money. Like their children, the parents do not generally associate working the land with an identifiable profession which would require the acquisition of technical knowledge and would lead to social advancement.

This lack of self-recognition is perceived by children in rural areas who, when asked 'What does your father do?' often reply 'He doesn't do anything.' This negative perception of their food-producing activity reinforces their belief that anything is better than living off the land. As a result, children turn away not only from farming, but also from the lifestyle that is connected to it, and many of them, for better or worse, go and try their luck in the city. The assessment of the National Plan for Childhood showed that the fathers of approximately 45 per cent of children living on the streets were farmers.[49]

In 2009, 80 per cent of the population in Burkina Faso was living in rural areas. The farming sector employed 92 per cent of the working population and produced close to half of the country's exports. Farming makes it possible to meet the nation's basic food needs in the absence of other possibilities for production on a large enough scale.

In the future, education should then also include ways of teaching both parents and children to appreciate the value of the skills and knowledge that are tied to food-producing farming activities. These might then no longer be discredited and could be performed without shame alongside other modern-day activities.

An Increase in Temporary and Informal Work

The four life stories in part one are set in a context of increasing temporary work in France and higher levels of informal work in the other three countries.

In France, wage or income inequalities have remained steady over the last 20 years, but inequalities in exposure to temporary work have considerably increased and run much deeper than in most other western countries.[50] A study conducted in 2005 among a representative sample of people in poverty connected with ATD Fourth World indicates that illiteracy remained a sad reality, since one fifth of them found it difficult to read a newspaper, write a letter or count.[51] Close to one in five were considered disabled, which indicates a serious trend that emerges from this study: the growing risk of assimilating extreme poverty with disability.

There was a 51 per cent rate of unemployment among the people surveyed, five times the national average. Of those working, 65 per cent only had access to specific types of employment such as temporary work, government-assisted contracts, fixed-term contracts or part-time open-ended contracts and various internships. Often, these people were employed in highly insecure jobs as sandwich sellers, cleaners, maids, letterbox advertising distributors, unskilled workers on construction and public works sites, car park attendants or delivery men. These workers were not unionised with nobody to protest on their behalf or demand that they be reinstated if they were laid off, which is why they so often said they felt as if they were 'treated like animals'. This study paints the picture of a disqualified population that is excluded from the usual systems of education, business and workers' struggles, and forced to depend on public benefit and mutual aid organisations to survive.

In developing countries, an overwhelming number of jobs performed by very poor families are in what is called the 'informal' economy, which is not regulated by laws and administrative procedures, but rather by family and community ties.

The International Labour Organisation (ILO) considers informal work to include all paid work, performed by self-employed or by salaried workers, which is neither recognised nor protected by existing laws and regulations. Most workers in the informal economy have no permanent job, receive no protection from the social welfare system nor work benefits (holidays, etc.), have no representation and no power whatsoever to negotiate with their employer.

The size of the informal work sector is difficult to determine since its definition varies from one country to another and available figures can only serve as indicators. According to the World Bank, the informal economy made up 60 per cent of total GNP in Peru and 43 per cent in the Philippines.[52] There are no figures available for Burkina Faso where 90 per cent of jobs are in the farming sector, which is not considered as informal work. In sub-Saharan Africa 29 per cent of children were working, compared with 16 per cent in Latin America. In sub-Saharan Africa, South America and South East Asia, the ILO affirms that the proportion of informal work in overall employment has not fallen but, rather, risen over the last decade.

There are several reasons why the informal economy is growing more rapidly than the formal sector. The first reason is linked to demography, since the formal job market is having trouble absorbing a very large population increase and massive migration towards the cities.

Between 1970 and 2005 the French population grew by 25 per cent, rising from 50 million to 62.8 million inhabitants. Over the same period, populations in Burkina Faso and Peru more than doubled, from 5.3 million to 13.2 million inhabitants and from 13.1 million to 27.9 million respectively. Likewise, the population of the Philippines leapt from 36.5 million to 83 million inhabitants, one of the highest rates of population growth in the world.

Moreover, more and more women began working, either by choice or out of necessity. Finally, the massive rural exodus greatly contributed to the expansion of the informal economy as impoverished peasants and their children came to seek out better opportunities in the cities and, once there, created their own jobs to survive. In 2008, for the first time in history, 3.3 billion people, or over half of the world's population, were living in urban areas.

Rural poverty is not the only reason for migrating to the cities. A study of the dynamics of migration in the Philippines shows that schooling is the main reason for migration to the cities, either because of the lack of schools in rural areas or because standards are better in the cities.[53] This is borne out in Mercedita's life story in her return to the capital from the countryside for her children's schooling. Grants for private school enrolment fees or for costs associated with transport, equipment or uniforms are easier to obtain in Manila than they are in the provinces.

Rural impoverishment in Burkina Faso and elsewhere has been cited as a factor that contributes to the weakening of parental authority. It is also a main cause of the massive rural exodus observed in Peru, the Philippines, and in many African countries, and illustrated in the life stories. There are numerous reasons for peasant impoverishment in these countries. The first reason is no doubt the ideology of Third World development through industrialisation, since for decades this has driven national policies and international aid to neglect support for food-producing agriculture. In its 2007 report on global development, the World Bank acknowledged this negligence which has led to underinvestment in farming for decades, and to a spectacular drop in public development assistance devoted to agriculture. 'Over the last fifteen years it has been halved', exclaims the Director General of the United Nations Food and Agriculture Organisation indignantly.[54]

Some developing countries have neglected their farmers: in sub-Saharan Africa, 4 per cent of public expenditure is allocated to them, whereas they contribute 30 per cent of GDP and represent 75 per cent of the population.[55] While food production per capita has greatly increased in Asia, it is constantly falling in Africa, where three quarters of the land is cultivated without the use of fertilisers or improved seeds and the soil is among the most depleted on the planet.[56]

In many countries, the farming sector is also affected by climatological and environmental disasters. Since 1970, countries in the Sahel region have suffered intense drought, as the result of a 30 per cent drop in rainfall which is probably due to global warming.[57] Another reason that must be stated is lower agricultural prices. This ongoing trend has persisted for decades. It is caused by the incoherence and iniquity of rich countries offloading their surplus onto world markets while, at the same time, imposing a reduction in customs barriers in developing countries and restricting imports from them.

Finally, the increase in informal employment occurred against the backdrop of growing debt in Third World countries and trade liberalisation. In particular, the foreign debts of Burkina Faso, Peru and the Philippines increased and gave rise to Structural Adjustment

Policies (SAPs) which were implemented in conjunction with the World Bank and the International Monetary Fund (IMF) between 1980 and 1999. At the same time, high agricultural subsidies in rich countries weakened agriculture in poor countries. Given this context, the rise of an informal economy for survival 'is firstly a response to multiple failures: failure of the plans for development through industrialisation, failure of the constitutional State and its institutions, and failure in the generalising of social rights'.[58]

Promoting Decent Work

The World Confederation of Labour was justifiably concerned about the fact that decent work was almost totally absent from the Poverty Reduction Strategy Paper objectives that the World Bank and the IMF negotiated with the governments of 60 to 80 developing countries. The ILO reminds us that decent work should be at the very centre of global, national and local strategies for economic and social progress, since it represents a way to achieve sustainable development based on fairness and inclusion.

According to this UN agency, there are four elements in the promotion of decent work:

- *the right to work*, since productive work is the best way out of poverty
- *rights*, and, more precisely, the application of the core labour standards defined in international labour agreements (trade union freedom, protection of workers' rights to belong to trade unions and bargain collectively, prohibition of forced labour and of the worst forms of child labour, etc.)
- *social protection*, which protects people against poverty
- *social dialogue*, since it is crucial for employers, trade unions and associations to be involved in strategies for reducing poverty.

Peruvian economist Hernando de Soto, who has been studying the informal economy for several decades, believes that in order for it to become legal, some of the unwritten rules of the informal sector need to be incorporated into national legislation. The law must be based on a social contract that takes into account the practices and interests of the poor; all too often, this is still not the case.[59]

Over the last few years, some important advances have been made when it comes to recognising that decent work is the best way to fight against poverty, hence the goal of full, productive employment and decent work was added to the Millennium Development Goals in 2007.

Over the last 30 years, micro-credit, which was invented in Bangladesh by Muhammad Yunus, has been developed in many countries to improve the situation of people working in the informal economy, especially women. Its inventor has greatly contributed to making people realise that when the poor are given greater financial capabilities they are the most determined fighters in the struggle against poverty. He believes that we will progress much faster once decision-makers realise that poor people are their partners and not spectators or enemies.[60]

If his own determination to reach the poorest is undeniable, his many disciples do not share the same level of commitment, some even charging exorbitant interest rates. As micro-credit becomes more widespread, it is no longer always adapted to people living in extreme poverty.[61] In Bangladesh, since 2002, large-scale alternative programmes have been implemented for those considered to be 'ultra poor': day labourers, domestic servants, beggars, people who cannot afford two meals a day, farmers without land, and so on. These programmes are based on three areas of intervention:

- granting disadvantaged households a small amount of capital goods (a few animals or a plot of land, for example) which they can put to productive use in order to generate a small income
- a few weeks' training to teach them how to make the most of this capital
- a survival allowance for the period before the capital goods begin to generate an income.[62]

Rather than micro-credit, these are micro-donation programmes, aimed at several hundreds of thousands of families. In Burkina Faso, careful observation of local practices convinced the ATD Fourth World team that families such as Paul's could rarely find the means to reimburse micro-credit, and therefore, to support the economic activity of Paul's family, micro-finance in the form of micro-donations was more beneficial.

One other important area that is the subject of serious study is the creation of social protection systems in developing countries; these could be essential in strategies for combating poverty and extreme poverty. In 2004, the World Commission on the Social Dimension of Globalisation stated that a minimum level of social protection for individuals and families needed to be accepted as an undisputed part of the socio-economic 'floor' of the global economy.[63] This universal social safety net could comprise four elements:

- health care coverage
- family benefits that would allow children to attend school
- a minimum social benefit that would protect those who are fit to work from falling into deep poverty
- benefits to cover the risks of old age, permanent or temporary disability and the loss of a spouse.

Depending on the level of protection required, according to studies carried out by the ILO, financing such a safety net would cost between 2 per cent and 6 per cent of global GDP, and countries should remain responsible for providing most of the funding.[64] It would be available to low-income countries, as long as they received international aid for a transitional period.

In practice, incorporating small-scale farmers and fishermen, as well as illegal and intermittent workers from the informal sector, into a social protection system poses serious technical and economic problems. In addition, the proportion of children in the population is often very high and places a heavy burden on the funding of the system.

Still in their early stages, a number of studies are under way looking at how social security systems in the developing world are changing and the problems they encounter.[65] Community-based micro-insurance systems, tontine systems, etc. have become more widespread in sub-Saharan Africa since the 1990s, and mutual benefit heath insurance schemes are experiencing strong growth in India and Bangladesh. Bilateral aid agencies are financing new experimental systems. Thus the Netherlands Ministry for Development Cooperation is financing the implementation of basic health coverage for several thousands of workers in Nigeria's formal and informal sectors. It is based on the principle of involving the private sector and progressively increasing the insurance premium so that, over time, the programme finances itself. The German international cooperation agency GTZ is also financing a pilot project for providing additional resources to very poor households, with or without children, in a district of Zambia.

The fact that these types of programmes, aimed at the poorest populations and countries, are becoming so widespread raises the question of the sustainability and predictability of Official

Development Assistance (ODA) from rich countries, a question which the governments of these countries avoid answering. Recent history does indeed show that they do not keep their promises. ODA to Africa, which G8 leaders pledged to increase by US$25 billion by 2010, is estimated to have increased by only US$12 billion (in 2004 prices) between 2004 and 2010.[66]

Access to Decent Housing

The four life stories show the extent to which the poorest households are forced to live in a harmful environment, including living on the streets without privacy or protection, exposed to bad weather, noise and exhaust fumes. Similarly in urban slums, families are subjected to, among other things, permanent darkness, a lack of air circulation which leads to suffocating heat, nauseating smells and rats. In rural Burkina Faso, the drought that has affected the Sahel region for the last 30 years is one of the reasons why Paul's village is so poor. In Cusco, the Rojas Paucar family and many others have built their houses in a dangerous area that is subject to landslides during periods of heavy rain. As emphasised by the former United Nations Secretary-General, it is a fact that 'poor people already live on the front lines of pollution, disaster and the degradation of resources and land.'[67]

Migration

In each of the four life stories there are migrations to escape poverty or to seize new opportunities. In Burkina Faso, Peru and the Philippines, these migrations take place within the same country, which shows that in every case ties with the rural environment are maintained by those who move to the city. In the Philippines story, the family's move between Manila and the provinces demonstrates the extent to which the cost-benefit analysis of each move yields uncertain and changing results.

International migrations also play an important role. In Burkina Faso, Paul's family, like that of a whole generation of Burkina Faso families, has made the most of the opportunities on offer due to the once enviable development of its Ivory Coast neighbour, now so scarred by the effects of political instability. Financial support is sent to the families, as explains the father of another child met in the city: 'Nobody lives solely off what they have in the village. Everyone has someone somewhere else who sends them something from time to time.' The conflict that first erupted in the Côte d'Ivoire in 2002 led to many Burkinabes fleeing the country.

In Farid's story, we observe several moves back and forth between France and Algeria: his father emigrating to France, his son being sent back to Algeria with the extended family and Farid leaving Algeria for France and ending up on the streets.

The relationships between migration, globalisation and poverty is a greatly debated issue, including the complex nature of internal and international migrations, the importance of remittances sent by immigrants to their families, and the problems of managing migratory flows and of acknowledging the rights of immigrants. There were an estimated 214 million international migrants in the world in 2010, representing an increase of almost 40 million in the first decade of the twenty-first century, and over double the number of international migrants in 1980.[68] The Philippines 2009 census recorded nearly 2 million 'Overseas Filipino Workers' and that the money these people send their families comprises 12 per cent of the country's GDP.[69]

Gender Dimension of Basic Ties and Basic Services

In Burkina Faso, while Paul's mother does not know how to read and write, his father does; nevertheless, both his mother and grandmother clearly occupy an important place in his life. Neither his elder sister nor his younger brothers went to school. In the Philippines and Peru, the parents enrol both their sons and daughters into the education system, only for the elder siblings, regardless of their sex, to give up school in order to help pay for their younger siblings' schooling.

In all of the stories, women have access to informal work. However, this does not mean that certain prejudices and taboos do not remain: in Peru, Andean culture can lead to husbands refusing permission for male doctors to touch their wives, nor do they wish them to use contraception, sometimes leading to domestic violence.

In the *Voices of the Poor* study conducted by the World Bank among poor families in some 50 countries, Deepa Narayan states:

> Under increasing economic pressure, men in many parts of the world have lost their traditional livelihoods and women have been forced to take on additional income-earning tasks while continuing their domestic tasks ... Many men react to their loss of power as breadwinner by collapsing into drugs, alcohol, depression, wife-beating, or by walking away.[70]

Families pay a high price for these changes in roles and responsibilities which are traditionally attributed according to sex. Nevertheless, this challenge to traditional male power does not seem to provoke an increase in domestic violence against women. On the contrary, such violence seems to have dropped markedly in South America and Asia, but slightly less so in Africa, both because men are more dependent on their wives and because the standards of what is acceptable have changed as a result of campaigns led by, amongst others, NGOs and churches.[71]

Lack of Right to Health Care

An inability to pay for medicines or hospital bills features in every life story except that from France. This is because health costs are covered by a social security system in France. Moreover, the French example mentions other social welfare provisions: adult disability benefit and a housing allowance, offering a level of financial security that is completely absent from the other stories. Accessing such benefits was however a long and complex process, and support from people who were competent and willing to help was crucial.

The difficulties in gaining access to health care are evident throughout Mercedita's story in the Philippines, including both infant mortality and premature adult death. According to the national survey on demography and health conducted in 2003, the risk of a child dying in the Philippines was much higher than in any other country in South-East Asia. In 2010, out of 1,000 newborns, 32 die before reaching the age of five. Families living in poverty are at even greater risk: for the poorest 20 per cent of the population, the mortality rate of children below the age of five is three times as high as for the wealthiest 20 per cent of Filipinos.

Poverty increases vulnerability in many ways, including mother and child malnutrition, insufficient access to healthcare services, unhealthy living conditions, shortage of available drinking water and a lack of information regarding health.

The Rojas Paucar life story illustrates how health problems can seriously threaten the fragile balance of a family. Like many disadvantaged families this includes turning to traditional medicine for treatment, only reluctantly resorting to the local health centre or hospital when the illness worsens in spite of traditional treatments. Lack of money to pay for hospital expenses leads families to resort to asking friends and family for help. Access to health care is not free in Peru, even though in 2002 Alejandro Toledo's government adopted measures to help young mothers with low incomes. Public health institutions and centres were supposed to exonerate people who were considered destitute, but due to a lack of subsidies from the Ministry of Health, low-income families must continue to pay part of their hospital and treatment expenses. According to a study conducted by the Lima-based Economic and Social Research Consortium, 65 per cent of Peruvians had neither social security benefits nor health insurance in 2005, and had to pay for consultations, operations and medication when they were ill.[72] Even though the costs may be minimal, extremely disadvantaged families can find themselves unable to pay them. The lack of basic equipment in public institutions often requires patients to supply such things as gauze and cotton wool, which is yet another hurdle for the poorest among them.

This situation is common in many developing countries. In the Philippines, 20 per cent of poor households are covered by health insurance.[73] As a result, they only use health services in an emergency and must pay for the treatment they receive.[74] In July 2008, the Cheaper Medicines Bill was signed into law, adopting similar measures to those in neighbouring countries. Until then, some medicines could cost from two to seven times as much as in other countries in the region, which meant that people living in poverty were unable to receive suitable treatment for chronic illnesses such as tuberculosis.

Ten years of ATD Fourth World action for the health of small children in deprived districts of Antananarivo in Madagascar have revealed the same problems relating to costs and staff attitude, and the same feeling of being misunderstood and humiliated in hospitals. The medical staff are often from the middle or upper class and have been trained to practise Western medicine, whereas those who come from an extremely poor environment turn to traditional medicine for treatment and only go to hospital as a last resort. Experience has shown that by organising well-planned meetings in locations and at times that are carefully chosen, it is possible to bring these two worlds closer together and to combine the knowledge of traditional medicine with that of Western medicine for the benefit of both parties.[75]

CITIZENSHIP TIES

Promoting New Forms of Participatory Democracy

What do the four life stories tell us about the citizenship ties of people living in poverty or in extreme poverty? This bond is based on belonging to a nation which has obligations towards its members and recognises that they have certain rights, a nation in which the role of the government can vary immensely, though it is always decisive.

To have rights, one must be legally registered, but this is not enough. In rich countries, it remains very difficult for the most underprivileged populations to be politically represented, since these people are in the minority and often discredited. The same is true in poor countries where democracy is fragile, where the poorest find themselves confronted with governments that are under the influence of the most powerful, and whose leaders lead lives far removed from that of the people. But the forms of participatory democracy promoted by various organisations (NGOs, trade unions, religious institutions, etc.) bring them recognition and an opportunity to influence certain government decisions.

Legal Registration

The four life stories show how difficult it is for the most disadvantaged to get the official documents they need in order to live as citizens with rights. In Peru, members of ATD Fourth World often help very poor parents to register their newborn children with the proper authorities and obtain a birth certificate. These procedures are so long, complicated and costly that people have trouble navigating them on their own, especially when the parents are separated and they have to be located. Peruvian law stipulates that parents have 30 days to register the birth of a child and that this declaration must be made in front of witnesses who, like the parents, must present their identity papers. The obligation to show all of this identification can present an obstacle.

The family often lacks the time and resources to perform the necessary administrative procedures. Sometimes the parents are simply so afraid of being rejected and humiliated that they do not go to the registry office. The situation is similar in the Philippines, where Mercedita often had to use her children's christening certificates instead of their birth certificates to enrol them in school.

This situation is so common in developing countries that in 2011 UNICEF estimated that only 51 per cent of the estimated total of births were registered.[76] Yet, other than being the first legal recognition of a child's existence, birth registration is vital to ensure proper planning of necessary facilities such as schools and health clinics. In most countries, a birth certificate is compulsory in order to enrol a child in school, be treated in a health centre, and so on.

Following a campaign launched by UNICEF, with support from the countries in question, registration rates of children aged between zero and 59 months increased during the 2000–09 period. They now reach 83 per cent in the Philippines and 93 per cent in Peru, but only 30 per cent in those countries that are considered the least developed – of which Burkina Faso is one. The percentage of registrations is always higher in cities than in rural areas.[77]

Significant progress has been made in Burkina Faso by reducing registration fees and mobilising many local associations, especially women's groups. In the Philippines, a law was passed which gives a man's biological children the right to use their father's name while waiving registration fees and the penalty fees that usually apply to retroactive registrations. In Peru, bylaws were passed in three districts for birth certificates to be delivered free of charge.

Representing the Interests of People Living in Extreme Poverty

The four life stories demonstrate how hard it is for the most disadvantaged to make their voices heard and have their interests taken into consideration, whether it be in their neighbourhood, at school, in health facilities, in municipal urban planning, in the media or in the political arena. They illustrate an observation that is widely documented: that all over the world, government spending on health, education and the environment benefits those who are not poor much more than they do the poor, who receive only crumbs from the table and manifestly lack the power to change their situation.[78] During electoral campaigns, of course, candidates trying to win votes give a lot of attention to disadvantaged neighbourhoods and communities. In the Philippines, for example, this attention often goes hand in hand with allegations of vote-buying or intimidation of these communities; over the last few years, these have become a recurring characteristic of local and national elections.

In the Philippines, each district is administered by a *barangay*, through which inhabitants can obtain documents and defend their rights. But the community of families living under the Quirino Avenue bridge is not recognised by any of the neighbouring *barangay*, and this not only means it is excluded from any democratic representation, but also that its members are faced with sometimes insurmountable difficulties when they need to obtain a proof of address, medical assistance, places in school for their children, permission to vote or recognition of the fact that they are citizens of Manila.

Hence, to protect its interests, the community created its own association, the SMIT, which represented it in negotiations with local authorities. However, without the legal status of a *barangay*, the SMIT was not able to stop the implementation of a city-wide 'beautification' plan which, in April 2005, led to the eviction of all the families living under the bridge without any guarantee of rehousing. Today the SMIT no longer exists. Since 2006, it has been through participation in ATD Fourth World adult forums that the inhabitants have been able to organise themselves to cope with demolitions and rehousing and to designate members of the community to represent them in negotiations with local authorities.

In Peru, the inhabitants of El Mirador are united in a neighbourhood association that is managed and run by the landowners. The tenants, who rent a house at a moderate price, and the caretakers, who do not pay rent, are not allowed to take part in the association's meetings or in any of its decisions. They meet amongst themselves, but they have little influence.

In rural areas, it is the most dynamic people who lead the village meetings and decide, for example, which lands to cultivate. Generally, the poorest farmers do not attend because they do not own any land and believe that what they might say would not be taken into account.

The violence that shook France in 2005, including the neighbourhood in which Farid, Céline and their child live, bears witness to the anger of some of the younger residents at being excluded from the economic and cultural development they see elsewhere. The vandalising of schools is evidence of the rage of young people who feel they have been abandoned by the education system. People living in the underprivileged urban areas of France feel that they are not properly taken into account in the country's policies, which tend to favour the middle class and reveal a major democratic deficiency.

International Relations and Fragile Democracies

In order to be understood properly, the growth of the informal economy in Third World countries and the difficulties faced by the education, health and welfare systems, as they are illustrated in the four life stories, must be placed within an international context.[79]

For several decades, the indebted countries of the south have been paying greater amounts to the north than they receive in return. According to the Organisation for Economic Cooperation and Development (OECD), ODA from donor countries totalled

US$129 billion; Third World country foreign debt servicing (payment of interest and amortisation instalments) amounted to US$475 billion according to World Bank figures from 2009.

This situation 'is the very expression of the structural violence in the current world order', wrote Jean Ziegler, former United Nations Special Rapporteur on the Right to Food.[80]

But situations in developing countries differ extraordinarily. Indeed, in 2004 the amount of debt service paid by Burkina Faso only represented 9.7 per cent of the amount of ODA it had received, while it was 5.6 times greater than the ODA in Peru, and 25 times greater in the Philippines.[81] The reason for this is that Burkina Faso benefited from the debt reduction initiatives for the Most Heavily Indebted Poor Countries, which were implemented in 1996 and again in 2005.

Considered middle-income countries, Peru and the Philippines did not benefit from these measures. In 2004, the total value of Peru's foreign debt was equal to half of its GDP, while the amount of debt service it was compelled to pay was twice as much as government spending on education and 2.8 times higher than government spending on health.[82] In the Philippines, the State's foreign debt has been well in excess of the country's GDP since 2001. The growth of this debt has resulted in an increase in the amount of interest to be paid, which reached 33.2 per cent of the state's budget spending in 2005 and led to deep cuts in spending on education and health.[83]

The history of this debt and of the policies implemented to reduce it is already a long one. In the late 1970s, the increase in Third World debt led the Bretton Woods institutions – the World Bank and the IMF – to implement a new policy. Together, in the early 1980s, the World Bank and the IMF granted new concessional loans to Third World countries, subject to certain conditions, which were negotiated and recorded in SAPs.

Burkina Faso, Peru and the Philippines negotiated loans which were granted in exchange for putting SAPs into place. These recommended strategies such as reducing state expenditure in order to allow countries to repay their debts, encouraging export agriculture, liberalising trade by reducing import duties and privatising state-owned companies and public utilities. The running costs for state services were reduced, but so was spending on health and education. This led to large-scale redundancies in a number of countries. In many cases, loans were granted to dictators or to corrupt governments, which helped them to hold on to power and grow richer. Many NGOs from the north and south are asking for the cancellation of these 'odious' debts that have impoverished the contracting countries.

Implementation of the SAPs very quickly met with strong resistance. Criticism came from within the very institutions that had implemented the SAPs and was made public by Joseph Stiglitz, former chief economist for the World Bank, who denounced the ineffectiveness and the ideological nature of the recommended strategies.[84] In most cases, they led neither to growth nor to the development promised, and the countries' debt increased. A few years later, the World Bank itself acknowledged the failure of the policies that had been adopted and abandoned SAPs in 1999.[85]

To show their willingness to 'put the governments of the south back in the driver's seat' and reduce the number of conditions, the Bretton Woods institutions implemented new concessional loans called Poverty Reduction and Growth Facilities that were to be combined with Poverty Reduction Strategies. The importance of spending on education and health was recognised, and governments were encouraged to define their strategies for reducing poverty in consultation with civil society.

An added challenge for countries reliant on cash crops, such as Burkina Faso, is world price volatility. The drop in the price of cotton, the country's main export, constitutes a significant economic challenge.[86] This highlights the inconsistency of rich countries, which allocate money to ODA while heavily subsidising their own agriculture and forbidding countries in the south to do the same. The United States, the world's leading exporter, spends over US$3 billion per year on supporting its cotton producers, putting the least developed countries at a serious disadvantage.

The ILO claims that in sub-Saharan Africa, the added value per worker is 13 times lower than that of workers in the developed world.[87] There is a strong argument here, not least from a recent report of the Human Rights Council, that the protection of food-producing agriculture, which is an element of the food sovereignty of countries, needs to become part of the range of generally accepted measures in trade agreements, along with the introduction of clauses for protecting human rights.[88]

Participatory Democracy

The four life stories show that helping the most disadvantaged and sharing in their lives must be a long-term project, for it is only with time that trust can be built. Once this trust is established, it is much easier for people to talk about their lives, their thoughts and their hopes. These stories also highlight the different means by which they can make themselves heard by experts and authorities, both individually and collectively.

In each of the life stories, financial aid in the form of loans or donations, often for small amounts, are asked for. The fact that the ATD Fourth World teams who handle financial aid are so careful can seem shocking when they are faced with people who have nothing. In reality, the main aim is not to compensate for the chronic lack of resources that occasional aid can never replace, but rather to maintain a long-term relationship with no strings attached. The goal is to create the right conditions so that the structural causes of the problem can be addressed together, by claiming one's rights and creating ways to generate rights.

In very poor environments, responding too generously to requests for money would generate a higher demand and this would transform the team into a financial aid department, steering it away from its primary mission. Nevertheless, refusing to grant urgent financial aid can endanger the relationship with the applicant, who may feel misunderstood and abandoned to their poverty. In some cases, not fulfilling these requests can endanger the life of the applicant or of their loved ones. So the answer is almost always to give a small amount of help, which provides a temporary solution to the problem encountered, without creating a sense of dependency between the beneficiary and the donor.

In all four life stories, gatherings to commemorate the World Day for Overcoming Extreme Poverty, each 17 October, appear as powerful moments in participatory democracy, where the most disadvantaged are in the spotlight.

In Manega, Burkina Faso, and in Manila's Rizal Park in the Philippines, as well as 28 other locations around the world, monuments have been erected displaying the words that are engraved on the Commemorative Stone in Honour of the Victims of Extreme Poverty which was inaugurated in Paris on 17 October 1987:

Wherever men and women are condemned to live in extreme poverty, human rights are violated. To come together to ensure that these rights be respected is our solemn duty.

Father Joseph Wresinski.[89]

In 1992, the General Assembly of the United Nations designated 17 October as the International Day for the Eradication of Poverty. A few years later, the Philippines declared it a national day.

Following a United Nations organised consultation on how to extend the reach of the International Day for the Eradication of Poverty, a report from the United Nations Secretary General stated:

> The most important feature of 17 October is the visibility that it provides to those who normally are unseen and unheard by the rest of society; it reaffirms their status as full and equal citizens … making a contribution to society that is often overlooked. Their testimonies demonstrate the ways in which poverty and extreme poverty persistently undermine the ability of people to fulfil their obligations and access their human rights … As a rallying point for people from many different walks of life, the day provides an occasion for a dialogue that leads to a better understanding of the responsibilities of each stakeholder in creating a society based on respect for the dignity of each of its members.

Case studies show the power this day has to transform both people living in poverty, who gain self-esteem and the respect of others, and people from other social circles, who overcome some of their prejudices, which can lead them to new actions. Public authorities and the media often attend this day but their presence, although very desirable, must be carefully prepared in order for it to be fruitful.[90]

RE-ESTABLISHING BASIC TIES TO ACHIEVING RECOGNITION

Analysis has shown that if basic social ties are broken or terribly damaged at the family or community level, at school and at work, and on the level of citizenship, the individual or his family cannot gain access to their fundamental rights. Re-establishing basic ties therefore appears to be a necessary condition for gaining access to rights and, more than that, a necessary condition for gaining recognition in the sense of the word as it is currently used in sociology and political philosophy.

Philosopher Axel Honneth developed a theory of recognition by analysing feelings of contempt, humiliation and attacks to one's dignity – all of which are feelings of non-recognition. According to him, many social confrontations are not limited to conflicting interests and can be better understood by looking at these feelings of belittlement which generate a struggle for recognition.[91]

The image that people have of themselves is dependent on how others see them. Honneth believes that three principles of recognition determine each person's legitimate expectations in modern societies:

- *Love in the sphere of intimacy*
  This covers all of the strong emotional bonds that nourish our relationships with our family, spouses and friends. We know how important mothers and fathers are in the development of personal identity and autonomy, and it is through experiencing love that each of us is able to build self-confidence.
- *Equality in the legal sphere*
  This gives each person the feeling of having the same rights as others, in order to develop a feeling of self-respect.
- *Recognition of usefulness in the community sphere*
  This gives each person the feeling that they are useful and can contribute to the community, and that this can help build self-esteem.

This analysis has the advantage of expressing the struggle for recognition positively, rather than negatively as the struggle against disqualification or exclusion. It emphasises a very important aspect of each person's legitimate aspirations, which are too often ignored by economists. The struggle for recognition is evident throughout the life stories we have analysed, but it does not sum up the struggle against extreme poverty, which is a combination of extreme material poverty and social exclusion.

What allowed Farid and Céline to overcome extreme poverty was the understanding and support they received, and the recognition of their value, their dignity and their efforts. But it was also getting access to housing and a decent job. Paul overcame extreme poverty by renewing his ties with his family and reconciling with his relatives, but also by gaining access to housing and employment. By participating in ATD Fourth World activities and by writing their life stories, Mercedita and the Rojas Paucar parents gained recognition for their tireless efforts and their dignity, their desire for a close-knit family, their daily struggle to give their children a school education and their solidarity with their neighbours. But this recognition from a limited number of people left Mercedita without access to her basic rights to family life, health, a decent job and housing. It leaves the Rojas Paucar parents without any opportunity to overcome extreme poverty. This experience is very painful for them and for all those who have fought alongside them, because they are all faced with their own powerlessness in spite of the intensity of their efforts and the time committed to them.

Establishing and strengthening social ties that are a source of recognition is therefore a necessary condition in the struggle against extreme poverty. But this condition in itself is not sufficient. As philosopher Nancy Fraser points out, we must 'envision social arrangements that can redress both economic and cultural injustices'. Only by working to 'unite redistribution and recognition ... can we meet the requirements of justice for all'.[92] How globalisation and democracy can contribute to achieving this is the subject of the next chapter.

NOTES

1. Paul Bouchet, 'Le rôle du droit en question', *Revue Quart Monde*, Vol. 186, No. 2 (May 2003).
2. Serge Paugam, *Les formes élémentaires de la pauvreté*, Paris: Presses Universitaires de France, 2005, pp. 79–80.
3. Hélène Garner, Dominique Méda and Claudia Senik, 'La place du travail dans les identités', *Economie et Statistique*, Vol. 393–394 (November 2006).
4. Paugam, *Les formes élémentaires de la pauvreté*, p. 10.
5. ATD Fourth World, *How Poverty Separates Parents and Children: A Challenge to Human Rights*, Paris: Fourth World Publications, 2004; ATD Fourth World, *Valuing Children, Valuing Parents*, London: ATD Fourth World, 2004.
6. Maria Maïlat, Romanian anthropologist and novelist, cited in Maryvonne Caillaux, *Contre vents et marées. Réflexions sur la famille*, Paris: Éditions Quart Monde, 2006, pp. 63–4.
7. To read about the resilience of people who have suffered great traumas, see works by Boris Cyrulnik, *Les nourritures affectives, Un merveilleux malheur,* Paris: Éditions Odile Jacob; *Talking of Love on the Edge of a Precipice*, London: Allen Lane, 2007.
8. Quoted by Jean-Louis Saporito, *Smiles Worldwide*, Paris: Les Arènes, 2007, p. 21.
9. Xavier Godinot, *Les travailleurs sous-prolétaires en France*, Paris: Éditions Science et Service – Quart Monde, 1985.
10. Paul Vercauteren, *Les sous-prolétaires, essai sur une forme du paupérisme contemporain*, Brusels: Éditions Vie Ouvrière, 1970.
11. Amade Badini, a presentation given to the seminar *Writing the Life Stories of Families Living in Poverty*, 7–10 October 2004, and cited in ATD Fourth World, *Contribution to the Moving Out of Poverty Study: Family Monographs from Burkina Faso and Peru*, Paris: Fourth World Publications, 2005, p. 63.
12. Majid Rahnema, *Quand la misère chasse la pauvreté*, Paris: Fayard/Actes Sud, 2003, p. 228.
13. S.M. Miller, 'The American Lower Class: A Typological Approach', *Social Research*, Vol. 31, No. 1 (Spring 1964).
14. Thierry Torche and Pascale Pichon, *S'en Sortir, Accompagnement sociologique à l'autobiographie d'un ancien sans domicile fixe*, Saint Etienne: Publications de l'Université de Saint Etienne, 2007, p. 58.
15. Serge Paugam and Mireille Clémençon, 'Détresse et ruptures sociales', *Observatoire sociologique du changement et Fédération nationale des associations d'accueil et de réadaptation sociale (Fnars), Recueils et Documents*, Vol. 17, (April 2002).

16. Patrick Declerck, *Les naufragés. Avec les clochards de Paris*, Paris: Éditions Plon, 2001.

17. Gérard Bureau, 'Familles en grande pauvreté aujourd'hui en France', *Revue Quart Monde*, Vol. 203, No. 3 (August 2007).

18. Johan Schölvinck, 'Foreword by the United Nations', in ATD Fourth World, *How Poverty Separates Parents and Children*, Paris: ATD Fourth World, 2004, p. 9–10.

19. Secrétariat permanent du Comité National chargé du suivi et de l'évaluation du Plan National d'Action pour l'Enfance, *Etude sur la situation des enfants et des femmes vivant dans des circonstances particulièrement difficiles au Burkina Faso*, p. 16.

20. ATD Fourth World and UNICEF, *Reaching the Poorest*, Paris: Éditions Quart Monde, 1996.

21. Ibrahim Zougmoré, 'Pourquoi les enfants quittent-ils leur famille?', *Revue Quart Monde*, Vol. 189, No. 1 (February 2004).

22. Ibid., p. 18.

23. Ibid., p. 20.

24. Majid Rahnema, *Quand la misère chasse la pauvreté*, p. 163–79.

25. Amade Badini, presentation given to the seminar *Writing the Life Stories of Families Living in Poverty*, cited in ATD Fourth World, *Contribution to the Moving out of Poverty Study*, pp. 8–9.

26. UNICEF, *The State of the World's Children 2011*, New York: UNICEF, 2011.

27. Laure Pasquier-Doumier, *L'évolution de la mobilité scolaire intergénérationnelle au Pérou depuis un siècle*, DIAL Working Paper, 2003, p. 25.

28. UNICEF, *The State of the World's Children 2011*.

29. Nicolas Lynch Gamero, a presentation given to the seminar *Writing the Life Stories of Families Living in Poverty*, 7–10 October 2004, and cited in ATD Fourth World, *Contribution to the Moving Out of Poverty Study: Family Monographs from Burkina Faso and Peru*, Paris: ATD Fourth World, 2005, p. 28.

30. United Nations Development Programme, *World Development Report 2010*, New York: UNDP, 2010.

31. Joseph Ki-Zerbo, Cheikh Hamidou Kane, Jo-Ann Archibald, Edouard Lizop and Majid Rahnema, *Education as an Instrument of Cultural Defoliation: A Multi-Voice Report*, in Majid Rahnema and Victoria Bawtree (eds), *The Post-Development Reader*, London: Zed Books, 1997, pp. 152–60.

32. Mamadou N'Doye, *Cultures africaines, défis et opportunités pour le développement*, in Jean-Eric Aubert and Josee Landrieu (eds), *Vers des civilisations mondialisées ? De l'éthologie à la prospective*, La Tour d'Aigues: Éditions de l'Aube, 2005, p. 117.

33. Speech given on 17 October 2000, on the occasion of the International Day for the Eradication of Poverty, and cited in ATD Fourth World, *Contribution to the Moving Out of Poverty Study*, p. 11.

34. Amade Badini, presentation given to the seminar *Writing the Life Stories of Families Living in Poverty*, cited in ATD Fourth World, *Contribution to the Moving Out of Poverty Study*, p. 11.

35. Claude Dalbera, Jean-Jacques Friboulet, Valérie Liechti and Anatole Niameogo, *La mesure du droit à l'éducation. Tableau de bord de l'éducation pour tous au Burkina Faso*, Paris: Karthala, 2005.

36. Cited from an interview with Professor Badini undertaken by the ATD Fourth World team in Ouagadougou in 2005.
37. Jona M. Rosenfeld and Bruno Tardieu, *Artisans of Democracy: How Ordinary People, Families in Extreme Poverty and Social Institutions Become Allies to Overcome social Exclusion*, Lanham, MD: University Press of America, 2000.
38. Fourth World Movement/USA, 'Unleashing Hidden Potential', *Fourth World Journal*, September 2001, January 2002, May 2002, September 2002 and November 2003.
39. Pierre Merle, *L'élève humilié*, Paris: Presses Universitaires de France, 2005.
40. Claude Pair, 'L'école devant la grande pauvreté', *Revue Quart Monde*, Vol. 174, No. 2 (June 2000).
41. Joseph Ki Zerbo, *A quand l'Afrique, Entretiens avec René Holenstein*, La Tour d'Aigues: Éditions de l'Aube, 2004, p. 177.
42. Xavier Godinot, *Les travailleurs sous-prolétaires en France*, Paris: Éditions Science et Service – Quart Monde, 1985.
43. Nasser Tafferant, *Le bizness, une économie souterraine*, Paris: Presses Universitaires de France, 2007.
44. www.unhabitat.org/
45. Erhard Berner, 'Legalizing Squatters, Excluding the Poorest: Urban Land Transfer Programs in the Philippines', Paper presented at Workshop on 'Urban Poverty Alleviation in Asia – Challenges and Perspectives', Kaiserslautern, 17–19 July 2006.
46. Fondation Abbé Pierre, *L'état du mal-logement en France*, Paris: Fondation Abbé Pierre, 2011.
47. Nicolas Sarkozy, speech delivered to the Economic and Social Council of France on the occasion of the International Day for the Eradication of Poverty, 17 October 2007.
48. Ibid.
49. Secrétariat permanent du Comité National chargé du suivi et de l'évaluation du Plan National d'Action pour l'Enfance, *Report on the National Plan for Childhood*, 2005 p. 28.
50. Eric Maurin, *Les nouvelles précarités*, in Pierre Rosnavallon, Thierry Pech, Eric Maurin and Pierre Veltz (eds), *La nouvelle critique sociale*, Paris: Éditions du Seuil, 2006, p. 22.
51. ATD Fourth World Research and Training Institute, *Ecouter donne la parole, enquête 2005*, Paris: ATD Fourth World, 2005.
52. Friedrich Schneider, 'Size and Measurement of the Informal Economy in 110 Countries around the World', Paper presented at a Workshop of Australian National Tax Centre, July 2002.
53. Agnes Quisumbing and Scott McNiven, *Migration and the Rural-Urban Continuum: Evidence from the Rural Philippines*, IFPRI FCND Discussion Paper 197, 2005, available at www.ifpri.org
54. Jacques Diouf, 'Se nourrir plutôt qu'être nourri', *Le Monde Diplomatique*, October 2007.
55. Kofi Annan, 'Pour une révolution verte en Afrique', *Le Monde*, 11 July 2007.
56. Manuel Castells presents the evolution of food production per person over ten years in *End Of Millennium*, Cambridge, MA: Blackwell, 2003, p. 117.
57. Christiane Galus, 'Trente années de sécheresse au Sahel', *Le Monde*, 30 November 2004.

58. Bruno Lautier, *L'économie informelle dans le tiers monde*, Éditions la Découverte, 2004, p. 112.

59. Hernando de Soto, *Le mystère du capital. Pourquoi le capitalisme triomphe en Occident et échoue partout ailleurs?*, Paris: Flammarion, 2005.

60. Muhammad Yunus, *Vers un monde sans pauvreté*, Paris: Éditions JC Lattès, 1997.

61. United Nations General Assembly, 53rd Session. *Report of the Secretary General on the Role of Microcredit in the Eradication of Poverty*, A/53/223, 10 August 1998.

62. Refer to the programme *Challenging The Frontiers of Poverty Reduction: Targeting the Ultra Poor* initiated by the Bangladesh Rural Advancement Committee.

63. World Commission on the Social Dimension of Globalization, *A Fair Globalisation: Creating Opportunities For All*, Geneva: International Labour Organisation, 2004, p. xiii.

64. Wouter Van Ginneken, 'Social Security and the Global Socio-Economic Floor: Towards a Human Rights-Based Approach', a presentation given to the Annual Conference of the Research Committee on Poverty, Social Welfare and Social Policy of the International Sociological Association, *Social Policy in a Globalising World: Developing a North-South Dialogue*, 6–8 September 2007.

65. Blandine Destremau and Bruno Lautier, 'Social Protection and Social Rights Regimes in Developing Countries: Towards the Construction of a Typology', a presentation given to the Annual Conference of the Research Committee on Poverty, Social Welfare and Social Policy of the International Sociological Association, *Social Policy in a Globalising World: Developing a North-South Dialogue*, 6–8 September 2007.

66. Organisation for Economic Cooperation and Development, *OECD Development Co-operation Report 2010*, Paris: OECD, 2010.

67. 'Annan Faults "Frightening Lack of Leadership" for Global Warming', *New York Times*, 16 November 2006.

68. International Organisation for Migration, *World Migration Report 2010 – The Future of Migration: Building Capacities for Change*, Geneva: IOM, 2010.

69. Article in *Philippines Online Chronicle*, January 2010.

70. Deepa Narayan, *Voices of the Poor: Can Anyone Hear Us*, New York: Oxford University Press for the World Bank, 2000, pp. 175, 203.

71. Ibid., pp. 125–32.

72. *Le Monde*, 5–6 August 2007.

73. National Statistics Office Philippines] and ICF Macro, *Philippines National Demographic and Health Survey 2008: Key Findings*, Calverton, MD: NSO and ICF Macro, 2009.

74. World Bank, *Filipino Report Card on Pro-Poor Services*, Report No. 22181 – PH, Washington, DC: World Bank, 2001.

75. Chantal Laureau, Caroline Blanchard and Xavier Godinot, *Rendre les services de santé accessibles aux plus pauvres. Dix années d'action à Tananarive, Madagascar*, in Agence Française de Développement and ATD Fourth World, proceedings of the seminar on Extreme Poverty and Development in June 2006.

76. UNICEF, *The State of the World's Children 2011*.

77. Ibid.

78. World Bank, *World Development Report 2004: Making Services Work for Poor People*, Washington, DC: World Bank and Oxford University Press, 2003.
79. A more comprehensive account of the evolution of this situation is available from Serge Michaïlof, *A quoi sert d'aider le Sud?*, Édition Economica-Agence française de développement, 2006, pp. 1–36.
80. Jean Ziegler, *L'empire de la honte*, Paris: Fayard, 2005.
81. Figures from the International Debt Observatory, available at www.oid-ido.org/rubrique.php3?id_rubrique=3
82. Ibid.
83. Social Watch, *Social Watch Report 2006: Impossible Architecture*, Montevideo: Social Watch, 2006, p. 241.
84. Joseph Stiglitz, *Globalisation and its Discontents*, New York: W.W. Norton and Company, 2002.
85. World Bank Independent Evaluation Group, *Assessing World Bank Support for Trade, 1987–2004*, Washington, DC: World Bank, 2006.
86. International Development Association and International Monetary Fund, *Heavily Indebted Poor Countries (HIPC) Initiative and Multilateral Debt Relief Initiative (MDRI) – Status of Implementation*, Washington, DC: IDA and IMF, 2007, p. 56.
87. International Labour Organisation, *Global Employment Trends: Brief, January 2007*, Geneva: ILO, 2007, p. 2.
88. Human Rights Council of the United Nations General Assembly, *Report of the Independent Expert on the Effect of Economic Reform Policies and Foreign Debt on the Full Enjoyment of All Human Rights, Bernard Mudho*, A/HRC/4/10, 3 January 2007.
89. For further information, visit www.oct17.org/en
90. ATD Fourth World, *Making the Most of October 17*, a report of the seminar held in Montreal, Canada in May 2006 following resolution A/RES/60/209 paragraph 55 of the General Assembly of the United Nations.
91. Axel Honneth, *The Struggle for Recognition: The Moral Grammar of Social Conflicts*, Cambridge: Polity Press, 1995.
92. Nancy Fraser, 'Social Justice in the Age of Identity Politics: Redistribution, Recognition and Participation', The Tanner Lectures on Human Values, paper delivered at Stanford University 30 April to 2 May 1996.

6
Democracy, Globalisation and Extreme Poverty

Xavier Godinot

More than 220 years ago, reformers argued that it was possible to put an end to poverty and described the measures by which this could be achieved. Inspired by scientific progress, by the promise of growing international economic activity, and by the revolutions which had taken place in France and the United States, at the end of the eighteenth century political thinkers, such as Paine and Condorcet, maintained that all citizens could be protected from the vagaries of life by systems of insurance and social security. The idea that it is possible to put an end to poverty thus dates from the birth of democracy in the West.

Current debates about globalisation and poverty are still strongly influenced by the ideological arguments of those times.[1]

The Duke of La Rochefoucauld-Liancourt, a reporter for a committee for the eradication of begging appointed by the Constituent Assembly in 1790, wrote:

> We have always remembered to give charity to the poor, never to recognise the rights of the poor over society ... Public charity is not kindness, it is a duty, it is justice. Where there exists a class of people without subsistence there exists a violation of the rights of humanity.[2]

Two centuries later, on 17 October 1987, Joseph Wresinski inaugurated a Commemorative Stone in Honour of the Victims of Extreme Poverty on the Plaza of Liberties and Human Rights in Paris, on which was engraved:

> Wherever men and women are condemned to live in extreme poverty, human rights are violated. To come together to ensure that these rights be respected is our solemn duty.

The twentieth century was marked by the triumph, and then the failure, of the great ideologies of world transformation, regardless of which side of the political spectrum they came from. In the name of equality for all and the construction of a classless society, communism created totalitarian regimes which were among the most oppressive ever seen. In the name of science, the hygienist and eugenicist movements organised the forced sterilisation of millions of people, often from the most disadvantaged backgrounds. In the name of neoliberalism, policies imposed by the governments of industrialised countries and developing countries have thrust hundreds of millions of people into poverty. Under all of these regimes, the fight against poverty is constantly threatening to turn into a ferocious fight against the poor.

This chapter seeks to address three questions:

1. Is globalisation an opportunity or an obstacle, given that 'the elimination of poverty' has become a focus of national and international policies?
2. Which social movements do the most underprivileged populations need to support them in their struggle to gain access to fundamental rights?
3. What *personal* transformations are needed to allow the *social* transformations to occur which are necessary for the eradication of poverty?

GLOBALISATION AND THE FIGHT AGAINST POVERTY

The term 'globalisation' designates the development of interdependent ties between human beings, human activities and political systems on a worldwide scale. The links between countries, businesses and individuals are interconnected in such a way that events and decisions in one part of the world have an effect, to a greater or lesser degree, on other parts of the world.

The economist Daniel Cohen distinguishes between three major globalisation cycles.[3] The first is linked to the discovery of America by Christopher Columbus, followed by sixteenth-century European expansion. The second globalisation took place in the nineteenth century; this was based on:

- the Industrial Revolution
- colonisation, which brought a number of countries into a shared political arena
- inventions, particularly the steam engine and the telegraph.

It was followed during the first half of the twentieth century by a period of economic protectionism and two world wars. During the 1970s and 1980s a third cycle of globalisation opened which continues today.

In the fight against extreme poverty and the implementation of human rights, globalisation brings both opportunities and risks.

Two Schools of Thought: Economic Liberalism and Human Rights

The Universal Declaration of Human Rights, adopted on 10 December 1948, was a major act of globalisation by which the United Nations General Assembly recognised that all human beings, wherever they lived, had universally defined tangible rights. The preamble states that the declaration is 'a common standard of achievement for all peoples and all nations'. The law, which is at the heart of this project, must ensure protection so that all human beings may have 'freedom of speech and belief and freedom from fear and want'.[4]

Amartya Sen has underlined the intellectual error which sees democracy essentially in terms of votes and elections, rather than in a larger perspective of public debate. For Sen, democracy is indeed a universal value; this does not mean that it receives universal approval – no value has this privilege – but it does mean that people everywhere have good reason to consider it as a universal value.[5]

The 1970s saw the emergence of the information technology revolution, which was the starting point for the restructuring of capitalism in the world. The globalisation which resulted from this is characterised by three interdependent phenomena:

1. New information and communication technology makes it possible to communicate across the world at ever faster rates and ever more cheaply.
2. Trade and cross-border investments are increasing, as a result of the reduction in customs tariffs and protectionism.
3. Financial deregulation promotes the circulation of capital, which is growing at a phenomenal rate.

The same technology and the same products are available everywhere, but the principal vector of globalisation is finance, because it standardises the principles of making profit from capital. New types of company have appeared:

- multinationals, whose decision-making centres remain in their country of origin
- transnationals, whose decision-making centres are more scattered.

Numbering 7,000 at the beginning of the 1960s, multi- or transnational corporations reached 70,000 in 2005, generating two thirds of the world's trade. The power of their shareholders has become dominant, and employees are sometimes considered as simply one of the company's expendable variables.

The Washington consensus

The fall of the Berlin Wall in 1989 and the implosion of the USSR in 1991 signalled the collapse of communism and the victory of economic liberalism. The dominant ideology of the last 20 years of the twentieth century, interchangeably referred to as 'economic liberalism' or 'neoliberalism', can be characterised by what the economist John Williamson called the 'Washington consensus'.[6] According to its creator, this expression defined the policies of the Washington-based institutions which provide aid to developing countries:

- the World Bank
- the International Monetary Fund (IMF)
- the Inter-American Development Bank
- the United States Treasury.

The Washington consensus consisted of a ten-point series of reforms, initially formulated for implementation in Latin America, but which rapidly became a model for the entire developing world. It gave precedence to monetary and financial management criteria over social criteria for government policies, including:

- fiscal discipline and the reorganisation of public spending priorities
- liberalisation of commercial exchanges, interest rates and investments
- privatisation of public companies and services.

In reality, it often led to a reduction in the role of the state, even to weakening it in the long term. This consensus has become a thing of the past, and today the debate is centred around the future role of international financial organisations.

Over the last few years, the international context has changed with the rise in power of China, whose trade with Africa increased fourfold between 2001 and 2005. The Washington consensus could be followed by the 'Beijing consensus'. There is nothing to say that it would be more favourable to the full exercise of human rights for all.

Opposing Schools of Thought

Two opposing schools of thought continue to exist – seeing globalisation through the prism of human rights on the one hand, and the law of the market on the other. Theorists such as Milton Friedman and Friedrich Hayek have given an almost metaphysical power to the latter. Hayek argues:

> It is a fundamental illusion to believe that human reason is capable of defining the rules of methodical organisation with a fixed objective. Man is not master of his destiny and never will be.[7]

In contrast, the Universal Declaration of Human Rights defines a project where humanity unites to outline the society that it would like to create.

The dominant neoliberal ideology, and its suspicion of legislation in general, led the United States government, the leading financial contributor to international institutions, to weaken the role of UN agencies in the 1990s by withholding financing of their projects while continuing to pump money into the Bretton Woods institutions (namely the International Monetary Fund and the World Bank), which are not legally subject to the requirements of human rights compacts. As a result, the United Nations Conference for Trade and Development, which traditionally strives to defend the interests of the poorest countries, saw its role progressively eroded. Governments of states that are members of the Organisation for Economic Co-operation and Development (OECD) make recommendations to multinational corporations, but these are not binding.

Nevertheless, the globalisation of human rights has also made progress. A recent study shows that non-governmental organisations have played a decisive role in promoting an integrated approach to human rights and issues of development.[8] The World Summit for Social Development in Copenhagen (1995) was a key moment in this evolution, promoted by a broad coalition of NGOs. On the fiftieth anniversary of the Universal Declaration of Human Rights in 1998, the UN Secretary-General reaffirmed that the implementation of human rights is the ultimate aim of the United Nations.[9] Since then, a number of UN agencies have adopted an approach to poverty based on human rights and have promoted development based on human rights. These include the Office of the High Commissioner for Human Rights, UNESCO,[10] UNICEF and the United Nations Development Programme (UNDP).

People who Live in Extreme Poverty

Surging inequalities

In 2004, the UNDP Human Development report noted rapid progress in reducing poverty in some countries but also that an unprecedented number of countries saw development slide backwards in the 1990s. It found that people in 46 countries are poorer today than in 1990. In 25 countries more people go hungry today than a decade ago.[11] The *Atlas du Monde Diplomatique* (produced by the French newspaper *Le Monde*), trying to identify the winners and losers of globalisation, criticised 'surging inequalities'.[12]

It is one thing to observe these growing inequalities, it is another to know whether they are due to globalisation or to other causes. François Bourguignon, director of the Paris School of Economics and former Chief Economist at the World Bank, outlined a partial answer in an article about the increase in these inequalities, both in developed and developing countries.[13] He suggested three reasons to explain the growing increase in salary inequality:

1. The increased demand for skilled workers created by technical progress, and their growing scarcity worldwide, has resulted in an increase in their remuneration.
2. The modification of social norms in terms of remuneration, linked to the loss of influence of trade union organisations, which has been seen all over the world. Previously, employees presented a united front to employers or shareholders, whereas individualism now dominates and salary disparity is openly tolerated. This is not only a 'spontaneous' evolution. Some multinational companies are resolutely anti-union; Wal-Mart, which employs more than 1 per cent of the US workforce, is one example. Furthermore, the number of union members who

are assassinated, attacked or imprisoned is particularly high in the emerging economies of the Americas, Asia and Oceania.[14]
3. The growing international mobility of highly skilled workers tends to progressively standardise salaries and wage earners' social models.

Despite the rise in salary disparity, the inequality of disposable income has recently decreased in countries such as Brazil and Mexico, and has changed little in France, Germany or Canada, thanks to ambitious redistribution policies. These have made it possible to limit the unequal consequences of globalisation. Other means could also play a role, such as a quicker and more efficient response from education systems to the need for a skilled workforce. In the absence of at least one of these solutions, social tensions could easily impede the globalisation process; for instance, the return of protectionism in certain countries.

Millennium Development Goals

In December 1999, 1,000 trade unions and NGOs proclaiming 'The world is not for sale' transformed the meeting of the World Trade Organisation in Seattle into a fiasco. Many see this event as the birth of the anti-globalisation movement.

At the turn of the millennium, the *Jubilee 2000* campaign to cancel Third World debt handed a petition of 22 million signatures to the members of the G8. The context was ripe for attempting to create a synthesis between the market forces approach and the human rights-based approach to development and the fight against poverty.

The Millennium Declaration, adopted in September 2000 in the presence of representatives from 189 member states of the United Nations, confirmed the aim of 'freeing the entire human race from want'. This text states:

> The central challenge we face today is to ensure that globalisation becomes a positive force for all the world's people. For while globalisation offers great opportunities, at present its benefits are very unevenly shared.

Nevertheless, a certain ambiguity pervades, with confusion between 'poverty' and 'extreme poverty'. The Declaration aims to 'free our fellow men, women and children from the abject and dehumanising conditions of extreme poverty' and to 'create an environment

... which is conducive to development and to the elimination of poverty'.[15]

Eight Millennium Development Goals (MDGs) have been defined, to be achieved by 2025; 18 interim targets are to be reached, mostly by 2015 or 2020. Goal 1 is entitled 'Eradicate extreme poverty and hunger'. Two targets linked to it, to be achieved between 1990 and 2015, are to reduce by half both the proportion of the population whose revenue is less than one dollar per day and the proportion of the population suffering from hunger. (The other goals are: 2. Achieve universal primary education; 3. Promote gender equality and empower women; 4. Reduce child mortality; 5. Improve maternal health; 6. Combat HIV/AIDs, malaria and other diseases; 7. Ensure environmental sustainability; 8. Develop a global partnership for development.)

The principal strength of the MDGs is that, for the first time in many years, they have allowed many and varied stakeholders to unite behind the same objectives. Public opinion has breathed new life into official development assistance. Many NGOs have formed national and international coalitions which continue to campaign for governments to respect Goal 8, in particular, by developing a global partnership to reduce Third World debt, to increase the quality and quantity of official development assistance, and to put in place fairer international trade rules.

However, experience has shown that top-down policies never reach the hard core of extreme poverty: households which accumulate lasting insecurities in all the areas of their lives. Concern remains over the way in which certain goals infer an abandonment of the most disadvantaged populations, allowing the most dynamic elements to 'escape poverty' while leaving others worse off. A number of MDGs are universal; others are partial, such as Goal 1, which aims to reduce by half the proportion of the population in a situation of extreme poverty. Such a statement can appear legitimate because it is not possible to do everything immediately. The risk is that *a reduction in the scale* of extreme poverty would leave the problem of *eradicating* extreme poverty untouched. Seen from the point of view of the populations which suffer from great poverty and hunger, such an objective, far from being a mobilising influence, can result only in division and the fear of being left behind.

The MDGs are based on the supposition that the richest countries will respect their commitments to supplement the financial capacities of the most disadvantaged countries, in order to put in place a vast social safety net for the poorest populations. These countries have a right to aid and the ideal financing mechanism for this would be international taxation. We have, so far, only seen a tentative attempt at this with a tax on airline tickets.

The Secretary-General of the United Nations has said:

> In the Millennium Declaration of 2000, world leaders set forth a bold and inclusive new vision for humanity. Pledging to channel the fruits of globalisation to benefit all people, leaders committed themselves 'to spare no effort to free our fellow men, women and children from the abject and dehumanising conditions of extreme poverty' ... We must recognise the nature of global trust at stake and the danger that many developing countries' hopes could be irredeemably pierced if even the greatest anti-poverty movement in history is insufficient to break from 'business as usual'.[16]

In 2010, a report on progress towards the MDGs, based on data collected by 25 international organisations, showed that improvements had been made and were still possible in most areas of the world, but that much remained to be done.[17]

The universal poor

Using an index that defines poverty and extreme poverty in monetary terms to represent the evolution of poverty overall, can be called into question for at least three reasons.

1. *Different forms of insecurity do not overlap, either in Europe or in developing countries.*
A study of different dimensions of poverty was conducted among the inhabitants of Antananarivo in Madagascar, a country with one of the lowest Human Development Index ratings. Different forms of insecurity only very partially overlap for these inhabitants: 2.4 per cent of them experience seven forms of insecurity, whereas 78 per cent are affected by at least one form of insecurity. A similar observation has been made in European countries.[18] Focusing only on the monetary dimension of poverty results in the emergence of a specific sub-group that is not representative of the poor population; the poorest in the population accumulate insecurities over the long term in a number of areas of life.

2. *The definition of monetary poverty thresholds is arbitrary.*
For many years, the World Bank adopted an absolute poverty measurement which was widely used:

- People in developing countries living on less than US$2 per day are poor.
- People in developing countries living on less than US$1.25 per day are extremely poor.
- No one lives on less than US$1 per day in industrialised countries.

Taking into account the inevitably arbitrary character of a threshold at US$1 or US$2 per day,[19] it is difficult to say whether monetary poverty has increased or decreased over the period in question. According to these criteria, extreme poverty decreased between 1981 and 2004 because the number of people living on less than US$1 per day dropped from 1.5 billion to 980 million. But, over the same period, the number of people living with less than US$2 per day increased from 2.5 to 2.6 billion.[20] Furthermore, the international poverty threshold requires complex calculations which experts themselves are obliged to revise. The UNs *Millennium Development Goals Report* of 2007 reported that new estimates of the relative cost of living in different countries made it necessary to revise the threshold, which could modify the understanding of the scale and the distribution of poverty in the world.[21] In 2008, the extreme poverty threshold has been shifted from US$1 to US$1.25 a day, whereas the poverty threshold remains unchanged.

3. Annual revenue is not a reliable poverty indicator.
French and European statistical work has shown that annual revenue, as declared by households, shows a disconcerting instability over the short term, which makes it impossible to use it as a reliable indicator of the numbers that fall into and climb out of poverty. The very reliability of the monetary indicator is questioned by the experts of the official European statistics organisations, who acknowledge themselves to be 'in complete opposition with the practices adopted by the international instances'.[22]

For all these reasons, many reject the idea that poverty and extreme poverty can be perceived in a one-dimensional manner and reduced to a question of money. The majority of experts recognise that – far from being neutral – indicators reflect the definition given to poverty, the value judgement projected on it and on the poor, and the philosophical and ideological framework which this process is part of.[23] From this perspective, it is not surprising that a bank with its headquarters in Washington defines poverty in terms of dollars, nor that inhabitants of other countries virulently reject the imposition of this definition.

Who is included in the poverty statistics?

The way that monetary poverty is measured in the European Union is no more satisfactory. According to the European Council of 1984, the poor are:

> persons, families and groups of persons whose resources (material, cultural and social) are so limited as to exclude them from the minimum acceptable way of life in the Member State to which they belong.[24]

We are talking here about the definition of 'absolute socio-historic poverty', recognising the need for a basic minimum in a specific country at a given time. However, the threshold of monetary poverty used by Eurostat is closer to a relative measure: those whose income is less than 60 per cent of the median income are considered to be poor. Once again, this is a technocratic indicator defined by specialists, without consultation with the populations living in poverty and the associations which represent them.

More than 20 years ago, Amartya Sen was already pointing out that this type of indicator had the curious tendency to remain unchanged whether all revenues doubled in a period of prosperity or halved in a period of recession. With such indicators, he argued, poverty can quite simply never be eliminated, and poverty reduction programmes can never really succeed.[25] These indicators cannot measure absolute poverty, which we can all see has not disappeared, just by walking the streets and travelling on the underground systems of major European cities. There are three major problems with the indicator:

1. It establishes an arbitrary level of monetary poverty, whereas it should be capable of measuring degrees which range from insecurity to extreme poverty.
2. It measures relative poverty and, therefore, is neither a real indicator of poverty nor a real indicator of inequality.
3. It is based on statistical enquiries which only count households in normal housing – excluding not only the homeless, but also those living in collective housing, in hostels, prisons,

psychiatric hospitals, retirement homes and so on, as well as illegal immigrants. So people who live and die on the streets each year are too poor to be taken into account in the statistical enquiries about poverty in Europe.[26] Such a situation is ethically and scientifically unacceptable. In France, the government institution which investigates poverty and exclusion estimated in its 2005 report that those excluded from the statistics on ordinary households represent 2 per cent of the population and that the majority of them would, in all probability, be amongst the poorest.[27]

In December 2001, the Laeken European Council adopted a Social Protection Committee report setting out commonly agreed and defined indicators for social inclusion. It concluded by saying:

> The Social Protection Committee recognises the importance of increasing the involvement of excluded people in the development of indicators, and the need to explore the most effective means of giving a voice to the excluded.[28]

Since then, the European Anti-Poverty Network, the international movement ATD Fourth World and other associations have worked to achieve this.[29] The next challenge is to create a forum for dialogue where social science specialists, populations in situations of great poverty and other stakeholders can share their knowledge and expertise.

Three Economics Professors: Three Strategies

How to eliminate extreme poverty in a generation

As Special Advisor to the UN Secretary-General for the implementation of the MDGs, and one of the youngest economics professors at Harvard, Jeffrey Sachs was a staunch promoter of the project to achieve 'the end of poverty',[30] the title of his bestseller published in 2005.

To counter the indifference or the scepticism of many, Sachs asserts that extreme poverty, which kills 20,000 people every day, can be eliminated in 20 years. The project to 'put an end to poverty' follows two intertwined objectives:

1. To enable 1 billion people in the world to escape from extreme poverty, targeting those who earn less than US$1 a day, often

against a background of political instability, while having to fight disease, isolation and environmental difficulties, as well as the lack of access to water, sanitation, medical treatment, education and technology.

2. To make it possible for all the world's poor, including the 1.6 billion people who in 2001 lived on less than US$2 per day, to 'ascend the ladder of economic development'. Sachs says that it is essential to make it possible for these people to get a foot on the first rung of the development ladder so that they can pull themselves above the purely subsistence level and take control over their lives and their futures.

Sachs rejects a certain number of prejudices relating to corruption and throws back at the western countries their argument of poor governance, calling attention to the ravages of slavery, colonialism and the consequences of the Cold War. At the beginning of the twenty-first century, he reminds us, Africa is poorer than at the end of the 1960s, when the IMF and the World Bank started to intervene on the continent.[31]

In contrast to the unique recipe proposed by the Bretton Woods institutions, he pleads for 'clinical economics' which, like medicine, would adapt solutions to each country, carefully monitoring their implementation and constantly evaluating the results. In his view, the principal challenges facing the world are not overcoming laziness or corruption, but taking into account such features as geographical isolation, the prevalence of disease or the vulnerability to extremes of climate in the poorest countries and populations.

These populations are already active and have a realistic perception of their own condition and ways of improving it; they are simply too poor to resolve their problems on their own. They are the victims of the 'poverty trap', a vicious cycle of poverty that is particularly visible in countries with high rates of malaria or other diseases absent in the West. Malaria keeps these countries in poverty. As a result, the potential market for a vaccine is not enough to motivate pharmaceutical companies to undertake the enormous investments in research that are needed.

To enable these countries to reach the first rung on the ladder of economic development, it is necessary to make essential investments in six fields:

1. human capital, such as health, nutrition and training
2. business capital, via machines, equipment and transport

3. infrastructure, in the form of roads, energy, water and sanitation, ports and airports, and telecommunications
4. the environment, through arable lands, healthy soils and biodiversity
5. public institutions, especially commercial laws, the judicial system, government and police services
6. research and development in the form of the scientific and technological expertise which increases business productivity and helps to improve the environment.

Sachs proposes that national poverty reduction strategies should be based on the MDGs, and that donors should draw up agreements with poor countries to finance these strategies. He underlines the need for substantial progress at a global level:

- The debt of the most heavily indebted poor countries should simply be cancelled.
- The popular slogan 'trade not aid' is false for the poorest countries. Trade on its own will not satisfy the essential needs of isolated villages in Africa; they need 'trade *and* aid'.
- The liberalisation of agricultural trade is essential, with the progressive suppression of the enormous subsidies that the rich countries grant their farmers.
- Science must be applied to development, by allocating more resources to meet the research and development needs of the poorest countries in the areas of health, agriculture, energy, climate and conservation of biodiversity.
- Global warming, for which the rich and emerging countries are the main culprits, will have its greatest consequences on the poorest countries and substantial progress must be made in the reduction of pollution and the monitoring of the climate.
- The role of the United Nations in worldwide social and economic regulation must be strengthened.

Sachs asserts that the MDGs can be entirely financed by the Official Development Assistance (ODA) already promised by the donor countries, if they keep their promises. Finding the civic and moral energy for all this may appear daunting, but he reminds us that the *Jubilee 2000* campaign for debt cancellation originally met with strong resistance. However, by becoming a mass movement which collected 22 million signatures from 60 countries, the campaign obtained impressive results.

Sachs recognises that, between 1990 and 2001, globalisation made it possible to cut the number of people living in extreme poverty by 200 million in India and 300 million in China. However, he criticises governments for their failure to institute a legal framework for the activities of multinational corporations. Economic reasoning, he writes, justifies the market economy as long as the rules are fair.

The failure to end poverty

As a former research economist at the World Bank, William Easterly, Professor of Economics at New York University, argues that western efforts to help the rest of the world – spending US$2,300 billion in development assistance over the last five decades – have 'done so much ill and so little good'.[32] Despite this colossal investment, the West has been unable to provide children from the poorest countries with medicines costing 12 cents per dose to stop them from dying of malaria and incapable of providing poor families with mosquito nets costing four dollars each. Rich countries cannot hope to make any progress if they do not address both these tragedies.

The fundamental reason behind the west's failure in its efforts to help developing countries is that, like the colonialists of old, they think that they know best what is good for others. Their aid strategies have two major faults:

- they do not enable the reactions of the needy populations to be recorded
- nobody is held accountable for aid failures.

The real victories over poverty, Easterly demonstrates, have been based on indigenous initiatives. Planners are almost always wrong, because they ignore cultural, political and bureaucratic complexity; they fail to reach the poorest or to provide them with real aid. 'The right plan is to have no plan', is Easterly's solution.[33]

Easterly says that for decades the IMF awarded loans to bankrupt states run by notoriously corrupt leaders, and pleads for an end to 'the pathetic spectacle of the IMF, World Bank and other aid agencies coddling the warlords and kleptocrats'.[34] The growing insistence from donors on 'good governance' should not blind us to the fact that attempts at changing political culture from the outside result in demonstrations of good governance – like the 2,400 reports each year that Tanzania must produce for its donors – rather than in real changes.

It is not by chance that the major economic success stories of recent decades – Japan, China, Taiwan, South Korea, Thailand – have occurred in countries which have never been successfully colonised by the West. The only laggard in the region is the Philippines, which was colonised.

Easterly asks for the ODA to be completely rethought, with a change in attitudes, objectives and methods. Like Sachs before him, he emphasises that ODA will not put an end to poverty. Only endogenous development based on the dynamism of individuals and businesses in a market economy can do that.

The West seeks to help the people living in poverty rather than their governments. It should therefore restrict the objectives of its own agencies, increase accountability and invest more effort in recording the reactions of the populations through greater representation, greater participation and more democratic procedures.

Reaching the bottom billion

Paul Collier, a former director of the Development Research group at the World Bank and Professor of Economics at Oxford University, focuses on the billion inhabitants of 57 countries which, at the turn of the millennium, were poorer than in 1970. He calls them 'The Bottom Billion'.[35] Seventy per cent of them live in sub-Saharan Africa, the others in Haiti, Bolivia, Central Asia, Laos, Cambodia, Yemen, Burma and North Korea. Collier shows that they experienced a tiny growth in per capita income during the 1970s followed by a decrease in this income during the 1980s and 1990s. It is not that these countries have followed a poor growth model; they have not experienced growth at all. Without economic growth it is impossible to put an end to poverty and extreme poverty.

The gap between these countries and the rest of the world has continued to widen since the 1980s and the danger is that they may lose all hope of their children living in a society which has caught up with the rest of the world. The better-off amongst them will continue to flee to more developed countries, leaving behind them vast areas of chaos which are safe havens for criminals and terrorists.

To characterise the situation of these countries, Collier draws on the idea of poverty traps used by Sachs, but applies it to four other areas:

- countries being financially impoverished by interminable civil wars
- failure of natural resources

- being landlocked with bad neighbouring countries
- bad governance in a small country.

As a result of the traps, these countries missed the globalisation train in the 1980s and it is very difficult for them to get on board, now that other countries such as China and India have taken their place using the competitive advantage of their cheap workforce. Change must come from within the poorest countries, but the policies of western countries could make it easier for them to achieve this.

Collier considers that Sachs, the flag bearer for the left, has overestimated the importance of ODA; Easterly, flag bearer for the right, has overestimated not only the negative effects of ODA but also the ignorance and the powerlessness of the West. Collier proposes some innovative solutions using a wide spectrum of policies to support the struggles of people within the poorest societies, who are battling against powerful groups opposed to change.

Action to reduce poverty

Both aid and growth are required yet 'the constituency for aid is suspicious of growth, and the constituency for growth is suspicious of aid'.[36] Public opinion is powerful. The support of citizens from wealthy countries can be decisive in the struggle to reduce poverty, provided that attitudes change.

Collier suggests using three instruments to make the changes that are needed:

- military intervention
- laws and charters
- commercial policies to thwart marginalisation.

Although military intervention is obviously very unpopular, the intervention of the British Army in Sierra Leone in May 2000 within the framework of a UN mandate put an end to the reign of terror of the warlords in that country and opened a new route towards peace and democracy.

Five international charters

For decades, banks in rich countries have taken the money of criminals and dictators from the poorest countries, becoming – however indirectly – supporters of such regimes. In July 2005, following the *Make Poverty History* campaign, the G8 summit at Gleneagles in Scotland announced that ODA would be doubled.

All means must therefore be employed to ensure that this aid is not diverted by corruption.

Collier notes that behaviour is generally guided by norms rather than laws. Norms are voluntary and effective, because they are imposed by peer pressure; for instance, Eastern European countries agreed to adhere to the *Community Acquis* in order to become members of the European Union.

Collier proposes five international charters, which could be used as instruments by those who are fighting for greater justice in the poorest countries. If their governments refused to adopt the charters, they should be held to account. If reformers won power in these countries, they could adopt them; it would subsequently be politically difficult to abandon them.

1.   *Income from natural resources*
Income from oil, or from other extraction industries, must be available for the development of the producer countries.

2.   *Democracy*
There is a need for transparent elections and also a need to ensure that opposition can be freely voiced. In particular, television and radio stations should be free of government monopoly.

3.   *Budgetary transparency*
Create strong pressure from civil society for change by making public the fact that 30–90 per cent of subsidies intended for schools or health clinics do not reach their destination.

4.   *Post-conflict situations*
Provide guidelines to donor countries and draw lessons from the Truth and Reconciliation Commissions.[37]

5.   *Investment*
Guarantee that private investment, whether domestic or foreign, will not be confiscated by governments.

Commercial policies

Collier argues that commercial policies must be redefined to avoid the marginalisation of the poorest countries: by subsidising their own agriculture, wealthy countries weaken that of the countries that they are also trying to help.

Exports from the countries which are home to the 'bottom billion' must be protected from Asian exports and their position within the World Trade Organisation should be re-examined.

Questions that Remain Unanswered

Professors Sachs, Easterly and Collier have moved the debate forward. However, examining them in the light of the life stories from the first part of this book reveals some unanswered questions.

Poverty in rich countries

Jeffrey Sachs states that 'poverty does exist in rich countries, but it is not extreme poverty'; extreme poverty can be found 'only in developing countries'.[38] This excludes Farid and Céline in France (Chapter 3) like tens of millions of other people who are prisoners of poverty in the west. In the most deprived areas of the United States extreme poverty still kills people every day. Although the Millennium Declaration does not state that it only applies to developing countries, it is implicit in most interpretations. There are several explanations for such short-sightedness. The World Bank believes that no one in the richest countries lives on less than US$1 per day, and the statistics of Eurostat only measure relative poverty. But it can be argued that a person who is homeless in Paris, London or New York is in a situation of extreme poverty even if they earn more than US$1 a day by begging.

William Easterly and Paul Collier fail to address the question of great poverty in rich countries. Collier believes that the MDGs represent great progress but they 'track the progress of five of the six billion people on our planet' whereas efforts should be concentrated on 'the bottom billion', living in the 57 countries he lists. He argues that 'We need to narrow the target and broaden the instruments.'[39]

The 'bottom billion' that Collier designates according to their country of residence does not correspond to those Sachs had identified by their daily income of less than one dollar per day, regardless of the country where they lived. In this narrowing of the target, the families of Mercedita in the Philippines (Chapter 2), and Benigno and Alicia Rojas Paucar in Peru (Chapter 4), are excluded. With them are excluded hundreds of millions of poor people who live in poor or middle-income countries which have experienced differing levels of growth over the last decades. Only Paul and his fellow citizens in Burkina Faso (Chapter 1) are potential beneficiaries of these policies. The irony is that Paul has already found a way out of his extreme poverty.

The three authors understand the need to take account of the complexity of societies in a global context in the fight against extreme poverty. However, they exclude populations thrown into poverty from their analysis and their political recommendations.

- Sachs argues that the poorest populations must climb onto the first rung of the development ladder that the industrialised countries have already climbed. The Western development model is presented as having already put an end to extreme poverty.
- Easterly argues that the white man should rather clean up his own backyard and recognise the serious inadequacies of his economic models and his democracies.
- Collier considers that priority should be given to countries without economic growth. The implicit reasoning being that those countries which do have economic growth will thereby eliminate extreme poverty; this has yet to be proven.

In countries with strong demographic growth, economic growth is a required condition for overcoming poverty. The growth of inequality in all countries, and particularly those in eastern Asia, where the proportion of consumption by the most underprivileged dropped dramatically between 1990 and 2004, clearly indicates that not everyone benefits from economic growth, and that some risk being completely left by the wayside.[40]

Social exclusion

The issue of social recognition is not acknowledged by Jeffrey Sachs. William Easterly has shown that it does not only involve the relationship between individuals but also between the West and developing countries. If the West were prepared to accept that it does not have the solutions that developing countries should implement, but that both parties must look for them together, their relationship could be transformed. Joseph Wresinski said:

> We must have the humility to recognise that in terms of human rights and democracy, there are no masters: we are all apprentices who have a lot to learn and to do … The global approach to human rights from the depths of poverty places us all at the same level.[41]

Guidelines on Extreme Poverty and Human Rights

The *Draft Guiding Principles on Extreme Poverty and Human Rights* was adopted by the United Nations Sub-Commission on the Promotion and Protection of Human Rights in September 2006. Drawn up during regional seminars on different continents in consultation with people living in extreme poverty, this project states:

> Poverty persists in all countries of the world, regardless of their economic, political, social and cultural situation ... poverty and exclusion from society constitute a violation of human dignity; and that urgent national and international action is therefore required to eliminate them ... implementation of such policies and programmes without the participation of the persons concerned and their associations and organisations constitutes a violation of the right to participate in public affairs ... public and private bodies working to reduce extreme poverty (whether in industrialised or in developing countries) ... are duty-bound to make their programmes public, disclose their working methods and objectives as well as their funding, and account for their activities.[42]

SOCIAL MOVEMENTS AND THE ERADICATION OF POVERTY

In France, during the second half of the twentieth century, two major figures brought into the public arena the urgent need to fight poverty in partnership with those who were experiencing it: Henri Grouès, known as Abbé Pierre, founder of Emmaus International, and Father Joseph Wresinski, founder of the international movement ATD Fourth World. These two visionaries created movements whose first members were people experiencing extreme poverty; these were movements without religious or political allegiance, which could in no way be defined as 'charitable works'.

The Innovative Contribution of Joseph Wresinski

Wresinski created a political project, developing a strategy and a philosophy. His thinking on the subject of extreme poverty and the means of overcoming it was born of experience. The child of poor immigrant parents, he was already running errands at the age of four. He suffered from the absence of his father and was subjected to the taunts of his peers because of a slight limp.

As an adult, he committed himself totally to the inhabitants of the emergency housing camp at Noisy-le-Grand, near Paris. His determination to live in Noisy-le-Grand, sharing the lifestyle of the poorest, became not just the basis of his life but one of the founding tenets of the movement that he was about to create. Wresinski went on to lead this new movement and to become a member of the Economic and Social Council of France. He spent time with both the elites of the world and also with those living in extreme poverty; he never stopped learning from all of them.

Professor André Gueslin, specialist in the history of poverty in France, says, 'Joseph Wresinski managed to place the accent on the role of exclusion in extreme poverty; that is to say, the cultural and political dimensions, which were little known until then.'[43]

The ATD Fourth World movement breaks with the tradition of giving assistance. In the past, religious charities were concerned with providing immediate aid. Progress was made with the creation of Emmaus by Abbé Pierre, which transformed the beneficiaries of aid into workers at the service of the organisation. Father Joseph, who had experienced extreme poverty, went even further: his policy objective was the conquest or the recovery of rights.[44]

The creation of a new collective identity: the Fourth World

In 1969, after twelve years spent living with the people in Noisy-le-Grand, working alongside them and others in extreme poverty, and corresponding with academics from a number of continents, Joseph Wresinski forged the notion of the 'Fourth World'. In the book he published with the sociologist Jean Labbens, Wresinski wrote:

> The Fourth World is the underclass; a population deprived of culture, unqualified or barely qualified, often under-employed, the least represented because trade unions do not reach them, because social service organisations only find out about them when they put them into care, and because their interests have less weight than those of others in the programmes of political parties.[45]

His definition is very similar to that which Michael Harrington gave to the 'have-nots' of America in 1962:

> [those who] do not, by far and large, belong to unions, to fraternal organisations or to political parties. They are without lobbies of their own ... As a group, they are atomised. They have no face; they have no voice ... Only the social agencies have a really direct involvement with the other America, and they are without any great political power.[46]

The invention of the expression 'Fourth World' was the culmination of determined efforts to rid society of the negative identities imposed on the most underprivileged families. They were often categorised at the time as social cases, maladjusted families, difficult families or misfits they were labelled as deprived, disintegrated and, sometimes, as beyond redemption. (The story of this quest would later become the subject of a book.[47])

The term 'Fourth World' borrows from the terms 'Third World' and 'Fourth Order'.

The term 'Third World' was invented in the 1950s by Alfred Sauvy, at the time of the Cold War between the capitalist and communist blocs. It designated the group of countries that had broken their colonial chains and had gradually become considered as the receptacle of all the poverty in the world. At a time when industrialised countries were 'marked by a great silence about the poor in general',[48] the distant poor of the Third World suddenly appeared, suffering from hunger while the West was living with plenty. By coining the term 'Fourth World', Wresinski's intention was to draw the attention of his contemporaries to the poverty within western democracies which had become invisible to them.

The term 'Fourth Order' originated during the French Revolution to designate a category of people who were not guaranteed political representation. In France in 1789, when the Estates General were called into session, bringing together the representatives of the three estates, or orders, of the realm – the Nobility, the Clergy and the Third Estate – Dufourny de Villiers published a pamphlet of the Fourth Order, noting that the poorest were not taken into consideration in the *Cahiers de Doléances* (a list of grievances drawn up by each of the three estates). He asked for poor workers, the infirm, the destitute and the wretched to have real political representation:

> I will not only ask why there are so many unfortunates but why this enormous class is rejected from the nation? Why does it not have its own representatives?[49]
>
> His question remained unanswered.
>
> Bolstered by its new identity and the questioning that it caused, the ATD Fourth World volunteer corps became unreservedly engaged in political action and protest.[50]

The working class and the underclass

The Industrial Revolution of the nineteenth century caused the question of mass pauperism to resurface. Resisting repression and all sorts of difficulties, the workers movement took shape as a collective force due to the influence of skilled workers and intellectuals.

Marx and Engels distinguished a 'proletariat' amongst the poor from a 'lumpen proletariat':

> In all big towns, [this] forms a mass sharply differentiated from the industrial proletariat, a recruiting ground for thieves and criminals of all kinds living on the crumbs of society, people without a definite trade, vagabonds, men without hearth or home.[51]

Thus, 'the story of the working class and the story of the underclass have diverged', comments Wresinski.[52] Theoreticians have questioned the manner in which the working class movement considers the underclass:

> Is it not true that by rejecting this population from the working class, by refusing to show any solidarity with or understanding of the downtrodden ... the leaders of the workers' movement, keen to maintain their respectability, have propelled the extreme poor towards social oblivion and, through a lack of generosity, have weakened the universal reach of their struggle?[53]

Wresinski observed that, 'beyond a certain level, poverty no longer leads to revolution. The poor person himself becomes the instrument of his impoverishment.'[54]

A people of the Fourth World?

Wresinski radically renewed the question of whether impoverished populations are forever destined to be the objects of measures decided by others, and never the subjects of their own decisions and projects.

Members of ATD Fourth World and its volunteer corps – a group of men and women who choose to spend their lives living alongside the most disadvantaged – called for an alliance with the weakest which would fight for their cause in professional and social circles. The poor and the non-poor are encouraged to join forces in a project of personal and collective transformation, the ultimate aim of which is the eradication of extreme poverty and freedom for all.

Far from being seen as the marginal residue or inevitable waste product of any society, those who are overwhelmed by extreme poverty are at the very heart of the ATD Fourth World collective project. Because extreme poverty has stripped these people of their self-esteem, giving them a negative identity, the non-poor must show them the recognition they need if they are to become subjects and actors. A turning point is needed from both sides; that is to say, a profound internal change or another way of seeing life in general and one's own life in particular, similar to that experienced by Geneviève de Gaulle after meeting families in the Noisy-le-Grand emergency housing camp (see Introduction).[55]

Alain Touraine, the father of 'sociology of action', asks:

What, exactly, is the turning point which allows the excluded person to become an actor? Is it the fact of being taken into consideration or is it being able to show dissent and express one's point of view? Both are necessary.[56]

The Fourth World University Research Group has described and analysed the stages which open the way from shame to pride. This process of transformation begins with an encounter between the excluded and people who show them recognition, making them realise that rejection is not necessarily inevitable. Then, through attending meetings and taking part in public forums, these victims of exclusion become aware that they are not alone in their situation, which frees them of their feelings of guilt and shame. The next stage is a growing awareness that they can become the defenders of a cause; coupled with learning to speak in public, this is a liberating experience. The life story of Farid (Chapter 3) is a good illustration of these stages, resulting in the creation of an activist. Farid was proud to be part of delegations representing his peers at the European Economic and Social Council in Brussels, and to talk to the press about his situation.

This 'people in movement' is neither a social class nor a group of social classes, but the collective actor of the passage from exclusion to recognition. The Fourth World University Research Group writes:

The People of the Fourth World is composed of individuals with a common aim ... dedicated to its main goal which, for the poorest, represents a hope and a path that leads from the shame of poverty to the pride of belonging to this People; and, therefore, how it also incorporates all those who are working towards the same goal, even if they have no personal experience of poverty.[57]

ATD Fourth World offers people from all social, philosophical and religious backgrounds a way forward, and a search for other ways of being. On its utopian side, ATD Fourth World asserts the need to apply human rights to all human beings, including the most impoverished; on its ideological side, it confirms the need to eradicate extreme poverty and put an end to the process of social exclusion. We need to add an ethical dimension to this model by taking the most impoverished as the reference point against which all personal and collective progress should be measured.

Reaching out to and representing the poorest

In order to be the instrument for representing and liberating all those who suffer from social exclusion, the international movement ATD Fourth World must ensure that it remains loyal to the populations for which it was created and adapts to the demands of its times. Wresinski's great fear was that the movement would distance itself from the most disadvantaged populations, or manipulate and betray them. Considering such tendencies as being inherent to all human organisations, he sought to counter them with the spirit and the institutions that he created.

The creation of a volunteer corps was a first response. This body is unusual in the NGO world, notably because of its methods of recruitment and remuneration.

The 'Charity Business' has developed enormously over recent decades, driving NGOs to become ever more professional in their fieldwork and in their fundraising. Many believe that they must offer attractive salaries in order to recruit competent managers, even if those salaries remain below the levels offered by business.

In contrast, ATD Fourth World maintains a recruitment policy based, not on job descriptions and generous salaries, but on a lifestyle choice including proximity to the most disadvantaged populations. Salaries, close to the legal minimum wage in the industrialised countries, are calculated to allow members of the volunteer corps to live decently, if simply; they all earn the same salary, regardless of their position, qualifications or length of service, although their family circumstances or responsibilities are taken into account. Volunteer corps members are encouraged to live in disadvantaged areas.

Making such active choices remains attractive for many, and the ATD Fourth World volunteer corps currently counts around 400 members. Working in this way serves to maintain the radical nature of the organisation.

A further challenge is to avoid oligarchy. Political scientists have demonstrated the existence of an 'iron law of oligarchy', which inevitably results in the confiscation of power by the permanent and senior members of an organisation, assigning a passive role to the rank and file.[58]

Wresinski responded to this issue by saying:

> Our role is to learn what the weariest can teach us. As long as we continue to learn, our place alongside the poorest will be legitimate. It is those who suffer the most who remind us that we have joined forces with them and demand it of us.[59]

In November 2004, a general assembly bringing together ATD Fourth World delegates from 30 countries, adopted this text:

> Our priority is to reach out to the poorest and most ignored people, be alongside them, and create links with them and between them … When the most excluded people can contribute their knowledge and experience to society as equals, extreme poverty will be overcome … [ATD Fourth World] was founded with the conviction that since people have created the conditions for extreme poverty and social exclusion, people can and should make a serious and long-term commitment to eliminating these conditions.[60]

To succeed in this, it is essential for a spirit of enquiry about the lives of the poorest to become a way of life. In this sense, the expression 'the poorest' does not designate a population in extreme poverty but refers to an intention and a constant effort to seek out people who are even poorer and excluded than those already encountered. It is from this perspective that the Fourth World University Research Group stated:

> Basically, representation is rendering present the issues of those who are absent within all bodies where decisions are made, such as political parties, trade unions, associations etc. Our research showed us that this can be achieved with reference to the poorest, not by classing them as a social group in their own right, but by adopting an attitude which constantly seeks out the excluded amongst the excluded.[61]

The political representation that should be promoted is thus not that of a category of people, which would result in corporate representation, but that of a struggle against extreme poverty and exclusion, which concerns us all.

Access to fundamental rights

ATD Fourth World sets up pilot projects to test new ways of enabling populations living in extreme poverty to gain access to their fundamental rights. The projects are set up in specific locations, often in partnership with other organisations and agencies, and take place over a fixed period of time. Usually, pilot projects associate research with action in order to advance understanding, to learn by experience and be able to reproduce it elsewhere, or even to generalise it.

Since the end of the 1960s, ATD Fourth World projects have addressed issues in the fields of:

- children's development[62]
- access to knowledge and culture, health and social protection[63]
- work and professional training[64]
- public speaking[65]
- increased access to culture and education
- training of professionals.

These projects are financed by public authorities or by private foundations. It is vital that this does not lead to an assumption that society in general can delegate their responsibility for abandoned populations to NGOs. The antidote is to involve public and private partners in the implementation of these projects, both in human and financial terms.

In information societies, knowledge is at the heart of the processes of domination, exploitation and exclusion; these exist wherever knowledge is produced, transmitted and acted upon. At the foot of the social ladder, those who do not participate in either the production or the appropriation of knowledge are excluded. To combat this exclusion, it is therefore essential that the most disadvantaged not only benefit from the knowledge transmitted by community, school and university, but that they are associated with the production of knowledge. When their knowledge gained from life experience is combined with knowledge born of action and personal commitment, alongside academic knowledge, everyone's knowledge is enriched.

One current pilot project concerns access to decent employment and to new information and communication technology. It involves around 150 youths and adults amongst the most disadvantaged inhabitants of a poor district of Antananarivo in Madagascar. This four-year project is being run in partnership with the company Telma (Telecom Madagascar), in part funded by the French Development Agency.

Building new agreements in political arenas

To combat extreme poverty and the processes of exclusion, it is necessary to determine who is responsible for them.

Wresinski did not designate a specific social category or institution which was responsible for extreme poverty. Rather it arises from a violent social order, built on attitudes of indifference, ignorance and disdain, which can be found in people of all social classes. In 1983, he produced a report commissioned by the Minister for Planning in France in which he wrote:

> Our society accepts as self-evident that the maximum of collective insecurity be heaped on the members who have the least means to counter it. This de facto agreement is at the root of the longevity of extreme poverty.[66]

Majid Rahnema, in his research on the causes of extreme poverty in the modern world, also wonders how to identify the real culprit behind this systematic destruction of entire populations and their ways of life. He says:

> There is no tyrant to kill. The enemy is nowhere and everywhere ... Despite the supposed conspiracy theories pitting the North against the South, whites against people of colour, Christianity against Islam, the vast majority of those caught up in this economic mega-machine want nothing more than to offer their support for the resolution of these problems.[67]

The struggle against extreme poverty and exclusion does not imply switching roles and places, but a change in rationale. Wresinski stated:

> True liberation will give those who are rejected the means to be free without becoming, in turn, the oppressors. If we accustom the poor to despise the rich, we change the masters by creating new slaves.[68]

Fighting extreme poverty means creating agreements in which the rules of the game are radically transformed. This implies alliances with a variety of individuals and partners with specific objectives. If the enemy is everywhere and nowhere, then potential allies are too. Even in the institutions which implement disastrous policies, there can be allies. The objective of eradicating poverty must become part of us and be written into laws and international conventions. It cannot be achieved unless the most underprivileged populations are accepted as partners in the conception and the implementation of fundamental rights for all.

The adoption of the Wresinski Report, *Chronic Poverty and Lack of Basic Security*, by the Economic and Social Council of France in February 1987 was the prelude to a series of legal breakthroughs. It is recognised as the foundation for a number of historic measures, including basic social benefits, access to healthcare, training, culture, a return to employment. The framework law on the fight against poverty and social exclusion of July 1998 also took root in the Economic and Social Council.[69] The creation of an inter-association forum on housing rights in 2003, the work of the High Committee for Housing the Underprivileged and a number of media campaigns led to the law of March 2007 instituting a legally enforceable right to housing.[70]

With other partners, ATD Fourth World continues to lobby for the European Union to consider the most underprivileged populations as essential partners, and to listen to their contribution to the debate on the purpose of the European Union. Also for any European Constitution to include the objective of the eradication of great poverty and social exclusion, both in Europe and in the rest of the world.[71]

ATD Fourth World works within the United Nations system, in partnership with the NGO Committee on Social Development[72] and the International Trade Union Confederation. The International Day for the Eradication of Poverty is the focus of activity. One successful achievement was the adoption of the *Draft Guiding Principles on Extreme Poverty and Human Rights* adopted in 2006 by the United Nations Sub-Commission on the Promotion and Protection of Human Rights in Geneva.

PERSONAL TRANSFORMATION AND SOCIAL TRANSFORMATION

Christopher Winship, Professor of Sociology at Harvard University, defined Wresinski's unique contribution as follows:

He calls us to understand poverty in a profoundly different way, not just as destitution or oppression but as social isolation. This isolation is created by us all to the degree that we live apart from the poor and fail to understand that their fate is ours.[73]

This approach is radically different from that of the economists examined earlier, and calls their whole approach into question: if extreme poverty is the result of social exclusion as much as extreme material and cultural poverty, then perhaps economic, scientific and technological progress alone are not enough to eradicate it. What personal and collective transformations are required to move from the exclusion to the recognition of impoverished populations?

Exclusion Through the Ages

The sociologist Serge Paugam draws attention to the phenomenon of exclusion:

> Each society contains its element of undesirables, of human beings whose humanity we end up doubting and who should be removed in one way or another.[74]

In his study of the history of poverty in Europe, Bronislaw Geremek shows that poverty has always inspired contradictory feelings: compassion and repulsion from individuals; organisations for aid and repression from the authorities.[75]

Compassion and charity have inspired the creation of numerous institutions over the centuries to relieve the suffering of populations hit by poverty or extreme poverty, including mendicant orders and countless religious congregations at the service of the poor, general hospitals and public assistance.

However, at all periods and on all continents, the fear of disorder, insecurity, epidemics and criminality focuses on the populations which are the furthest from the established norm. These populations are disqualified, demonised and devalued to the extent that they are considered to be useless to society. Science or religion can appear to rationalise the idea, thus making it irrefutable. By the radical inferiority which is given to them, the victims are no longer considered as fully-fledged human beings but as subhuman, the detritus of humanity stripped of their rights. This is how slavery and apartheid were justified. This is how western societies considered vagrants before the Industrial Revolution, and the pitifully poor of the nineteenth century, opening the way to banishment, capital punishment, imprisonment, forced labour and deportation to the colonies.

In traditional societies, identity was conferred at and by birth. Recognition was linked to status, which was linked to birth. Today, recognition no longer depends as much on who we are as on what we do. Members of modern society must fight for recognition, which is won by demonstrating social capacities.

Fear and Loathing of People in Extreme Poverty

Many terms are used across the world today to describe the most impoverished people.[76] In Egypt they are known as *madfoun* – the buried, or the buried alive; in Ghana, *ohiabrubro* – the destitute poor, without work, ill and with no-one to look after them; in Brazil, the *miseraveis* – the destitute; in Russia, the *bombzi*, the homeless; in Bangladesh, the *ghrino gorib* – the despised or hated poor. In Africa it is said that they are possessed by demons or witches, that they are mentally ill and leprous; in Latin America they are known as thieves, homosexuals and inhabitants of the most violent districts; and in South Asia as low caste, rag pickers and the landless.

The ethnologist Patrick Declerck says:

> It is impossible to understand anything about the paradoxes in the help for the homeless if we don't appreciate to what extent they are, consciously or not, the objects of the hatred and vindictiveness of the public. The general message is twofold, contradictory and paradoxical: they are frightening and they are poor victims. Get rid of them, they stink. Help them, they are suffering.[77]

How Evil becomes Commonplace

The fear which grips one at the sight of a homeless person seen in the street is frequently hidden or denied; it is taboo in a society which glorifies 'winners'. Denying the shock and, as a result, the suffering which the encounter with extreme poverty provokes is to blind oneself to the defensive reactions that each person constructs for protection. There are many such reactions. The most common are escape, ignorance and indifference, resulting in mass acceptance of injustice.

Stronger defensive reactions can be disdain or hatred or – on the contrary – compassion and acts of solidarity. Denying the fear that we ourselves feel is the first step in the process of making social injustice commonplace. For those who are in frequent contact with the destitute, such as medical and social workers and the police, denying the pain they feel at the sight of the suffering of these people can lead to emotional coldness, denial and retaliation.

Denying the suffering of the other is a second stage in the process of making evil commonplace. Christophe Dejours[78] shows that to rationalise their behaviour, individuals can 'suspend their ability to think', choosing to wear 'voluntary blinkers' by falling back on all sorts of stereotypes, such as 'those who are unemployed, or in extreme poverty, are there because they want to be'.

When neither the fear that we feel ourselves, nor the suffering of the other, are recognised, there is a third stage in the psycho-sociological process of making evil commonplace: disqualifying the offending party and taking refuge in lies. Throughout history, downtrodden groups have been considered as cursed by God. After their disqualification, they may be relegated to places of punishment or abandon, or be subjected to different forms of exploitation, and even be victims of organised physical elimination, the ultimate manifestation of evil.

Attacking the Roots of Evil

Recognising one's own fear when faced with extreme poverty is the first step to being able to control it. Being able to talk about it, to talk about one's vulnerability with work colleagues or friends allows us to control it better and to master our reactions. Having recognised this existential fear, and the suffering that it provokes in each of us, one of the ways we can stop ourselves from succumbing to disdain or hatred of the impoverished is by learning to recognise the suffering that is tearing them apart. Recognising the suffering of others is to be moved by it, to become less indifferent and therefore more vulnerable – but also to become more human.

If we confront extreme poverty rather than fleeing from it, and listen to those who are experiencing it rather than seeking to silence them, it is impossible to deny their suffering. Face-to-face confrontation with them requires us all to wonder about the origins of this often unspeakable pain, and forces us to look for answers.

Feelings of dissatisfaction and revolt against this suffering can become powerful motors for action. Observing and analysing the violence done to the impoverished, lead to the denouncement of societies which make them into easy targets for the suppressed violence of any group.

Recent social psychology research confirms that a sort of 'anthropological cruelty' is latent within all of us, contained by barriers which are more social than individual. Experiments on groups of students have brought to light what Professor Philip Zimbardo calls 'the Lucifer effect': any normal person, subjected to particular situations or conditions, can abandon his moral scruples and actively cooperate in violence and oppression.[79] The history of the Nazi regime provides abundant proof.

The rejection of the impoverished is conditioned by prejudices which, for centuries, have legitimised and perpetuated indifference, ignorance and disdain. Wresinski never ceased to denounce such prejudices and vigorously contested the idea that all societies produce waste, an inevitable residue. He regretted that history was read, and society analysed, solely in terms of a balance of power, hiding the totally powerless from view.[80]

Wresinski questioned the age-old distinction between the 'good' and 'bad' poor, which was upheld by progressive parliamentarians at the time of the French Revolution. Whilst they asserted, for the first time, the rights of the poor man over society, some of these parliamentarians considered that the 'bad poor' should be deprived of these rights.[81]

Two centuries later, Wresinski retorted:

> The poorest have always been the bad poor and not for reasons of congenital immorality, as mankind has repeated for centuries. They have been, and still are today, the bad poor because it is impossible for anyone, once below a certain level of poverty, to live according to the surrounding community's standards of good behaviour.[82]

He also contests the simplistic nature of the discourse which asserts that there are the rich on the one side, seeking only their own profit, and on the other side the poor, wanting justice and fraternity. This reinforces social barriers rather than helping to overcome them.

A New Perspective on Relationships

The equal dignity of human beings is the moral and ethical foundation of human rights. But recognising the human beings who have been the most disfigured by extreme poverty as our equals in dignity and in rights requires a difficult and continual personal effort. Wresinski confirmed the urgent need to do this in order to respond to their deepest aspirations:

> What the most impoverished constantly seek is consideration. He who has always had it cannot imagine what it is not to have it.

The manner in which one is recognised by others, is dealt with and is honoured is worth more than bread.[83]

Fabrice Matsima, who has personal experience of exclusion in France, gives a vivid picture of what it feels like:

Some people give you this withering look and it turns you to stone and kills you. In their eyes we are immediately branded and labelled, and that label is difficult to shake off. But if someone looks at you in a positive way, it makes you feel alive again, as if you had drunk water from a spring. It feeds your brain and your entire body. It gives you the strength to carry on.[84]

Being recognised by others gives us the force to go forwards. But getting very close to the poorest, in order to recognise them as equals – similar in humanity yet at the same time different – requires us to become poor ourselves, in one way or another. In all eras and in all civilisations, some people have chosen a certain simplicity to fight extreme poverty. It means learning to live without superfluous items in order to content oneself with the essential, a choice at odds with the general trend in a consumer society.

René Cassin, one of the principal authors of the Universal Declaration of Human Rights, states that it is a document which aims to turn us towards the service of others. Each individual must feel that he is indebted to, and the guarantor of the rights, of other individuals in a spirit of human rights and responsibilities.[85]

The great figures in the fight for human rights – Mahatma Gandhi, Martin Luther King, Nelson Mandela, Abbé Pierre and Joseph Wresinski – all drew from the best of the great philosophical and religious traditions to feed their convictions. Social injustice can endure only with the cooperation of populations. The greatest possible number of people must refuse to cooperate with a social order which perpetuates extreme poverty; citizens must move from an attitude of collaboration or resignation to a posture of resistance.

How can such a change be performed, how can it be made easier, and consolidated? The book *Artisans of Democracy*[86] is devoted entirely to these questions. It analyses twelve stories of alliances between people with very diverse responsibilities and poor people, then draws conclusions about the 'stages of their journey'. The internalised recognition of the suffering and fragility of the people who endure extreme poverty is often the source of an alliance with them, of a commitment to act because of them.

Encountering extreme poverty opens new perspectives and results in the discovery that beyond the extreme conditions which disfigure them, human beings maintain an equal dignity and deserve esteem and friendship. This discovery enables us to look deeply into the most fragile parts of ourselves, to accept our own powerlessness without the fear of being destroyed. Reinvesting in these secret areas, which are normally hidden, allows individuals and institutions to rediscover their humanity and free the stifled aspirations which are dormant within them: to become more civilised and to contribute to a more humane and less violent world. This exchange creates deep and enduring connections between excluded and included.

In order to eradicate extreme poverty, Wresinski suggests not only considering the poorest as our equals, but taking them as the reference point of our own progress:

> The message we are bearing has a universal character. Man is the most important. The more he is abandoned, despised, crushed, then the more value he has.[87]

This proposition is comparable to a Copernican revolution, shattering the usual perspective of the understanding of the relationship between men, just as Copernicus and Galileo revised the representation of the world, by proving that the earth turned around the sun and not vice versa.[88]

Wresinski suggests that what is considered to be the most marginal should be placed at the centre of our vision, that what is thought of as of secondary importance must become essential. The heart of his message can be summed up like this: the poorest themselves hold one of the keys to our freedom, if we accept them as partners and guides. Because nobody can free themselves alone, and nobody can free others, we must free ourselves together. We can choose to accept or to refuse this proposition. But it can no longer be ignored as the core proposal for building a society free of extreme poverty.

NOTES

1. Gareth Stedman Jones, *An End To Poverty?: A Historical Debate*, London: Profile Books, 2004.
2. François-Alexandre-Frédéric de La Rochefoucauld-Liancourt, *Premier rapport du Comité de mendicité. Exposé des principes généraux qui ont dirigé son travail*, Paris: Imprimerie Nationale, 1790.
3. Daniel Cohen, *La mondialisation et ses ennemis*, Paris: Hachette, 2005.

4. Preamble to Universal Declaration of Human Rights, adopted and proclaimed by the General Assembly of the United Nations, A/RES/3/217 A, 10 December 1948.

5. Amartya Sen, 'Democracy as a Universal Value', *Journal of Democracy*, Vol. 10, No. 3 (July 1999), and article by Amartya Sen in *The New Republic*, 4 October 2003.

6. John Williamson, 'From Reform Agenda to Damaged Brand Name: A Short History of the Washington Consensus and Suggestions for What to do Next', *Finance and Development*, IMF (September 2003).

7. Quoted by Jacques Ribs, 'Droits de l'homme et mondialisation', *Revue Quart Monde*, Vol. 175, No. 3 (September 2000).

8. Celestine Nyamu-Musembi and Andrea Cornwall, *What is the 'Rights-Based Approach' All About? Perspectives from International Development Agencies*, IDS Working Paper 234, November 2004.

9. Kofi Annan, address given to United Nations General Assembly, SG/SM/6827 HR/4393, 10 December 1998.

10. See UNESCO's *Small Grants Programme*, within its Poverty and Human Rights framework.

11. United Nations Development Programme, *Human Development Report 2004*, New York: UNDP, 2004, p. 132.

12. Le Monde Diplomatique, *L'Atlas*, Paris: Armand Colin, 2006.

13. Article by François Bourguignon in *Le Monde*, 12 December 2007.

14. Le Monde Diplomatique, *L'Atlas*, pp. 64–5, 146–7.

15. United Nations General Assembly, 55th Session, *United Nations Millennium Declaration*, A/RES/55/2, 18 September 2000.

16. United Nations General Assembly, *Report of the Secretary-General on the Work of the Organisation*, A/61/1, United Nations, 2006, pp. 4, 9.

17. United Nations, *Millennium Development Goals Report 2010*, New York: UN, 2010, p. 4.

18. See *Economie et Statistique*, Vol. 383–384–385 (December 2005), particularly Mireille Razafindrakoto and François Roubaud, 'Les multiples facettes de la pauvreté dans un pays en développement: Le cas de la capitale malgache'.

19. All the more so as the value of the dollar has dropped sharply over the last few years.

20. Deepa Narayan and Patti Petesh, *Moving Out of Poverty: Cross-Disciplinary Perspectives on Mobility*, New York: Palgrave Macmillan and the World Bank, 2007, p. 1.

21. United Nations, *Millennium Development Goals Report 2007*, New York: UN, 2007, p. 7.

22. Daniel Verger, 'Bas revenus, consommation restreinte ou faible bien-être: les approches statistiques de la pauvreté à l'épreuve des comparaisons internationals', *Economie et Statistique*, Vol. 383–384–385, (December 2005), p. 27.

23. Blandine Destremau and Pierre Salama, *Mesures et démesure de la pauvreté*, Paris: Presses Universitaires de France, 2002, p. 110.

24. European Community, *Council Decision of 19 December 1984 on Specific Community Action to Combat Poverty*, 85/8/EEC.

25. Amartya Sen, 'Poor, Relatively Speaking', *Oxford Economic Papers*, Vol. 35, No. 2 (July 1983).

26. An eminent sociologist and poverty expert at the OECD, when asked at the end of the 1990s to take these populations into account in his statistics, claimed that it would be too expensive and too complicated to do so.

27. Observatoire National de la Pauvreté et de l'Exclusion Sociale, *Le rapport de l'Observatoire National de la Pauvreté et de l'Exclusion Sociale 2005–2006*, Paris: La Documentation française, 2006, p. 43.

28. Social Protection Committee, *Report on Indicators in the Field of Poverty and Social Exclusion*, October 2001, Council document No. 13509/01.

29. See Gilles Hacourt and Ludo Horemans, *Projet européen d'indicateurs de pauvreté à partir de l'expérience des personnes vivant en situation de pauvreté. Rapport final*, Brussels: European Anti-Poverty Network, September 2003; Service de Lutte Contre la Pauvreté, la Précarité et l'Exclusion Sociale, *Une autre approche des indicateurs de pauvreté*, Collective Report, March 2004.

30. Jeffrey Sachs, *The End of Poverty: Economic Possibilities For Our Time*, New York: Penguin Press, 2005.

31. Ibid., p. 189.

32. William Easterly, *The White Man's Burden: Why the West's Efforts to Aid the Rest Have Done So Much Ill and So Little Good*, New York: Penguin Press, 2006.

33. Ibid., p. 5.

34. Ibid., p. 368.

35. Paul Collier, *The Bottom Billion: Why the Poorest Countries Are Failing and What Can Be Done About It*, New York: Oxford University Press, 2007.

36. Ibid., p. 183.

37. Truth and Reconciliation Commissions are panels which have been set up in more than 25 countries following periods of dictatorship or repression. They work towards national reconciliation by allowing victims to express themselves and the perpetrators of abuses to recognise their guilt towards those victims.

38. Sachs, *The End of Poverty: Economic Possibilities For Our Time*, pp. 18, 20.

39. Collier, *The Bottom Billion: Why the Poorest Countries Are Failing and What Can Be Done About It*, pp. 189, 190, 192.

40. United Nations, *Millennium Development Goals Report 2007*, p. 8.

41. Joseph Wresinski, *Lutter contre la misère, c'est lutter contre la plus flagrante des violations des droits de l'homme*, in Mouvement International ATD Quart Monde, *Rapport moral 1983–1984*, Paris: ATD Quart Monde, 1985.

42. Resolution 2006/9, *Implementation of Existing Human Rights Norms and Standards in the Context of the Fight Against Extreme Poverty*, in Human Rights Council of the United Nations General Assembly, *Report of the Sub-Commission on the Promotion and Protection of Human Rights on its Fifty-Eighth Session*, A/HRC/Sub.1/58/36, 11 September 2006.

43. See especially André Gueslin, *Gens pauvres, pauvres gens dans la France du XIXè siècle*, Paris: Aubier, 1998; André Gueslin, *Les gens de rien. Une histoire de la grande pauvreté dans la France du XXè siècle*, Paris: Fayard, 2004; André Gueslin and Dominique Kalifa, *Les exclus en Europe, 1830–1930*, Paris: Éditions de l'Atelier, 1999.

44. André Gueslin, 'L'impact d'un pionnier', *Revue Quart Monde*, Vol. 204, No. 3 (November 2007).

45. Joseph Wresinski in Jean Labbens, *Le Quart Monde, la condition sous-prolétarienne*, Paris: Éditions Science et Service, 1969.

46. Michael Harrington, *The Other America: Poverty in the United States*, New York: Touchstone, 1997, p. 6.

47. Fourth World University Research Group, *The Merging of Knowledge: People in Poverty and Academics Thinking Together*, Lanham: University Press of America, 2007, pp. 98–101.

48. Philippe Sassier, *Du bon usage des pauvres. Histoire d'un thème politique, XVIè–XXè siècle*, Paris: Fayard, 1990, p. 11.

49. Louis Pierre Dufourny de Villiers, *Cahiers du quatrième ordre celui des pauvres journaliers, des Infirmes, des indigens, etc., l'Ordre sacré des infortunés; ou Correspondance philanthropique entre les infortunés, les Hommes sensibles et les Etats-généraux: Pour suppléer au droit de députer directement aux Etats, qui appartient à tout français, mais dont cet Ordre ne jouit pas encore*, 1789, pp. 12–13.

50. Gilles Anouil, *The Poor are the Church: A Conversation with Fr. Joseph Wresinski, Founder of the Fourth World Movement*, Mystic, CT: Twenty-Third Publications, 2002, p. 139.

51. Karl Marx, *The Class Struggles in France: 1848-1850*, Marx/Engels Internet Archive, 1995 and 1999.

52. Anouil, *The Poor are the Church: A Conversation with Fr. Joseph Wresinski, Founder of the Fourth World Movement*, pp. 83–96.

53. Jacques Julliard, *Crise et avenir de la classe ouvrière*, Paris: Éditions du Seuil, 1979, p. 11.

54. Joseph Wresinski, in Labbens, *Le Quart Monde, la condition sous-prolétarienne*, p. 16.

55. See section 'An Encounter with Extreme Poverty', in Chapter 1.

56. Alain Touraine, 'Communiquer pour être', *Revue Quart Monde*, Vol. 166, No. 2 (April 1998).

57. Fourth World University Research Group, *The Merging of Knowledge: People in Poverty and Academics Thinking Together*, p. 114.

58. Erik Neveu, *Sociologie des mouvements sociaux*, Paris: La Découverte, 2005, p. 24.

59. Joseph Wresinski, address given to ATD Fourth World volunteer corps members during an evaluation and planning meeting, 19 August 1985.

60. Text from the International Movement ATD Fourth World General Assembly, November 2004.

61. Fourth World University Research Group, *The Merging of Knowledge: People in Poverty and Academics Thinking Together*, p. 439.

62. Alwine de Vos van Steenwijk, *Il fera beau … le jour où le sous-prolétariat sera entendu*, Paris: Éditions Science et Service, 1977.

63. François-Paul Debionne, *La santé passe par la dignité. L'engagement d'un médecin*, Paris: Éditions de l'Atelier and Éditions Quart Monde, 2000.

64. ATD Fourth World, *Finding Work: Tell Us the Secret*, Paris: ATD Fourth World Research Institute, 1996.

65. ATD Fourth World, *Participation Works: Involving People in Poverty in Policy-Making*, London: ATD Fourth World, 2000.

66. Joseph Wresinski, *Réfuser la Misère. Une pensée politique née de l'action*, Paris: Cerf et Éditions Quart Monde, 2007, p. 265.

67. Majid Rahnema, *Quand la misère chasse la pauvreté*, Paris: Fayard/Actes Sud, 2003, p. 205.

68. Anouil, *The Poor are the Church: A Conversation with Fr. Joseph Wresinski, Founder of the Fourth World Movement*, pp. 75, 160.

69. Jacques Dermagne, in a speech given to open the seminar *Extrême pauvreté et emploi décent* at the Palais d'Iéna, Paris, France, on 11 December 2006.

70. The *Loi du 5 mars 2007 instituant le droit au logement opposable et portant diverses mesures en faveur de la cohésion sociale* allows homeless people to take local authorities to court to guarantee their right to housing.

71. ATD Fourth World, *'What We Say Should Change Our Lives': Extreme Poverty, Involvement and Access for All to Fundamental Rights*, Paris: Fourth World Publications, 2006.

72. Committee of NGOs having consultative status with the United Nations Economic and Social Council (ECOSOC).

73. Christopher Winship in Anouil, *The Poor are the Church: A Conversation with Fr. Joseph Wresinski, Founder of the Fourth World Movement*, p. xiii.

74. Serge Paugam, *Les formes élémentaires de la pauvreté*, Paris: Presses Universitaires de France, 2005, p. 147.

75. Bronislaw Geremek, *Poverty: A History*, Oxford: Blackwell, 1997.

76. Deepa Narayan et al., *Voices of the Poor: Can Anyone Hear Us?*, New York: Oxford University Press, 2000, pp. 135–6.

77. Patrick Declerck, *Les naufragés. Avec les clochards de Paris*, Paris: Éditions Plon, 2001, pp. 24, 104.

78. Christophe Dejours, *Souffrance en France. La banalisation de l'injustice sociale*, Paris: Éditions du Seuil, 1998.

79. Philip G. Zimbardo, *The Lucifer Effect: Understanding How Good People Turn Evil*, New York: Random House, 2007.

80. Joseph Wresinski, *Refuser la misère. Une pensée politique née de l'action*, Paris: Cerf et Éditions Quart Monde, 2007, pp. 88–93.

81. François-Alexandre-Frédéric de La Rochefoucauld-Liancourt distinguished between 'the real poor [and] the bad poor, that is to say those known as professional beggars and vagabonds, who refuse to work and disturb the peace' in *Plan du travail du comité, pour l'extinction de la mendicité, présenté à l'Assemblée nationale, en conformité de son décret du 21 janvier [1790]*, Imprimerie Nationale, 1790.

82. Wresinski, *Refuser la misère. Une pensée politique née de l'action*, p. 165.

83. Joseph Wresinski, 'Quart-Monde et évangile', *Revue Igloos*, Vol. 87–88 (Winter 1975/Spring 1976), p. 23.

84. Fabrice Matsima, 'Si vous regardez l'autre comme quelqu'un qui vous ressemble …', *Revue Quart Monde*, Vol. 186, No. 2 (May 2003), p. 7.

85. Quoted in Daniel Fayard, 'Quand le plus pauvre donne l'intelligence du combat', *Revue Quart Monde*, Vol. 168, No. 3 (December 1998), p. 23.

86. Jona M. Rosenfeld and Bruno Tardieu, *Artisans of Democracy: How Ordinary People, Families in Extreme Poverty and Social Institutions Become Allies to Overcome social Exclusion*, Lanham, VA: University Press of America, 2000.

87. Joseph Wresinski, 'L'important est l'homme', *Revue Quart Monde*, Vol. 175, No. 3 (September 2000), p. 24.

88. Eugène Notermans, 'Une révolution copernicienne', *Revue Quart Monde*, Vol. 204, No. 3 (November 2007), p. 34–6.

Conclusion:
The Eradication of Extreme Poverty:
A Civilising Project

Xavier Godinot

As this book draws to a close, it is time to look again at what we have learnt.

According to historians, the very idea that extreme poverty could be eradicated dates from the birth of democracy in the West, when the economy was becoming increasingly global in nature and science was making great advances. During the 1790s, reformers affirmed that it was possible to put an end to extreme poverty and that poor populations had rights over society. A century and a half later, the preamble to the Universal Declaration of Human Rights considered that the highest aspiration of the common people was a world free from fear and want.[1] The Millennium Declaration of September 2000, adopted by 180 Heads of State and Governments, committed them to 'spare no effort' to put an end to extreme poverty by 2015.[2]

Yet it is difficult to distinguish between poverty, which must be reduced, and extreme poverty, which must be eradicated. Extreme poverty – a combination of destitution and social exclusion – undermines the very identity and dignity of human beings; that is why it must be eradicated.

UNDERSTANDING HOW PEOPLE SEE THE COURSE OF THEIR LIVES

The first part of this book, 'Resisting Extreme Poverty Every Day', immerses the reader in the life stories of people in situations of great poverty in four countries on different continents: Burkina Faso, France, Peru and the Philippines.

Understanding how the poorest see themselves and society is as difficult now as it was in the past. The contemporary perspective on poverty and development is conceived by experts from all fields who tend to look at society from the top down; it often stifles the voices of those in extreme poverty who have acquired a unique expertise about life by looking at society from the bottom up.

The stories in Part One are the fruit of this bottom-up experience. They are written by the people themselves in association with those living and working alongside them over the long term, with input from both local and foreign university professors. Writing these life stories was therefore the result of a long learning process, intimately linked to action. We can follow periods of crisis and of continuity of these people's lives and see them from their own point of view.

Great care was taken to ensure that they took a full part in the writing process and did not simply tell their stories for others to record. They gave their own interpretation of events and were able to modify the drafts and the final version. Two of the four stories tell of a rise in social status, leaving extreme poverty behind; the other two are an account of extreme poverty persisting over several generations, despite all the efforts made to escape from it, yet with strong hopes of a better future for the next generation.

Part Two of this book, 'Human Rights and Responsibilities: The Foundations for Living Together', places the shared lessons from Part One in the context of current debates on globalisation, democracy and the role of social movements.

All cultures seem to recognise the ethical principle that freedom and individual rights are counterbalanced by our responsibilities towards our neighbours, our country, humanity as a whole and the living world. But caution is needed in drawing conclusions from testimonies from four continents and four very different cultures. To understand extreme poverty and develop strategies for its eradication, the specific characteristics of each country must be taken into account; this is particularly the case when dealing with the question of 'national psyche' – that is to say, a country's specific social approach to poverty as defined by its past, its institutions and its economic situation.

The national psyche of France, where people who are classed as 'poor' form a disqualified minority, has been characterised by an extraordinary anxiety for the last 20 years. In a society which is fragmented and haunted by the fear of loss of social status, this has resulted in nearly half the French population believing that they could become homeless one day.

However, populations classed as 'poor' are numerous in the so-called 'middle income' countries, of which the Philippines and Peru are two, while they form the majority in Burkina Faso and other 'least developed' countries. These three countries have been profoundly affected by a long history of colonial domination which has persistently weakened the confidence of the population in their own abilities. Today, the specific situation of each country can be explained by historical, political and geographical factors; for instance, Burkina Faso has to overcome the challenge of a country with a high rate of illiteracy, no access to the sea, poor road infrastructure, frequent droughts and endemic diseases such as malaria.

RESOURCES AND OBSTACLES

Chapter 5, 'Basic Ties and Fundamental Rights', seeks to identify both the resources that people experiencing extreme poverty have to draw on and the obstacles they encounter. Analysing the four life stories in this way demonstrates that, in order to extricate themselves from extreme poverty, the individual or the family must be able to draw on basic ties which allow them access to their fundamental rights.

Four types of social ties between the individual and society are threatened by extreme poverty and therefore need to be reinforced:

- family ties
- community ties
- ties formed by organic participation
- citizenship ties.

Family and Community

The need to strengthen *family and community ties* is apparent in the four life stories. Preserving the family unit (however defined) and the happiness of its members appear to be values which are widely shared. But the conjugal bond is constantly threatened by insecurity and poverty, whilst the bond between parents and children is threatened by extreme poverty. Farid and Céline's child was taken into care at birth. Mercedita was first forced into having her baby son adopted, as she feared she would not have the means to bring him up, and then compelled to place her daughters in an orphanage to guarantee them the education she was unable to pay for.

All four stories demonstrate the importance of community ties in overcoming adversity. However, these ties are essentially made with people of the same social class, which appears to be both a refuge for its members and a barrier to contact with more affluent groups. While these ties help in resisting the daily grind of extreme poverty, they offer few outlets for escape.

In France, Farid constructed a life for himself by taking Céline as a partner, which protected him from the danger of falling into permanent vagrancy. Both then benefited from housing within the structure of a Family Support Programme, which helped them to find their way out of extreme poverty. In Burkina Faso, Paul extricated himself from the vicious cycle of life on the streets with the support of an experienced team who helped him to renew ties with his family and his village. Their stories confirm the sociological observation that people who have experienced parental love and benefited from a stable family life in their childhood are more able to break the cycle of extreme poverty than those who did not.

Paradoxically, the strength which the real family represents, despite often being mutilated by extreme poverty and reconstructed, has received little attention in programmes to overcome poverty.

Employment

The need to *find a home and decent employment* appears clearly in the four stories, all of which highlight the difficulties of the daily fight for survival in the informal economy which, with its multiplicity of poorly-paid activities, offers neither stability, regular income nor social protection. The possibilities of participation in the world of work come primarily from family or community ties.

The struggle for survival means that children are obliged to work from a very early age, making it more difficult for them to attend school. The low-paid, whether employees or self-employed, become poorer during their working life due to the progressive decline of their health and their capacity to work. Every time that Mercedita managed to put some money aside, either to build her savings or to reinvest in her own business, she was obliged to use it to cover medical costs.

Good health, access to housing and decent employment are clearly the keys for emerging from extreme poverty and, thus, the indivisibility of fundamental rights becomes apparent: the loss of one often leads to the loss of others and access to one often makes it possible to accede to the others. The examples of this are numerous. In France, Farid, who was in good health, found decent employment once he had been rehoused and given support through a two year programme to integrate himself into the world of work. In Burkina Faso, Paul's father and his uncles gave him access to an agricultural activity which generated earnings; his ability to read and count meant that he could find better-paid employment in a restaurant.

Despite these success stories, the general context remains very unfavourable for the most disadvantaged populations. In France in October 2007, 100,000 people were classified as homeless, 3 million were poorly housed and the employment rate for young people in the so-called 'difficult' neighbourhoods fluctuated between 30 per cent and 50 per cent. For their part, developing countries have not observed a reduction, but an increase, in informal employment, demonstrating the failure of the policies which have been implemented there. The main causes are the rapid demographic growth of these countries, the increasing number of women entering the employment market and a massive rural exodus, linked to the growing poverty of farmers.

The impoverishment of small farmers in a number of Third World countries, and particularly in sub-Saharan Africa, is mainly due to a lack of support for agriculture and particularly the production of food, linked to an ideology of development through industrialisation which has pervaded for decades. Climate and environmental disasters, added to the commercial policies of developed countries, are also at the root of this situation.

Development policies should therefore include increased support for food production and the promotion of decent employment, too often absent from the Strategic Frameworks for Poverty Reduction financed by the Bretton Woods institutions.

Micro-credit resources should be mobilised to this end, but alternative programmes are also required. The development of social protection systems should also be encouraged and supported in the numerous countries where they are currently absent.

Education

Improving the relationship between populations living in extreme poverty and formal schooling means reconciling *community education* and *school education*. The first education a child receives is through its parents, family and community. This education appears strongly in all the life stories but can sometimes clash with the values taught in schools.

The education system set up by the colonial powers in Africa was seen as an instrument of humiliation by the indigenous populations, so it is not surprising that they show a certain resistance to formal schooling, evident notably in the number of children who abandon their schooling.

In Burkina Faso, in the period 1996–2005, only 35 per cent of boys and 29 per cent of girls of primary school age actually attended lessons. And yet, if they ceased to denigrate traditional education, schools could have a vital role to play in minimising the contradictions between tradition and modernity.

The situation is markedly different in Peru and the Philippines, where 96.8 per cent and 90.4 cent respectively of children of primary school age were enrolled in 2009, although there is recurring criticism of the poor standard of education often on offer. In Peru, state schools in rural zones offered on average only one day of teaching per week at the beginning of the millennium.

Both teacher training and the level of salaries are often inadequate to accelerate the development of schools. Yet the life stories from Peru and the Philippines show that parents are ready to make considerable sacrifices for their children's education. It would be so much easier for them if primary and secondary education were genuinely, and in practical terms, free.

The problems are different in France: a recent official report criticised a primary education system that is 'resigned' to early failure, where there has been no improvement in results over the last ten years.

The most difficult task remains that of improving the relationship between impoverished populations and the education system. If education is to be offered successfully to the most disadvantaged populations, there must be more dialogue between educators and parents, and parents must be recognised as essential partners in the success of their children.

Citizenship

The analysis of citizenship ties shows the need to *encourage new forms of participative democracy*. The four life stories illustrate the difficulties for the most underprivileged to obtain the documents needed to exist as citizens with rights.

The obstacles to registering a birth are so great in developing countries that, in 2011, UNICEF estimated that only 51 per cent of the estimated total of births were registered[3] while, in Central and Eastern Europe, the right to register a birth has long been denied to the seven million members of the Roma population. Registration campaigns in this field have made significant progress.

The life stories show that, whether they hold the necessary documentation or not, the most deprived populations struggle to make their voices heard and to have their interests taken into account in their community, in schools, in the health system, in the media and in the concerns of the political classes.

The violence which shook low-income urban districts in France in 2005 was proof of the outrage felt by some of the young inhabitants of these areas at being excluded from economic, social and cultural development. Similarly, the housing crisis in France, particularly for the most underprivileged populations, reveals how poorly their needs and expectations are taken into account by representative democracy.

In the Philippines, Burkina Faso and Peru, citizens are faced with impecunious states and fragile democracies. The financial flow from the southern debt-laden states to the north, through the service of external debt in the Third World, has for years been many times greater than the money these states receive from the north through Official Development Assistance (ODA). This situation illustrates a structural violence in the world order, for which the self-interested lenders of the north and the corrupt regimes of the south are jointly responsible.

The Structural Adjustment Programmes, implemented and financed by the Bretton Woods institutions to reduce the debt in developing countries, have only made the situation worse. The commercial policies of the industrialised countries are often unjust towards those in the south. Nevertheless, the life stories demonstrate that it is possible to advance participative democracy with the most underprivileged populations and to train representatives from their ranks.

Establishing the basic ties in these four areas appears, therefore, to be one of the conditions necessary for access to fundamental rights, as well as being an essential condition for the recognition of the dignity of the most disadvantaged. But this recognition alone, coming as it all too often does from people of a similar social milieu, is too restricted and leaves Mercedita in the Philippines or the Rojas Paucar parents in Peru with no way out of extreme poverty.

It is only by uniting recognition and redistribution that the conditions needed for justice for all will be met. It is here that globalisation has a role to play in achieving universal human rights.

THE IMPACT OF GLOBALISATION ON THE MOST DISADVANTAGED

Globalisation is part of human history. The Universal Declaration of Human Rights, which was pronounced on 10 December 1948, was a major step towards the process of globalisation. The 1970s opened a new era of globalisation, with the growing number of multinational companies, the development of information and communication technologies and the expansion of trade and financial exchanges.

Today, two approaches to globalisation compete on the world stage:

- the market economy
- human rights.

While the market economy is extremely efficient at meeting the needs of solvent individuals by enabling businesses to make profits, it must continually create new needs in order to sustain itself. Without intervention from the state and from non-profit organisations, it does not allow the needs of the poorest populations to be met because they do not represent a source of profit in the short term.

The demonstrations against the World Trade Organisation in Seattle in 1999, and the *Jubilee 2000* campaign to cancel debt in the Third World at the turn of the millennium, demonstrated the need to find a compromise between the market economy approach to globalisation and the human rights approach, which are not necessarily antagonistic. Seeking to achieve this in launching the Global Compact, the United Nations Secretary-General invited major corporations, NGOs and public authorities to move from conflict to cooperation in order to implement human rights together.[4]

It was also the ambition of the Millennium Declaration, adopted in September 2000.

The Millennium Development Goals (MDGs) in many ways represent a change in strategy. For the first time, the United Nations General Assembly has made it possible for a large number and diversity of stakeholders to work together to achieve the objectives, subject to deadlines and defined targets of poverty reduction and an end to extreme poverty across the world.

Financial poverty indicators are both the most used and the most contested indicators of these defined targets. Recent European research has shown them to be unreliable, as the different types of insecurity only partially intersect; a multidimensional approach to household poverty is therefore essential. Furthermore, the implementation of objectives that are only partial – such as that of reducing the population living in extreme poverty by half between 1990 and 2015 – may well focus efforts on the categories of population the most able to 'find a way out' and leave those left behind even more disadvantaged.

Finally, the MDGs are based on the assumption that the rich countries will honour their commitments to supplement the financial capacities of the developing countries; this has yet to be proven to be the case. Thus, in June 2010, with five years remaining to the 2015 deadline, progress on the MDGs showed mixed results, indicating that improvements had been made but that much still remained to be done.[5]

Chapter 6, 'Democracy, Globalisation and Extreme Poverty', presented the theses of three eminent economists – Sachs, Easterly and Collier – who have studied the links between globalisation and extreme poverty; these were then examined in the light of the analysis drawn from the life stories. Their contributions are valuable but are also open to criticism when re-examined in the light of the life stories.

Common to their contributions is the importance they accord to social movements as a means of social transformation. Interest is currently growing in organisations whose membership includes people living in poverty, as opposed to traditional charitable or humanitarian organisations.

Joseph Wresinski developed an original philosophy and mode of action concerning the conditions under which these organisations can represent the poorest people in the public arena and the role they can play in the fight against extreme poverty. This was rooted in his experience as an immigrant child born into extreme poverty, as an adult immersed for ten years in the emergency housing camp of Noisy-le-Grand and, finally, as spokesperson for the poorest recognised at both the national and international level. What he built with others does not constitute a model to imitate but a legacy of questions and answers for specific contexts. Any individual or organisation seeking justice can draw on them to inform their thinking and their course of action.[6]

PERSONAL TRANSFORMATION AND SOCIAL TRANSFORMATION

If extreme poverty is not simply a problem of extreme material poverty, but also of rejection, disdain and social exclusion, then economic, scientific and technical progress are not enough on their own to eradicate it. The struggle against extreme poverty has dimensions which are not only scientific, economic and political, but also cultural and spiritual.

Current sociological and anthropological knowledge shows that exclusion has come down to us through centuries and civilisations.

Every society has its share of human beings whose humanity is questioned for a variety of reasons. Every person bears his part of 'anthropological cruelty' held in check by barriers which are less individual than social. The fear of disorder, insecurity, impurity, contamination and malediction is personified in populations which are the furthest from the established norm, and we seek to rid ourselves of them in one way or another, including by physical elimination.

Evil and social injustice become banal in a process founded on fear, where the violence, and sometimes extreme violence, imposed on certain categories of the population is eventually seen as normal. When neither the fear that one feels personally when faced with people disfigured by extreme poverty, nor their own suffering, is recognised, the conditions are ripe for those people to play the role of scapegoat, responsible for the ills that society cannot handle.

Age-old prejudices which distinguish between the 'deserving poor', who must be helped, and the 'undeserving poor', who must be punished, contribute to the legitimisation of the violence shown to these disqualified groups.

Conversely, the internalised recognition of the suffering, fragility and hopes of the people who are living in extreme poverty is often the origin of an alliance with them and of a commitment to act because of them. Meeting and acknowledging the people who have been the most disfigured by extreme poverty as one's equals, in terms of dignity and rights, requires difficult and continuous personal effort, made easier by support from a collective movement. This effort is essential if the excluded are to receive the much needed recognition which will give them the strength to go forward.

Being close enough to the poorest to recognise them as equals implies commitment and personal choices which go against the norm. Paradoxically, Wresinski asserts that the poorest hold one of the keys to our personal freedom and the progress of our societies.

Redefining Wealth

Faced with the challenges of today's world, it is no longer possible to conceive the struggle against poverty and extreme poverty without redefining wealth and what we consider valuable. The implicit objective of western development, which extends to globalisation, is a progression towards unlimited material abundance for all. The assumption is that by developing and stimulating what is superfluous, we enable each individual to gain access to the essentials. In this race, the difference between the essential and the superfluous disappears. Little by little it becomes apparent that this theory leads to a dead end.

Spreading the Western way of life across the planet poses important ecological problems. In a world where limited natural resources are under serious threat, it is essential to make strides in terms of sustainable development, according to the terms of the Brundtland report;[7] a substantial change is needed in the production and consumption methods propagated by the West. This transformation could occur in tandem with technical changes, a regeneration of values abandoned by the West, and a greater dialogue between cultures. Jean-Baptiste de Foucauld states: 'Abundance cannot be simultaneously material, relational and spiritual. There are always conflicts between these three dimensions.'[8] He proposes the concept of 'frugal and inclusive abundance'.[9]

'Live simply so that others may simply live', said Mahatma Ghandi. Majid Rahnema suggests that the efficiency revolution be completed by a sufficiency revolution, and reminds us that 'like the family, simplicity is always said to be declining but never disappears'.[10] The quest for simplicity, he reminds us, is deeply rooted in indigenous societies but also has solid roots in the West, from the Greeks to the Americans.

Amartya Sen has argued at length that development must not target growth in material wealth but in the freedom of individuals, which is substantially different. The sociologist Edgar Morin considers that more dialogue between cultures would greatly facilitate evolution towards a globalisation at the service of the human race, meaning a globalisation of understanding.

> Cultures must learn from each other, and the arrogant Western culture, which has positioned itself as the teaching culture, must also become a learning culture ... The West must integrate the virtues of other cultures in order to correct the unbridled activism, pragmatism, quantitativism and consumerism which it has unleashed at home and abroad. But it must also protect, regenerate and propagate the best of its culture which has produced democracy, human rights and the protection of the private world of the citizen.[11]

Today's globalisation is marked by a continuing battle between the differing approaches of economic liberalism and human rights, in which the former has often been the victor. Jeffrey Sachs and the economists who have discussed and completed his proposals underline the immense possibilities that the market economy offers, but also the need to correct its failings with a massive aid effort to developing countries, the modalities of which should be completely rethought. They also highlight the need to improve the legal framework of the economy for ethical and political reasons.

Joseph Wresinski reminds us that human rights indicate the road to follow to humanise globalisation; he suggests that the victims of extreme poverty should be a reference point for the effectiveness of rights for all. As the lawyer Mireille Delmas-Marty has suggested, significant progress could be made by using Human Rights law to:

> reconcile conflicting values, by asserting the indivisibility of fundamental rights as a whole, and to readjust the balance of power, by ensuring that States and businesses could be obliged to enforce them.[12]

Of course, this also applies to the Bretton Woods institutions.

This is a vast area of civic activity open to all who believe that the implementation of human rights is of greater value than reducing the world to a commodity. No agreement exists for a requirement to respect rights to be included in laws. Nevertheless, progress can be made through the voluntary signing of the various compacts, charters and guiding principles.

In this search for a different development model – one that places value on other forms of wealth – it is vital to structure correctly the objectives of economic development, environmental improvement and social cohesion. This is the very meaning of sustainable development.

Amartya Sen emphasises that one of the central problems is:

> the need for an integrated formulation ... The elimination of poverty and the consolidation and enrichment of the environment could be seen as different parts of an integrated task.[13]

In concrete terms this means that environmental protection programmes could be used to obtain decent employment and training for the most disadvantaged populations, whilst respecting local cultures. Currently these approaches are most commonly disassociated, and even antagonistic, as Pan Yue, the Deputy Director of the Chinese State Environmental Protection Administration, said:

> The pursuit of material gain seems to have become the only aim of society, and the result of this has been the decline in moral

standards. Our traditional culture, which places the accent on the harmony between man and nature, has been perceived as a straitjacket restricting economic growth.[14]

Inventing a model of sustainable development implies drawing on the best of the traditional values practised by numerous peoples; these have been stifled by the Western development model. The life stories demonstrate the importance of social values in Africa and Asia, and of reciprocity as experienced in Latin America. These values are part of the human heritage, which we must draw on to reinvent wealth today.

Instead of insisting on simple conformity to the dominant model, development programmes promoted by international institutions and governments could simultaneously encourage the recognition and support of cultures on the one hand, and the blending of know-how and cultures on the other.

The World Bank has recently published a collection of 60 contributions describing how African communities strengthen their capacity to lead their own development in the context of globalisation. These contributions show that communities are keen to combine their indigenous knowledge with modern knowledge and technology to obtain better results.

In the introduction to his progress report, the then President of the United Republic of Tanzania recommends to development experts, researchers and politicians that they:

> humbly learn from these cases. They [do not] seek to romanticize indigenous knowledge or traditions, or suggest that global knowledge is irrelevant. Rather, they show that indigenous and global knowledge working together in a democratic, self-determined way is the best combination to foster sustainable development.[15]

Renewing Democracy

As Amartya Sen has shown in his work on famine, representative democracy is not only a value in itself, as an option desired by numerous citizens who wish to be associated with the decisions that affect them, it also has a clear instrumental value in the fight against extreme poverty. This is demonstrated by the fact that in current times there are no longer famines in democratic countries, no matter how poor they are. All the famines of the last 50 years have occurred in countries under dictatorships, where the media are controlled and cannot report the needs and suffering of the starving. In such situations, the social distance between the governments and the starving is such that the deaths of the latter leave the former indifferent. In democratic countries, the incidence of serious food shortages immediately results in economic, social and political reactions which check the phenomenon.

Nevertheless, associative, trade union and political representation of the poorest populations remains uneven in all democratic countries. New approaches to participative democracy must therefore be developed. For example, the International Day for the Eradication of Poverty offers an opportunity which could be better exploited to create or intensify the dialogue between a large diversity of social classes. This day is one of the rare occasions in the year when people living in extreme poverty are visible and dare to address messages freely to the authorities. The fact that important people are present and take notice of them boosts the morale of the most disadvantaged, who go home with greater resolve to fight extreme poverty. The important figures who support this strategy of encounters acquire new perceptions which allow them to orient their actions and programmes better for fighting extreme poverty.

Throughout the world, many initiatives, often very simple ones, are being implemented to support the most disadvantaged in their efforts. It is important for them to be enhanced and to reinforce each other and inspire changes in social and economic policies.

> Whilst the poorest and those who associate themselves with them do not participate as equals in arenas where other citizens debate, and where tomorrow's society is being built, the struggle against extreme poverty will never be anything other than a marginal project. It will remain a fruitless exercise in catching up and repairing which will never achieve its objective, precisely because it is not at the heart of the challenges that society has adopted for its present and its future. Participative democracy is not only one of a number of tools for better sharing citizenship, it is also a prerequisite for the creation of a social existence jointly constructed by the diverse members of a society.[16]

FIGHTING EXTREME POVERTY: A SOLEMN DUTY

On reaching the end of this book, the reader may feel giddy or gripped by doubt. The eradication of extreme poverty is a particularly demanding goal, which requires concerted action on many different levels – economic, social, cultural, scientific, political, ethical and spiritual – implicating all elements of society. It is tempting to think that the simple citizen is powerless and to believe that if exclusion has existed in all civilisations, our era will not bring it to an end.

However, the life stories have shown that it is possible to overcome extreme poverty by joining forces with those who are experiencing it. Farid and Céline in France and Paul in Burkina Faso experienced the extreme poverty of those who live on the streets, and have now put that behind them because they met people who had made the eradication of extreme poverty a priority in their lives.

Although this association is essential, it is not enough on its own to overcome extreme poverty. As this book has shown, numerous changes are required. But if extreme poverty is an amalgam of poverty and social exclusion, any person, however powerless he or she may be, can help to diminish it by showing recognition to those experiencing it. Any act by which one recognises as an equal, in terms of rights and dignity, a person who is a prisoner of extreme poverty is an act which attacks extreme poverty by reducing social exclusion.

'Some people give you this withering look and it turns you to stone and kills you', says Fabrice Matsima. 'But if someone looks at you in a positive way, it makes you feel alive again, as if you had drunk water from a spring. It feeds your brain and your entire body. It gives you the strength to carry on.'

Those who wish to impose technocratic programmes which are predestined to fail, and those who believe they are powerless and claim that extreme poverty is inevitable, must be opposed by those who wish to build a fairer society, step by step, by joining forces with the most disadvantaged and by striving to achieve change.

Is not the progress of a society measured by the manner in which the weakest of its members are treated? As the philosopher Miguel Benasayag writes, it is no longer a question of acting 'for a promise, for a golden tomorrow ... but because justice is total in each act of justice'.[17]

Given that the eradication of extreme poverty is possible, it is an ethical, political and civic duty – 'a solemn duty' in the words of Joseph Wresinski – to enable every human being to live a decent life, where his fundamental rights are respected, and where he can exercise his responsibility to contribute to the wellbeing of his family, his community and of humanity.[18]

The eradication of extreme poverty points our lives towards ideals of freedom, justice and fraternity – goals which may appear unattainable today but which are the only source of all future opportunities, and before which humanity must never yield. It is a civilising idea which introduces new rules. We cannot do without that idea because it compels us to become more human and more consistent with our own ideals. Its far-reaching character is on a scale with the violations of human rights produced by extreme poverty and the expectations of those subjected to extreme poverty.

On 17 October 2005, a delegation of 15 people, led by ATD Fourth World, was received by Kofi Annan, the then Secretary-General of the United Nations in New York. Mrs Tita Vilarosa, who had lived for the last 15 years with her family in a cemetery in Manila, declared:

> Mr Secretary General, we stand beside you, the head of the United Nations, as you make a difference for the poorest in the world. Make us your partners as you move forward the agenda on security, development and human rights for all. Let's pool our knowledge together, yours and ours. Let us act now, no longer separately, but together.[19]

This invitation is also extended to every reader.

NOTES

1. Preamble to Universal Declaration of Human Rights, adopted and proclaimed by the General Assembly of the United Nations, A/RES/3/217 A, 10 December 1948.
2. United Nations Millennium Declaration, adopted by the General Assembly of the United Nations, A/RES/55/2, 18 September 2000.
3. UNICEF, *The State of the World's Children 2011*, New York: UNICEF, 2011.
4. Kofi Annan, address given to the World Economic Forum in Davos, Switzerland, SG/SM/6881, 31 January 1999.
5. United Nations, *Millennium Development Goals Report 2010*, 2010.
6. Joseph Wresinski's collected writings and publications have been collated and are open to consultation through the International Joseph Wresinski Centre, www.joseph-wresinski.org
7. The Brundtland Report, *Our Common Future*, was published by the World Commission on Environment and Development in 1987 and defined sustainable development and the policies needed to achieve it.
8. Jean-Baptiste de Foucauld, 'Quel nouveau regard sur l'exclusion?', *Revue Quart Monde*, Vol. 203, No. 3 (August 2007), p. 30.
9. Jean-Baptiste de Foucauld, *Les trois cultures du développement humain: résistance, régulation, utopie*, Paris: Éditions Odile Jacob, 2002.

10. Majid Rahnema and Victoria Bawtree, *The Post-Development Reader*, London: Zed Books, 1997, p. xvii.

11. Edgar Morin, *Les sept savoirs nécessaires à l'éducation du futur*, Paris: Seuil, 2000, pp. 114, 116.

12. Mireille Delmas-Marty, *Universalisme des droits de l'homme et globalisation économique*, in Martine Aubry (ed.), *Agir pour le Sud, maintenant!*, Éditions de l'Aube, 2005, p. 131.

13. Amartya Sen, 'Environment and Poverty: One World or Two?', an address given to the International Conference on Energy, Environment and Development: Analysing Opportunities for Reducing Poverty, 16 December 2006.

14. *Le Monde*, 23–24 July 2006.

15. Benjamin Mkapa, *Indigenous Knowledge: A Local Pathway to Global Development*, in World Bank, *Indigenous Knowledge: Local Pathways to Global Development*, 2004, p. 3.

16. Extract from an internal ATD Fourth World note by Gérard Bureau, 5 March 2008.

17. Florence Aubenas and Miguel Benasayag, *Résister, c'est créer*, Paris: La Découverte, 2002, p. 49.

18. 'Wherever men and women are condemned to live in extreme poverty, human rights are violated. To come together to ensure that these rights be respected is our solemn duty.' Joseph Wresinski, text engraved on the Commemorative Stone in Honour of the Victims of Extreme Poverty unveiled on 17 October 1987.

19. Cited by Catherine Moore, *The Day Mrs. Tita Villarosa Met Mr. Kofi Annan at the United Nations*, in Fourth World Movement/USA, *Fourth World Journal*, January 2006.

Index

Compiled by Sue Carlton